I Learn Better By Teaching Myself

and

Still Teaching Ourselves

Agnes Leistico

I Learn Better By Teaching Myself and
Still Teaching Ourselves
both by Agnes Leistico

Published by:

Holt Associates, Inc.
2269 Massachusetts Ave.
Cambridge, MA 02140

First printing of this combined edition, March, 1997.
ISBN 0-913677-12-4

Library of Congress Cataloging-in-Publication Data In Process

I Learn Better By Teaching Myself

Still Teaching Ourselves

I Learn Better By Teaching Myself

Agnes Leistico

Lovingly dedicated to my husband Dale and the children who brought about our family's learning adventures: James, Laurene, and Susan.

"I like to learn by teaching myself. I don't like someone else to teach me because I learn better by teaching myself."
Susan Leistico, age seven

Foreword

Have your ever considered yourself a homeschooling expert? Perhaps you have, but if you're like most parents, it's more likely that you've never really thought of yourself as an expert in the field. You teach your children, or you nudge them in the directions you think might be best for them, or you let them learn as they need and want to, and you hope for the best. You have days when everything goes well and great wonderful discoveries are made and learning is obviously taking place... and then you have days when everything drags along and nothing "academic" seems to happen, and you find yourself wondering if it's all going to work out.

That might not be the generally accepted description of an expert, but when it comes to home schooling your own children—how they learn best, and what they need most—you are the only *real* expert. It doesn't matter if you are just imagining what home schooling could do for your family or if you have been doing it for years - you are still the expert.

Other people's titles of "home schooling expert" are based on their own experiences with whatever parenting or training or reading or studying they may have done. You can base your expert title on the very same things, but with a specialty in your own family. This is an expert title that no one else can earn. You have lived with this youngster from his or her birth, and grown as a parent as your child has grown as a person. You've shared many experiences that make your insight uniquely valuable for your child's future. The people who are often considered the "experts" have plenty of valid information for you to select from and use, but their information must be filtered through this special expertise you have as a parent.

Home schooling experts write books, teach workshops, develop curriculums, edit newsletters, lead seminars, testify in court, organize conventions, and even publish magazines. These people have valuable information to share with people who are interested in teaching their own children. In writing, teaching, publishing, testifying and organizing they are demonstrating faith in *your* ability to be the real expert your family needs. And these people offer such a wide variety of options to choose from that it can be frustrating to select the "best" for your family.

Just how do you, as your family's expert, choose a book or a curriculum or a workshop from the ever-increasing choices available? How does one sort through the "home schooling experts" and their offerings to find those which might be right for your family and your approach to home schooling? The first step is to trust in your ability to be the real expert. You can start by determining your family's philosophy or motivation for home schooling. Examine your reasons for wanting to teach your own children at home, and list the methods your family feels comfortable with. Explore the subject, ask each other questions, discuss why you're home schooling, how it's working, and what changes various family members might like to see incorporated.

Knowing the approaches and methods that your family prefers will help when confronted with the wondrous selection of resources available at a curriculum fair, a home schooling conference exhibit hall, or through a home school supplier's catalog. Realizing what your family would like to work on will help in selecting workshops or seminars to attend, or in deciding which home schooling books to purchase. Envisioning the goals your family would like to achieve will make choosing the routes to those goals a fun and rewarding adventure for everyone.

As the Home Schooling Expert in your family, your decisions and selections will determine the direction and the ultimate consequences of your endeavors. Trust your abilities, believe in your own expertise, and then see what the "other experts" have to offer!

Mark and Helen Hegener
Publishers, Home Education Magazine

Introduction

Why do we allow adults greater freedom to learn according to individual learning styles than our children? More importantly, why don't we adults trust children to learn according to their personal interests? Could it be we turn many of today's American children away from learning long before they attain adulthood because we do not allow our children the freedom of choice in utilizing their personal learning styles? These questions have puzzled me. I realize there can be no easy answer. I take comfort in the knowledge that many noted educators also ask these questions and seek answers.

How can we encourage our children more effectively in their learning experiences? There is a widespread recognition that each person has a particular learning style that maximizes the quest for learning. This search for effective educational methods leads us to consider earlier proponents of various learning styles.

The noted author, educator, and home school pioneer John Holt advocated allowing children greater freedom in choosing what to learn when they were ready. Observing how young children learn to walk, to talk, and to function in social settings, he reasoned that this was a natural process and that later learning should flow just as naturally. Based on this he argued that learning involves the whole being of the learner. When self-esteem is left intact the child can wisely choose what learning is important and how to acquire it.

He is not alone in believing that children are the best judges of what should be learned, when it should be learned, and how it should be learned. Other noted educators have come to the same conclusion. Each has approached the question from different angles because each has had different backgrounds and insights and each approaches learning in varying ways. Maria Montessori emphasized the early childhood years and the respect for each young learner as an individual. Judson Jerome compared learning to gardening in which learning emerges when interference is avoided, nutrients are supplied, and pests are combatted.

Among other advocates of student directed learning experiences is Herbert Kohl, who addressed the need to consider the interests of the child for effective learning in his book, *The Open Classroom*. In *Deschooling Society* Ivan Illich contends that our society is inclined to believe the only valuable skills are those which are the result of formal schooling. Repeatedly we hear of educators and those vitally interested in education who state that the well-motivated or interested student usually needs no more assistance than that someone demonstrates on demand how to do what the student wants to learn to do. Students learn when they are interested in the subject.

Helen K. Billings, the founder of the Montessori Institute of America, devoted her life to promoting the concept that learning starts in early childhood and continues throughout a person's lifetime. She emphasized that student-initiated learning is the foundation for true education. She especially cautions adults to wait until invited into a student's activities as the learner's interest can wane at any semblance of pressure.

Carl Rogers came to the conclusion that only self-discovered, self-appropriated learning influences behavior. Noted author and educator David Elkind pleads for consideration of what he terms healthy education. His focus is on how a healthy education supports and encourages spontaneous learning processes. In his view, miseducation ignores the necessity of letting young students explore and understand their immediate world. Attempting to teach the wrong thing at the wrong time causes a loss of the positive attitude a student needs for learning. He joins many others in stating that it is important not to introduce information before the student shows an interest. The list of people advocating student-directed learning is long. Each has his or her variation of the theme that student-initiated learning is the most effective means of learning.

For purposes of this book the definition of interest-initiated learning will be that learning which the learner herself controls and initiates according to her own interests. Internal personal priorities guide her learning. Being entirely self-directed, the learner chooses when and how to learn about a given topic or skill. The teacher only enters into the learning process when invited to do so.

There are many books available now about homeschooling—what it is, how to start home schooling, why people home school, and the legal implications of home schooling—yet I have not heard of any which address how parents implement interest-initiated learning. This book attempts to fill this gap by showing the reader how our family tries to practice interest-initiated learning.

Our family is far from perfect. We have our good days mixed in with our bad days and we only imperfectly employ the concept of interest-initiated learning. My hope is that this book will encourage those readers already accepting of the idea to continue their own efforts to reach this ideal. And may those readers who oppose the idea of interest-initiated learning begin to understand what we are doing. I myself had to struggle with my own resistance to the idea that a student can learn without being told what and how to learn. My own children forced me to reconsider.

This book will present not only our story, but glimpses of how and why other families are practicing interest-initiated learning. Each family needs to approach interest-initiated learning in its own way as we are dealing with individual students in circumstances not duplicated in any other family. Take from this book what applies to your circumstances. Build on ideas presented to suit your family's needs. Above all, trust your own instincts.

There are three basic aspects to interest-initiated learning as brought forth in this book. One—it is that learning which the learner herself initiates and controls according to her own interests. Two—her own priorities (not imposed from the outside) guide the learner. And three—the teacher only enters into the process when invited to do so.

I do not claim to have many answers about why what is happening works, I just know it is working well for us. Our experiences and results will not be the same as another family's. In preparation for this book I have come more fully to the conclusion that the individual student/learner does know what is best for her. Too many of our students never have the opportunity to come to this realization. There are many theories and methods around. Each person has to study them and choose what works best. There is no single approach that works for everybody.

If all I do is instill in my youngsters a lifelong love for learning, I will have accomplished my goal. I firmly believe that interest-initiated learning is a means to this goal for us.

Agnes Leistico

Chapter One

Getting Started

In 1983 I met my first homeschool family. The mother and I were La Leche League leaders. We lived over 200 miles apart and were involved in a joint activity which required us to meet at each other's homes periodically. Up until that time I had never heard of homeschooling and from what I saw I was not at all impressed because the youngsters *seemed* to be doing nothing. "Schooling" meant blackboards, texts, worksheets, schedules, tests, and a certain amount of boredom to me at that time. These children always seemed to be reading something or doing some "foreign" activities the limited time I was around them.

This mother had secondary teaching credentials yet did not seem in the least worried that her youngsters weren't learning anything in my estimation. She tried answering my questions but we were on different wavelengths. While I accepted the fact that she was entitled to her own point of view, I was convinced she was harming her children's chances in later life to be successful and accepted.

Then when I learned that a friend living nearby had also begun homeschooling her son and daughter, I actively started resisting the idea. This was too much for me. I had great respect for both mothers but I could not accept their choice of education for their children. When two good friends of mine declared they were going to homeschool their little ones, I began to investigate why families choose to homeschool. But I was only willing to allow this in the case of little children. My own children were doing well in the local public schools. I felt that if parents were actively involved in their children's schools, problems could be worked out.

The first two families had older children and they were practicing what I now refer to as interest initiated learning. However, my friends Linda and Christine had children younger than mine who had never gone to school at all and they were following a curriculum more traditionally oriented under the auspices of a private school. This I could more easily accept at this stage.

In June of 1985 another friend organized a workshop on homeschooling. I would not consider homeschooling personally but I realized this was a movement in which several of my friends were interested. I felt I should learn as much as I could about the movement in order that I might better understand homeschooling.

A month later I attended the La Leche International conference in Washington, D.C., where I attended a session on homeschooling. I discovered the far reaching effects of the movement and that friends I had made in the La Leche League in both the U. S. and in Canada were now homeschooling. I began to realize there were numerous approaches to learning at home although most tended to be very loosely structured as opposed to what took place in my children's public school classes. In spite of all this exposure I was still convinced my youngsters were doing fine where they were.

Our oldest child, Jim, was reluctant to attend school in the third grade. When he was in kindergarten he could hardly wait to get to school each morning and cried when there was a holiday as he wanted to go to school. By second grade his enthusiasm had waned but I noticed no special problems. I thought he liked his third grade teacher. But there were so many days he complained of a headache or would say he did not feel well so that he would not have to go to school. Our doctor and the teacher both advised us to make him go unless Jim had a fever or some obvious symptom.

I felt this was wrong but many times ended up driving a very unhappy son to school. We lived within walking distance but sometimes the only way I could get him to go to school was to drive him. This led to more tears. Many times I allowed him to stay home but I was torn inside. My instincts told me it was a mistake to force him, yet "experts" were telling me I'd regret it later on if I did not make him go to school. As things turned out I have regretted forcing him go and have never regretted keeping him at home.

Fourth grade found a somewhat happier student although we still had days when he preferred to stay home. That year I allowed him to stay home without much fuss. Fifth grade seemed even better. There were some signs of stress which I chose to ignore as they appeared much less frequently. The one disturbing thing that occurred was that Jim started saying he did not like science. His teacher was science oriented. From what I could observe as a parent volunteer working in the classroom, the teacher was offering students a fascinating introduction to science. To this day Jim declares a dislike for science. Yet if you present him with a topic and don't label it "science," he enthusiastically digs right in.

Sixth grade was a disaster. Our district takes sixth graders from the neighborhood elementary school and places them with seventh and eighth graders on a separate campus. They now have a six-period day and move from classroom to classroom. Sixth graders were given a core teacher for three of their classes so they would not have to adjust to as many teachers.

Jim was miserable. Some of his teachers recognized this and tried to help us work out the problem. One teacher requested a counselor to see Jim in November. We later learned that it is not uncommon for some students to react negatively to the middle school. But because Jim was not a behavior problem, the counselor did not see him until January when the teacher had to send him to the counselor's office as he was so miserable.

Jim went into therapy. By mid February I decided he had to be homeschooled. The therapist did everything she could to dissuade me from bringing Jim home to do his studies. Yet she recommended that Jim had to be removed from the middle school even though there were no suitable alternatives to the middle school in Jim's case. (Within six months she had admitted the wisdom of bringing Jim home.)

I called the school district office to check into an independent study program. There was none available. I was referred to the County Schools office. When I told the woman I was looking into an independent study program for my sixth grade son her first question was "Who's your son's probation officer?" This floored me! I explained that he was not in trouble with the law. He was a straight A student well liked by every one of his teachers, and just needed an alternative learning situation. She had nothing to offer me.

This forced me into seriously considering homeschooling. Linda lent me all the back issues of *Growing Without Schooling*, John Holt's bimonthly newsletter for people interested in homeschooling. It took several days of constant reading, but I read every page searching for anything that would apply to older students. There was very little written then about working with older students so I had to rely on my instincts and whoever I could find to encourage me.

The local children's librarian at our public library was an enormous help. Pat was a retired teacher with an intense love for children and great understanding of the gifted child. Together we learned more about homeschooling. She was able to purchase appropriate books for the library on related topics. She encouraged us and was helpful in locating reading material in which Jim was interested.

A few months before we removed Jim from middle school I had learned that another friend had chosen to start homeschooling her ten-year-old daughter and five-year-old son. This amazed me as I never dreamed Karen would do anything that "drastic." Her husband was provost of the College of Creative Studies at the University of California at Santa Barbara. She just did not seem the type to me. Yes, I was guilty of stereotyping.

I knew that Karen was using the same homeschool organization as Linda and Christine so I wanted to look over her daughter's fifth grade materials. Besides, my husband was not at all convinced this would work. One evening we went over to their house to talk with them and to listen to Max's thoughts about his children learning at home and how he felt this would affect their chances to go to college. He told us of the Young Scholar's program offered at the College of Creative Studies for gifted children as early as seventh grade, urging us to consider the math program for Jim.

Because I had grave personal misgivings as to my ability to direct my children's studies, we chose to go with the same homeschool organization with which my friends were enrolled. This bought time for Jim. We enrolled him immediately, but it took a few weeks to gather the materials and to be assigned a teacher, and his only contact with the teacher was through the mail.

Jim needed the time he could get just to get in touch with himself once again. For about six months he would not pick up a book to read even for enjoyment unless he was directed to. His teacher was sympathetic and demanded only the minimum. He spent most of his days outside in our yard gardening and soaking up sun. I was quite involved as a parent volunteer in the two schools his sisters were attending so was not home for stretches of time each day. This turned out to be what he needed—time to be by himself for at least part of the day.

I wrote to a homeschooling friend living in Indiana. Pam had been homeschooling for four years.

> I desperately need to talk to someone doing it with teenagers to see how it works. Everyone I have met or known up to now has younger children. I did try to call you last weekend when I especially felt the need to talk to you about teenagers and homeschooling, but no one answered.
>
> Jim is doing nicely now that the pressure is off him. He gets along with Laurie again like he used to—what a blessing. And his intense emotional reactions have calmed down considerably. Last week he even went to the Outdoor School of Santa Barbara County Schools for a week of Science Camp offered for sixth graders. He had already paid for the trip last December but we did not know if he would actually go as the entire group is made up of students he knew from Middle School. But he did and came home tired but pleased with himself. It was a marvelous experience.

Pam's reassuring reply came promptly.

> In addition to his paper route and Kung Fu, Tim

(15) is taking a continuing education class at Purdue Calumet. The class is a private pilot ground school class. He's also doing volunteer work in the summer reading program at the library (part of the graduation requirements for Clonlara—volunteer work). The topper was he got a paying (real $!) job at the county swimming pool and works there four days a week. Yes, a home-schooling student can earn real money!

I tell you all this about Tim not only to let you know how crazy we are but to assure you (and myself sometimes) that homeschooling teens are "normal." The first year is really rough, Agnes, at least it was for me. I was so afraid they wouldn't continue to learn, but would forget everything they had previously learned—as if we always retain everything presented to us.

In the meantime I continued reading everything I could find about homeschooling methods. The more I read and talked with people, the more I realized the value of interest initiated learning. My confidence increased.

Because of important philosophical disagreements with the organization Jim had been enrolled in, I chose to take full responsibility for his education. I came to view education as a life experience that cannot be confined by time or textbook. I wanted Jim to know he got credit for every meaningful experience—something he had not been given before. In theory I was still resisting the concept of interest initiated learning, but in practice I was gradually accepting it.

It was only after I had been working with my youngsters at home for some time that I began to realize how my own background contributed to this educational endeavor. Learning has always played an important part in my life as a source of enjoyment and fulfillment. As Jim, Laurie and Susan came along I passed this on to them without realizing it until someone called it to my attention.

Growing up in a rural community, I attended one-room Highland School, where total enrollment for all eight grades never exceeded 20 students while I attended it. My father had attended the same school and for the first three years I had the same teacher he'd had. In the seventh grade four one-room schools in our mountainous district consolidated into a four-room school—still with an enrollment of less than 100 students.

It was quite an event to have to ride the bus to town to a high school with over a thousand students. Yet our little one-room schoolhouse produced an unusual number of honor students in high school. I remember one neighbor asking why this was so. Over the years little Highland School had produced several valedictorians. I attribute this to the positive learning experience we had in our little one-room school.

My grandfather had little formal education as he had grown up in a rural area of Missouri in the late 1800's. He had to devote most of his childhood to helping the family survive. In the early 1900's he came to California to establish his own large farm holdings. By the time my dad was born Highland School was established and he attended it on a regular basis. He was able to complete little more than a year of high school when his father became gravely ill and was not expected to live long. There were several sisters and a younger brother to care for, so my dad had to take over the ranch as a teenager.

Grandpa lived many more years. I was an adult when he died in his mid nineties. My impression of him to this day remains one of a man very much in tune with the world around him. He always had books and magazines around, and I often saw him reading. I loved to be around him.

My own father also reads extensively. He is a craftsman known for his innovative way of making tools fit a need or purpose. My mother was a registered nurse. She too is an avid reader. My brothers and I grew up in an atmosphere that encouraged learning all we could. My husband's father, too, had to leave formal schooling after the eighth grade. Yet he can hold his own with most people who have had a college education. The common thread between my father and my father-in-law is their desire to learn as much as possible and their love of reading a variety of materials.

My college years led me into teaching. But when I started teaching I was dismayed to discover that my students resisted my efforts to make them learn. The "methods" I had been taught just did not seem to work. Youngsters did not *want* to learn what I was teaching them. Yet when I worked with adults who came of their own choice I had a different experience. I found working with them enjoyable. Something was not working right with the youngsters so I gave up teaching them altogether.

When we were married I knew that I wanted to be at home with my children as they grew up. I joined La Leche League before Jim was born and soon became a La Leche League leader. As a leader I had to become knowledgeable as to all aspects of breastfeeding and to lead discussion meetings on breastfeeding and parenting topics. At last I had found my niche.

However I did not equate my work as a La Leche leader with my teaching efforts until just recently. Now I can see the relationship. These women came to the meetings because they had the desire to learn as much as they could about breastfeeding and parenting. They expected me to be a resource person and a guide but they did not want to be spoon-fed the information.

I led the meetings with the expectation that these were intelligent women who were interested in the topic and capable of drawing their own conclusions. They were free to come to the meetings when they wanted and when it met their needs. They knew I would accept them as individuals who would be making their own decisions as to the worth of my information to them. Now I ask myself why we can't allow our children the same freedom to acquire knowledge.

As Jim, Laurie and Susan grew from babyhood to toddlerhood, I just did what came naturally—which was to let them explore the world on their own terms. I tried to provide as many exploratory opportunities as possible. None of this was done with conscious thought as to its learning value.

My husband commented when Jim was about ten as to how comfortable the children were with using the library. His comment surprised me at the time because I had not deliberately set out to make them love the library. I love books so I am drawn to any library. This introduced Jim, Laurie and Susan to them. Each child could hardly wait for the time the library allowed them to have their own card. It is because the young-sters love going to the library that my husband has started making use of it himself. We have been fortunate to live near a library that has a good story time program for preschoolers. We surrounded ourselves with books we enjoyed with no particular thought as to educational value. Even before he learned to read, Jim would often fall asleep with a book in his hands. He still does occasionally. In fact, we all read before going to sleep almost every night.

Daily walks in our neighborhood started with Jim riding in a backpack. As the girls came along this continued. It was excit-ing for me to see common, taken-for-granted things anew through their eyes. Frequent visits to nearby parks and beach-es expanded our horizons. Garage sales became the source of many inexpensive and varied playthings. The favorite items related to daily living experiences. All three youngsters loved playing with their friends using their play kitchen set. Dolls and toy vehicles were also important to all three children. The conversations I overheard demonstrated the integral educa-tional and play value these items contained.

Television introduced us to even more opportunities. We do carefully select the programs we watch. When Jim came home for his studies this was a struggle. He wanted to retreat from the world, and television would have allowed this escape. He has a tendency to become mesmerized by television and I had to limit his viewing of programs. At first he resisted and tried to sneak some extra viewing time, but this rebellion did not per-sist very long. Now I notice he has much more discrimination in his viewing habits.

Jim came home for his studies in March. Laurie was doing well at her school despite a change in principals that had cre-ated a severe morale problem among the teachers that affected the students and parents. She is very outgoing and easily makes the best of a poor situation, so she started fourth grade that fall. I did not personally know the teacher she was assigned to but was hopeful it would work out despite unset-tling things I had heard about this teacher.

Five weeks later Dale and I went to Back To School Night. As we left the classroom Dale was the one to speak first. He wanted Laurie at home. The teacher, who had taught for almost thirty years, firmly stated that no child in her classroom was going to be ahead of or behind any other child in the class. Every child was expected to work the very same math problem and read the very same page as every other child in the class. She appointed "Captains" who were to tell her everything that went on in the room when her back was turned because "children at that age like to tattle anyway."

No wonder Laurie had been complaining that her fingers hurt because of writing so much and that she hated being a "Captain." It turned out that because Laurie was ahead of most of the class the teacher made her do more math problems (simple subtraction in this case). Every other teacher she had had encouraged her to work to her own capacity. None had required her to monitor the actions of her fellow students.

I knew from the experience of friends there was no appeal to this principal. He had belittled other parents and made school life harder on their youngsters when the parents had tried to improve a bad classroom situation. That November I wrote to a friend:

> Homeschooling is turning out to be so much easier on me than having Jim and Laurie in school. Time-wise, besides getting to be with them more, I find myself so much freer and not controlled by school activities. I did not notice it as much when they were all in the same elementary school but as they get older the demands on my time increased and were set by someone with no interest in family activities. And I am finding a side benefit in that I am brushing up on my own skills and learning new things. With the ages Jim and Laurie are they do most everything on their own. The only time I get myself hung up is whenever I start doubting myself and my own capability.

Susan was going to another public school in the district, a modified Montessori program which suited her well. She flourished in an environment which allowed her more freedom to choose her activities and she was stimulated by hands-on experiences. In kindergarten she participated in the IBM Writing to Read Lab. I was working in her classroom several times a week during kindergarten. In first grade she chose to write a "book" about the River Nile using high school books she picked up at the local school textbook depository. I was often in her classroom that year too.

But during first grade Susan started staying home "sick." When I talked to another mother in Susan's group I learned that her daughter was also refusing to go to school. We worked with the teacher who willingly worked with us to discover the cause. It turned out she had been ignoring her top group—since they were so capable—to spend more time with the four non-English-speaking students and with youngsters in the slower group. Once she again started spending time with Susan's group things smoothed out somewhat (what are we *asking* of our teachers)?

But I still noticed the spark going out of Susan. She started telling me that she needed more freedom to learn as she was ready and what she wanted to learn. She even wrote this down in a notebook. One day she told me, "School puts too much pressure on me. It makes me feel hot all over and uncomfortable. At school I can't learn what I want to when I want to."

Susan remained in the public school until the end of the first grade. But since then she has continued her studies at home and constantly expresses her appreciation. I am most grateful that she is able to tell me when something is not going well so we can adjust our own program to suit her present needs. Once when I was putting too much pressure on Susan to produce I found this note on my bedside stand next to the book I was reading:

> Dear Mom,
> I feel like I need a break (even if a short one) away. It's just I feel so cooped up here because I have to do a lot of stuff on schedule and have to do certain things. I don't have as much time to do stuff that I want to when I want to. I just feel so

cooped up. When I was in public school I remember
blinking back tears.

When a television news reporter visited our home for an
interview, Susan emphatically told him that freedom to learn
her own way best suits her educational needs. I resisted the
temptation to coach the girls in any way in preparation for his
interview. I realized I was taking a risk but I felt comfortable
enough with my girls to allow this freedom of expression.

The reporter asked the girls how long they expect to homeschool. Laurie responded she would like to go to high school.
Susan, on the other hand, stated that she thinks she will wait
until college. However this turns out will ultimately involve
their own decisions as they do know what they want.

A few years ago I would have been horrified at the thought
that a child can direct her own studies successfully. Now that I
look around and see some of the poor choices adults make for
children, and the ability children have to make intelligent
choices if allowed to, I have reconsidered.

My children have been labeled as "gifted." This is a label I
don't like when it connotes "my child is better than your child."
I do not consider my children as better, only as individual children with their own talents, strengths, and weaknesses. This is
a concept I have tried to impart constantly when speaking at or
participating in parenting or education-related workshops and
in private conversations.

I was delighted to receive a subscription renewal notice from
Gifted Children Monthly written by James Alvino, Ph. D., publisher, which states,

> It used to be thought that giftedness is some-
> thing a child was born with. Today we know other-
> wise. According to expert James J. Gallagher, "We
> can create giftedness through designing enriched
> environments and opportunities, or we can destroy
> it by failing to create those environments and
> opportunities."

My lifelong experiences have prepared me to implement the

idea of interest-initiated learning with my children. However, it is in retrospect that I discovered this fact. My background reading reinforced my thoughts as to what education is all about.

I came from a home where reading was important and went to a small one room school where I worked at my own pace and had plenty of tutors available. This laid the groundwork for me. I experienced teacher training that did not really teach me how to teach. This continued my education. I finally realized that "educational experts" do not have any more answers than I do as to how effective learning takes place. This forced me to the conclusion that I should truly start listening to my students. I now think that interest-initiated learning is most effective when the learner has not already been "programmed in the system."

Chapter Two

Choosing Our
Learning Materials

A child can make better sense of the world on her own than we can do for her through adult-produced curricula. My own children had to teach me the truth of this statement. I had been "schooled" to believe that certain trained adults are the only ones qualified to choose what is important to learn. Reluctantly I began to see the wisdom in listening to the student.

When we brought Jim home to do his schooling I did not believe I was capable of directing his studies. We enrolled him in a private school with independent study which could be done through the mail. I went to our school district textbook discard center to select what I considered appropriate books for Jim to study. I wanted to supplement the private school's textbooks on language arts, science, math, history, social studies, and music. Carefully I outlined a course of study for each subject. This contradicted my belief that I was incapable of directing his studies, although I did not realize this at the time.

Jim looked at what I had prepared without saying anything. He put the books in the box I gave him to file his school work. To please me he did some exercises I assigned in his U. S. History book. Eventually he stopped working on my assignments. His teacher's assignments fared a little better—but not much. I tried to work with him on some of the assignments I had given him. He did not want my help.

It was no wonder that he did not like the textbooks. I discovered by working with Jim how boring today's textbooks are. Publishers of textbooks claim that they are responding to the market, and to them this means that textbooks must present the subject in a manner that offends no one. They avoid the semblance of favoring one segment of our society over another. They claim they need to conform to current readability formulas.

Jim's new correspondence teacher used better quality textbooks than I found. This encouraged me to search for more interesting materials. To my delight I uncovered many sources for outstanding materials. Now I was in a dilemma. There was so much available that I became overwhelmed by my choices. Jim was not delighted over my discoveries. Someone else's choices did not interest him.

I started to observe his interests. Reading the back issues of *Growing Without Schooling*, I found a few articles on older students leaving the school structure to begin homeschooling. Parents, writing of their experiences, related that what their children needed most was time. They used the time to unwind, to heal, to dream, and to rediscover their interests. For some youngsters this required a year or more.

Sam, the son of my friend Laurie Struble, needed this time. I remember Laurie saying that it was a full year before he could handle learning activities as most people think of them. Sam started homeschooling in the fourth grade. He chose to attend one year of public high school but then returned to homeschooling. He passed the California High School Proficiency Test in April of 1988, and is now enrolled in classes at Allan Hancock College. When Laurie learned I was writing this book she wrote,

> Anyway, about how I got into homeschooling... I had no idea such a thing was possible when Sam was little. I diligently searched for the best school situation for him. He did okay in kindergarten (at public school) but the social situation was bad. It was such a tender age to be forced into a situation like that. So for the first grade we tried private school. The kids were basically nicer there but it was *so* strict, and pushed the kids academically. So it was back to the local public school for second grade. He did real well in school, but he didn't like it much and the social situation was still bad. So

for the third grade we tried another school which was the first year as a public school "back to basics" regime. It was terrible. That's when it all came to a head and we really started having problems. Sam was miserable. He'd wake up in the morning and say he wished he were sick so he wouldn't have to go to school. This bright, eager-to-learn little boy was totally burned out and tired of learning. The school system took his enthusiasm about learning away and "busy worked" him into the ground. He was a natural born reader, but for a year after he left school he wouldn't look at a book. And to this day he hasn't overcome his aversion to math.

Thus started our experience with homeschooling. And I became an immediate advocate. If ever a person were born to be "unschooled"' it was Sam. He did it all on his own. With his high linguistic intelligence, I never applied myself to "teaching" him, I just supplied him with books. He's a voracious reader and will study a subject in depth all on his own. A wonderful example of interest initiated learning. And he learns most of the material thoroughly and retains it well, unlike most of what he was "force fed" in school and quickly forgot.

Other than Laurie, I searched in vain for local families who were homeschooling older students. I wrote letters to any possible source I could uncover, but everyone I found had only younger children, and I was not yet convinced that Laurie's interest initiated approach was at all effective.

That spring Dale and I attended a conference devoted to parenting topics that changed the way I regarded learning alternatives. I presented a session on school readiness with an emphasis on kindergarten, and the discussion period clarified my thoughts as I responded to questions from participants. After my session I attended a panel session that explored available learning alternatives. Panelists discussed the advantages of public and private schools, homeschooling, and certain learning philosophies such as Waldorf and Montessori.

In the exhibit hall, at a booth for the Family Centered Learning Alternatives, we met Nancy Oh. I was beginning to suspect that Jim's independent study program was inappropriate for him, and Nancy showed us that it was possible to design a study program that considered the student's interests. Nancy and I became friends, and a month later she visited us while on her way to a homeschool conference. John Boston was sharing a ride with her to the conference, and I invited several friends to discuss homeschooling with John and Nancy. That discussion became my turning point, as John changed my mind about the effectiveness of student interest initiated learning.

John Boston is the administrator of the School of Home Learning (now Home Centered Learning). His program operates on the principle of "invited teaching," which means the role of the teacher is to assist the student in locating and using the kinds of materials, services, and people she needs in order to learn what she wishes to know. John has secondary level teaching credentials and a master's degree. He noticed that unless his students had a personal reason for taking his class they were not retaining what he taught them. This bothered him. When he attempted to set up programs matching the interests of his students he faced opposition from fellow teachers and the administration.

Stella and John Boston brought their son, Sean, home to study when he was in the fifth grade because he was so miserable in school. I can still hear John chuckle as he recalled his first attempts to "teach" Sean at home. John decided Sean needed help with spelling so he set up elaborate lesson plans to accomplish this. John's spelling improved. Sean was not interested in learning to spell. However, when Sean decided for himself that he needed to spell correctly, he taught himself.

John is a firm believer in interest initiated learning. In his quiet way he encourages others to be open to its possibilities. He founded Home Centered Learning because of his belief in a minimum of adult interference in the learning process. After five years of experiencing interest initiated learning with Sean, John wrote an article for *Growing Without Schooling*. He reported the results of allowing Sean the freedom to learn in their home and their community. Sean developed high level social skills, and a psychologist tested him. He lacked certain memorization skills but his abilities were of college entrance level. Activities in which he was interested sharpened his reading and math skills. He loved to work on his Honda motorcycle which in turn led to an interest in automotive mechanics.

Sean received his high school diploma from the School of Home Learning in 1987 and is now attending college. In 1988 Palomar College awarded him the Don Erbe Automotive Scholarship, an award established to acknowledge and encourage college students in the automotive field. It requires demonstration of high interest through outside participation and accomplishments. Sean is also on the college's honor roll.

John and Nancy pointed out that I had already been practicing interest initiated learning with my children—and with great success. From the time they were babies, I had surrounded them with many learning opportunities. Jim had entered the Lucky Supermarket "21 Days of America" essay contest in June, 1984 and won a trip to Washington, D. C. for the family. His teacher had told me that more than what he learned in school, my parenting style had enabled him to win the contest. Other teachers made similar remarks, but I did not believe them. It was only after John and Nancy pointed out the same thing that I understood.

I looked back over Jim's 1985-86 school year. He was in the local middle school until March and received all A's on his report card despite his learning frustrations and all the time lost due to illness caused by stress. His favorite class was music, where he learned to play the bell lyre. He liked his teachers and his teachers liked him. But he was under so much stress that he was not able to learn effectively.

One assignment stands out in my memory. For English he had to write a descriptive paragraph. He chose to describe Sherlock Holmes' distinctive hat, but he became extremely frustrated because of time limitations. I often read aloud in the evenings and he loved the Sherlock Holmes stories, and he wanted to go into depth on the topic of Sherlock Holmes. But there was no time nor credit granted him for pursuing this topic.

He resented the assignments his independent study teacher gave him, as feedback took so long. He mailed his assignments to the teacher every two weeks, and she was prompt in answering, but the assignments were sometimes four weeks old before he received a response. He was not particularly interested in the assignments anyway. There was no pressure put on him to complete them, and his teacher recognized the need for a period of healing. She used this time for the two of them to get to know each other.

At first I felt that the time from March to June was rather bleak. Then I began to realize the valuable learning experiences that had occurred. Jim started working out in the yard. He became interested in growing things. By that summer he planted a small vegetable garden. He was pleased with the results. His garden was an ordinary one by some people's standards, but we thought it was outstanding.

Jim became interested in weather. We ordered a four-way weather station that measured temperature, rainfall, wind direction, and wind speed. He faithfully recorded the rainfall. He and his grandfather, who lives two hundred miles north of us, compare our rainfall totals, and they often share weather observations. Weather conditions are important to my father because of his orchard, and so Jim learned about fruit ranching also.

I subscribed to the magazine *Gifted Children Monthly* (no longer published). If Jim got to the mail before I did I had to wait to read this magazine because he liked to read the "Spin Off" pages. Sometimes he even responded to some of their surveys and contests even though he has never enjoyed writing much. He did this on his own, without any coaching from me. The things I would encourage him to participate in usually did not appeal to him. Normally he did not read the rest of the articles in *Gifted Children Monthly*. However, I shared one article with him because of his interest in making money, and it was the beginning of his lasting interest in the stock market. The article, "Money Matters are 'Fun-ancials' for Children," was written by an attorney and financial writer whose special interest is investor education. She encourages teaching children how to invest their money, and her article shows how to invest $1,000 and then follow your investment, making changes as you go along to increase your investment. Jim read the article thoroughly and for almost two years formed his own portfolio, following its progress and reading the stock market section of our newspaper.

While he no longer keeps records on how his portfolio is doing, he still follows the ups and downs of the stock market. He loves to discuss the stock market with his grandfather, and they get into some interesting discussions on investing money. To this day Jim reads *The Wall Street Journal* when he visits his grandfather, and his dream is to set aside enough money to invest on his own.

One advertisement in *Gifted Children Monthly* caught Jim's attention. The Almaniac: The World Trivia Contest is a challenge not of what you know, but of what you can find out. The competition is stiff and the questions can be tricky, but all the answers are contained in the current *World Almanac* and *Book of Facts.* Four contests are featured each year, with two taken directly from the *World Almanac,* one using Rand McNalley world maps (for their Circumglobal Trophy Dash), and one using North American maps. Jim loved the intense research needed to complete the contests.

The contests covered a wide range of topics. Under sports one question asked: In which state is the football stadium of the greatest capacity? a) California, b) Michigan, c) Pennsylvania. The answer booklet was quite specific: California's Rose Bowl was the largest. If someone said Michigan they were quickly reminded that Michigan has the largest college stadium but the question was not limited to colleges. Careful research was necessary to answer their sometimes tricky questions. But the answer booklets even specify exact pages certain answers can be found on. For instance, in the same contest with the above sports question was one on religion: In terms of percentage of population, what is the most religious part of the world? a) Africa, b) Asia, c) Oceania, d) South America. The answer according to the 1986 World Almanac was Oceania. Its 79%

beats South America's 76%. The answer could be found on page 336 under Religion—Population, world.

Other topics in the 1986 contest included the Arctic, facts about the United States, the Presidency, science, astrophysics, and even a few questions on Individual Retirement Accounts. The map contests are even more of a challenge. For the fun of it I worked on one that featured actual railroad maps in a portion of China and learned fascinating facts about the geography of China.

The answer sheet is sent out promptly after the close of the contest. Each participant is given a final summary booklet and participants may challenge a given answer, with credit given for challenged answers and credit statistics about the participants. About 1,000 people participate each time, with the average age being in the mid-thirties, and very few participants under 20. Jim usually placed somewhere in the middle, though where he placed did not concern him. He just enjoyed the challenge, but because the contests are time consuming he has not entered since starting high school.

Jim did not want any assistance with any of the contests so I generally contented myself with browsing through them after he had sent his entries in. I was very impressed with the quality of these contests. Jim received a broad range of information through them and his research skills were definitely heightened.

Jim has a talent for mathematics. Susan does too. Dale, being an engineer, is strong in math skills. Laurie and I are more talented in writing skills than math. We enrolled Jim in the Young Scholar's Program at the University of California at Santa Barbara. UCSB College of Creative Studies created this program for middle school and high school students with aptitude in math, literature, science, and art. This program worked well for Jim and he was assigned a tutor for algebra.

Because the commute to the UCSB campus was difficult for us, Jim only participated for one quarter. Through a friend we located a local high school senior who came to our house twice a week. At first the young man was not certain he could tutor, but it did not take long for Jim and Mayur to develop a good working relationship. Mayur's father has a Ph. D. in mathematics, and he told Mayur that algebra was the keystone to all higher math. At first Mayur could not understand what his father meant, but one day he said to me, "At last I know what my father means. Now algebra makes sense to me. I see how it works with higher mathematics because of working with Jim."

Jim had 12 hours of instruction in algebra at UCSB and approximately another 30 hours at home. Yet he covered more than a year's worth of algebra, according to the high school counselor. He went directly into geometry in high school although our district requires incoming freshmen to take algebra. He also qualified to take advanced computer programming classes on the strength of his algebra experience.

Another math experience our youngsters have is keeping records for their newspaper routes. Upon acquiring their routes, both Jim and Laurie set up bookkeeping records that they are expected to maintain. Now that income tax laws have changed, even paper carriers need to file income tax and pay social security. When we set up their bookkeeping we did not realize how advantageous this was to become. Both of them now know their way around income tax forms because they are considered self-employed by the IRS. Dale has prepared our taxes for years and taken tax courses so he was able to help Jim and Laurie with theirs.

We have lively discussions concerning history, geography, and differing cultures throughout the world. We spent a whole year studying various holiday traditions throughout the world. Susan added her own information from a used textbook she acquired from discarded library books. I had outline maps that we marked up according to the countries involved. This turned out to be a painless, fun way to learn geography. Susan again added her own twist as she loved the maps which had mileage scales.

Spelling improved with each child the more they read. We all enjoy some variety of word puzzles, and this too has helped our spelling. The youngsters prefer the word puzzle books from the supermarket magazine racks such as Penny Press and Dell. Jim's particular favorite type of puzzles are the Logic ones. Susan especially enjoys doing the cryptograms. All three enjoy crossword and word search puzzles, but I quickly noticed that they did not enjoy word puzzles intended for children as much because they were too simple and uninteresting.

I did attempt formal spelling lessons but the three of them quickly let me know they did not consider the spelling lessons a learning experience. When their uncle visited us and wanted to send postcards to friends, he asked the girls to help him with many words as he is a notoriously poor speller. I could not help wondering where they had learned to spell so well since I had not taught them, but even the difficult words he asked of them came easy to the girls.

Pat, another homeschooling friend, told me one day of an experience she had with her eight-year-old Melissa. At that time Pat was following the Calvert lessons, and one of the spelling words was "apple." On every spelling test Melissa had no trouble spelling apple. One day Pat was getting ready to do her grocery shopping and she asked Melissa to add apples to the shopping list. At the store she noticed Melissa had misspelled "apple." When Pat asked her why she never misspelled it on her tests, yet had misspelled it on the list, Melissa told her that she had only learned to get it right on the tests. Once Pat let up on spelling tests she noticed a great improvement in Melissa's spelling.

California Education Code Section 51210 and 51220 list the required branches of study. The Education Code is specific only in certain areas; in other areas only broad categories of reasonable knowledge are specified. Grades one through six requirements include: English, mathematics, science, fine arts, and fire prevention. Social science, health, public safety and accident prevention, and environmental issues are more specific.

Social science is to include 1) the early history of California, 2) a study of the role and contributions of both men and women, black Americans, American Indians, Mexican, Asians, Pacific Island people, and other ethnic groups, to the economic, political, and social development of the United States, with particular emphasis on portraying the roles of these groups in contemporary society, and 3) a foundation for understanding the wise use of natural resources.

Health needs to include the effects of alcohol, narcotics, drugs and tobacco upon the human body, and physical education.

Public safety and accident prevention courses are to include emergency first aid instruction, instruction in hemorrhage control, treatment for poisoning, resuscitation techniques, and cardio-pulmonary resuscitation when appropriate equipment is necessary. Environmental issues to be covered are the protection and conservation of resources, including the necessity for the protection of our environment.

Because my youngsters love to read I find that I have no trouble whatever meeting the state requirements as to subjects to be taught. My primary function is to oversee that the requirements are met. Our community surrounds us with opportunities to meet the state requirements. Field trips our homeschool support group plans give us a social setting in which to meet many of these requirements.

Our town gives us many opportunities to study early California history first hand. We have one of the missions that form the California mission chain, and its restoration is nearly complete. The mission's docent program puts us in the spirit of mission days. La Purissima mission was chosen as one of only six historic areas in California for our state's celebration of the U. S. Constitution bicentennial in the joint state and Post Cereals "Pop into the Past" celebration. We enjoyed special activities that day. The girls dressed up in authentic Chumash Indian attire of the mission days for the event. The docents present many historical reenactments throughout the year at the mission.

Local Chumash Indians present aspects of early California Indian life. Laurie attended a four-hour session sponsored by the local museum on Indian skills and crafts. She made thread, prepared food, formed an arrowhead, and learned to start a fire using twigs during the day's activities. Periodically the local Parks and Recreation Department sponsors walking history tours which we have attended. This is a field trip we especially enjoy as the tour guide is so interesting and likeable.

We cover health and public safety issues by reading and discussion. Again there are many community resources available to us. We go on field trips to our fire station, water treatment plant, police station, and medical facilities. The Red Cross offers high quality first aid and babysitting courses of which we take advantage. The California State Department of Education requires AIDS instruction. I prepared a course on the subject only to discover all three youngsters were already well and accurately informed on the subject because of their observation and listening skills.

We often have informal spontaneous discussions. The youngsters present me with a synopsis of what they have absorbed. What an example they give me of the truth of what happens when you trust students to learn what is important. They show me my role as teacher is to guide and provide the resources.

Sometimes I will introduce a topic only to find that they are not interested, and nothing will make them learn if they do not find a subject interesting. I get immediate feedback that is unmistakable. In a formal school setting the demands on the teacher's time and attention made it impossible for them to freely express their lack of interest.

I fight a losing battle when I try to force my children to learn something that has no immediacy or meaning to their lives. I am still having to struggle with this, as the teacher and mother in me says that I know what is best for them. Yet every time I allow them to choose their own course of learning I am amazed at how well they have chosen for themselves. I do not necessarily know what or how my children should learn something unless I make the time and effort to listen to what they are saying by word and action.

In 1985 the State of California published the Model Curriculum Standards: Grades Nine Through Twelve. The emphasis is on reading skills because they foresee that more than half of the job openings in the future will require people with high-level skills in reading, comprehension, and thinking. With the schools' preoccupation on basic skills, researchers and teachers have noticed that while students have learned basic language arts and computational skills, they do not have a sense of how to use those skills to advantage in their lives.

Model Curriculum Standards acknowledges that these reading, comprehension, and thinking skills require cooperation. Home environment is the most influential element, and they even state that home is the first school. Those children who have homes where reading is enjoyed, literacy is valued, and interest in academic achievement is shown are the students who have a head start in educational institutions. After home, libraries are listed in the report as crucial to learning. Only then do the writers of this curriculum guide list educational institutions.

The teacher-student relationship is vital to the educational experience. The active and responsible agents in education must be the students. The authors state that nothing worth learning can be taught: "Students must themselves come to grips with major texts and with the difficult tasks of thinking and composing and articulating ideas into language."

Jim was searching for a job that will pay him more than his paper route does. He learned of the page position at our local public library so filled out the application form. During the process he realized how much experience he had accumulated and how many people were glad to serve as references for him. Besides his paper route he had tutored other children in our homeschool support group. The mothers could not praise him enough and the children he worked with still think he is the greatest friend they could have.

He went for his interview. After a half hour of talking with him, the library director and her assistant took him to a cart loaded with books patrons had returned. They told him to sort the books into categories. Jim's remark when he came home was, "That part was easy because it was just like sorting my baseball cards." He has thousands of baseball cards sorted into many boxes and knows exactly where each one is and its value. Until this happened my husband had been skeptical of any redeeming value to Jim's card collection.

Somehow we adults have to trust our children's choices of learning experiences. At times Jim has resisted my attempts to guide his studies. When I let him lead the way in curriculum choices, I notice he often surprises me and delights me with the results. His choices are usually better than mine because he knows himself far better than I do.

Chapter Three

Scheduling Our
Learning Opportunities

Nine-year-old Susan just announced to me that she is think-ing of a funny poem. While I am writing this she is engrossed in her composition. From experience I know that what she is pro-ducing is far better than any assignment that I could give her. Her pattern of literary accomplishments includes periods of barrenness followed by imaginatively written creations. Her imagination is vivid and lively, but she hates to be prodded into writing. Of the three youngsters she is the most adamant about not doing something she does not want to do.

At home she has the freedom to write creatively when she is ready no matter what day or time of day it is. Nothing squash-es her writing faster than telling her that she has to write something right now. No threats are severe enough to make her write something if she does not want to.

It is Friday. Susan has finished her poem and is singing to herself as she makes patterns with her Hama beads. She is delighted that I asked her permission to share her poem with you:

The Boring Day

Today is Saturday
It is such a boring day
I have no school, no written rule
I have no friends to talk to when class ends
I have no letters to write and also nothing to sight
I have no cards to sign and no letters to align
I have no calendars, books, letters, pledges to read because
I've just been freed
I have no friends to play with

I have no books/scripts to read because
I've just been freed
Today is such a boring day
I wish it would never end.

Observing my three youngsters closely has impressed upon me two important aspects of effective, long lasting learning. I notice these same traits in myself, and I've discovered several books and articles which also cite these two principles of learning.

First: there are individual learning rhythms of advance and retreat and of exploration and consolidation of ideas which often cannot be predicted or controlled. Second: students need both time and opportunity to reflect on the barrage of information to which they are exposed.

Are we sending wrong information to our children when we insist that only activities performed at certain times of the day or on certain days of the week count as "learning?" In a nationally televised interview in August, 1988, a National Education Association official declared that only learning which takes place during designated hours of the day compatible with state programs is valid.

In September, 1988, a local television station sent a reporter to our house for an interview on homeschooling. I did not coach the girls beforehand, but they proved to me that all our students need is our trust in them. The reporter stayed an hour and a half, taping most of that time. In the small portion of the interview which was televised that night on the news, both girls clearly expressed that they thought the greatest advantage they have in their present learning experience is the freedom to study what they want when they want. Both girls declared that that is the way they learn best.

One day I was chatting with a teacher who has a combination fourth, fifth, sixth grade class by choice. She is well known in the district as a superb teacher. She told me she wished she could either work with her own boys at home or find a program similar to what I do with my children. Then she related how the previous weekend the family camped at a local lake. Her youngest son spent about five hours with an elderly fisherman discussing fish and the art of fishing. Her closing statement was that those few hours were more valuable to her son than the previous month of school work had been, yet that experience would never show up on any school records.

My youngsters have their own individual learning rhythms. At first I worried about whether I was harming them by allowing them periods of reflection. I noticed that there could be long periods of time in which nothing seemed to be accomplished. These times of daydreaming and quiet reflection last for a few hours or even for a couple of weeks. Mostly they last for only a few days. Just when I start getting concerned the youngsters will astound me with the gigantic leaps in learning that have taken place during - and because of being allowed to have - their quiet periods.

During this time they usually strongly resist my efforts to impose any new materials or instruction I may have to offer. Instead they prefer to sit outside or in their rooms just staring off into space. Sometimes they will express boredom, but not too often. On the surface they do not seem to be doing much reading while in the phase, yet when I observe unobtrusively, I do notice that their choices tend to be more in depth reading than light reading.

Laurie struggles more than Jim or Susan with math concepts. However, once she grasps them, they stay with her. Multiplication of multiple digits was particularly difficult for her. No matter how many examples Dale or I used, she could not understand why you have to offset by one digit when you perform the addition operation in multiplication of multiple digits. We set aside math and went on to other topics. In the meantime she went into a reflective mood. We were preparing for a trip to visit grandparents in Minnesota so I figured there would be plenty of time to get back to math later on. Our first night on the trip we were eating supper at our motel restaurant when Laurie started doodling on her paper napkin. Her face lit up as she proudly proclaimed, "I got it!" She showed us her napkin filled with multiplication of multiple digits accurately done. There had been no outward indication that she had even been thinking of math all those intervening weeks.

Susan usually spends days at a time in her reflective moods

sitting out in our backyard. We have a particularly interesting yard as it is tiered in three levels and each level is different. There are marvelous fruit trees to climb and birds and other interesting creatures are attracted by our four fish ponds.

Susan will sit for hours observing the teeming life out there. She was the first one to notice that we had baby goldfish swimming among the hundreds of tadpoles. Never before had baby goldfish survived so at first we did not believe her. We had to admit that she did indeed know what she was talking about when she told us she had seen the goldfish mate and lay their eggs even though no one else had.

One evening eight-year-old Susan and I were watching the evening news. She turned and solemnly told me, "I like to make up my own mind about issues. That is why I read so much and listen to the news, so I can decide for myself what is true." From there she launched into a deep discussion about the Greenhouse Effect, a subject I had no idea she knew about. Her discussion demonstrated a deep understanding of the issues involved.

Susan often writes me notes. She gave me these unsolicited writings after going through some periods of daydreaming. Both were written at the age of eight:

> The light needs electricity from the battery from both sides so you have to touch the right ones together to turn on the light. You need bare wire so the electricity can get on the wire to go inside the light tube.

After her note she demonstrated her observation using a battery, wire, and a flashlight bulb.

> My explanation of how dinosaurs died. The plants started dying and became scarce, so since there wasn't any food, the plant eaters started to die. Soon the meat eaters discovered that and started eating each other. Soon there was only one left and with no food to eat it died too. What happened to the plants was it got too cold in some

parts of the earth and too hot in others, and the
land had started to shift.

In elementary school Jim developed an intense dislike for
anything labeled science. On our trip to Minnesota we stopped
at the Grand Canyon for two days. He was fascinated by his
surroundings but did not say much. Then we went on one of the
ranger-led geology walks. Since it was late in May Jim, Laurie
and Susan were the only youngsters on the walk of about fifty
participants. The ranger asked several geology related questions. Jim, who is usually very quiet and not given to answer
questions, raised his hand for every one of them and astounded
Dale and me by answering each one confidently. We had seen no
evidence of his choosing to study geology, yet even the ranger
was impressed with his knowledge.

While our days do have a certain amount of structure to
them, nothing is rigidly adhered to if something more interesting occurs. The youngsters get up at seven, fix their own breakfasts, do their chores, and then start the day's academic activities by eight. From eight to noon we concentrate on these academic activities according to each person's needs. The afternoon
usually finds a continuation of the morning's activities as well
as doing paper routes and outside activities such as Campfire
meetings. We have an early supper followed by a quiet evening.
Friends come and go throughout the afternoon and evening.
Bedtime is around nine. Normally, each one reads for awhile
before falling asleep.

In keeping with my philosophy that learning is not confined
by time of year, week, or day, I choose to "school" year round. If
some event which we consider valuable occurs on weekends,
evenings, or holidays, it counts for their learning accomplishments.

We have an excellent theatrical group connected with a local
community college that puts on outdoor performances on summer evenings. Susan developed an interest in Shakespeare all
on her own at the age of seven when she pulled my copy of *The
Complete Works of Shakespeare* from the bookcase. When she
was nine the PCPA Theater Group announced their presentation of *The Tempest*. Susan and I read the play aloud in prepa-

ration. She could hardly contain herself because of her delight as the play unfolded before her eyes that night. In fact she recognized one of the characters before I did when he came on stage. Laurie, on the other hand, saw no necessity to reading the play before we attended the performance. I have no doubt that the next time PCPA puts on a Shakespearean play, she will be the first to read the play.

One of Laurie's greatest pleasures is to put on a play, whether it is one she has made up or not. In 1986 we attended a conference for homeschoolers. A wonderful gentleman offered to work with the youngsters while the parents attended the sessions. Herb Hammer led them in producing short skits and plays; some were spontaneous and others were prepared. At the end of the day the children displayed their talents to the attendees. This was Laurie's introduction to the joys of putting on plays, and theater got into Laurie's blood.

We attended a four-day National Coalition of Alternative Community Schools conference in Escondido, California. Once again Herb led youngsters in putting on small plays for the four hundred participants in the conference. This cemented a very special relationship between Herb and our children, especially Laurie, and since then Herb has encouraged Laurie's interest in theater. He travels two hundred miles to attend performances that Laurie produces for our local homeschooling families.

One day Laurie saw a notice that the local Civic Theater group was auditioning for *The Best Christmas Pageant Ever*. The book, by Barbara K. Robinson, is one of our favorite stories. Both Laurie and Susan auditioned and were given parts. Laurie had a small speaking part but also was understudy for one of the major parts as the director was taking no chances of illness closing the play down. From October through the ninth and final performance in mid-December, we were at the theater around twenty hours a week.

We focused our learning experience around the play. After the close of the play one mother told me that her daughter's grades at school had suffered because of her involvement in the play. So often the truly valuable learning experiences do not count because they do not take place during school hours.

A homeschooling family with four boys, living on an island in the province of Ontario, Canada, spent the night with us while traveling through California. We compared our experiences and found that each year our approach to learning varies according to the needs expressed by the children. Mikell said that her first year was structured, but loosely. As she and the boys became more confident all structure to their days and activities was removed. They are in their fourth year and each year has been different. Now the boys are asking for some structure again.

These boys love life and love learning. It was inspiring to be around them. They could as easily discuss ocean life (something they had never seen before) as they could computers. They were fascinated with the history of California as it fit in with what they had been seeing on this trip. They could figure out mileage already covered and related costs despite not having had formal math classes.

Since California requires 180 days of school, I use a year round configuration. This means nine weeks of class and four weeks of break in record keeping each quarter. Just as many learning activities occur during the four week break as during the time of the nine week quarters. The main difference is that I am not keeping as detailed records of these experiences.

Even on days when they are sick, the children continue learning according to the energy available. While they were in school, I noticed that sick days were "do nothing" days. Now sick days are quiet activity days in which learning continues.

Each quarter I single out two or three major areas we will concentrate on. In this way I am assured that we are covering all the state requirements. At the same time I am exposing the youngsters to topics they might not otherwise have chosen or known about. Sometimes these topics are not enthusiastically received, but that is all right with me as I know that at least I have introduced them, and it is up to the youngsters to explore further if and when they choose.

One quarter we went into detail on the human body using the Invisible Man and Invisible Woman models, district textbooks, Dover anatomy books, and various newspaper and magazine articles. Each youngster reacted differently as I presented the material. That same quarter we worked on typing skills. This they found boring but I insisted that they work on it at least for the quarter as I consider typing skills important. Our third area of concentration was organizing a state-wide homeschool day with day-long meetings and workshops. The children each contributed to the success of that day. Those were our areas of concentration for that quarter, but reading, communication, and computational skills were not neglected.

Another quarter we used the TOPS science unit on magnetism while at another time we used the same science series on pendulums. Both of these units were popular, and the youngsters enjoyed all the hands-on activities provided. Susan went on from the magnetism unit to an interest in electronics, so we bought the Radio Shack Electronic Project Kit with 160 activities for her. She goes in spurts of interest. The kit will sit on the shelf for months, then she will use it extensively, writing up the results of her experiments in the book provided.

In our study of the contributions many different cultures have made to our American way of life, we devoted a quarter to using the Good Apple Activity Book entitled *Americans, Too!* This challenging book promotes understanding of American minorities through research-related activities. Since the girls avidly read the newspaper, I find that we get into some stimulating discussions on related topics.

During 1987 we devoted three quarters to studying American History and the U.S. Constitution as part of the Constitutional Bicentennial celebration. Because Jim had won the trip to Washington, D.C. in 1985, we could build on what we had seen during that trip. Since the youngsters were personally involved, they were much more interested. All three participated in essay and poster contests about the Constitution that year. Susan won an award from *Gifted Children Monthly* for her poster.

The book that Susan won for her poster is *Kids' America* by Steven Caney. This book is now a family favorite and a source of many hours of activities. Susan constantly refers to it. Among other things it contains articles on magic, weather forecasting, sign language, genealogy, frog jumping, and many more adventures. Along with activities you find beloved tales and legends.

During a contest sponsored by our public library, Laurie won several books for drawing a poster on the value of reading (within two days she had read the books). Her age group had the largest number of contributions so she was particularly pleased with herself.

My youngsters do not like using workbooks. All three youngsters have said that when in school they primarily wanted to get done with the workbook pages and did not really learn the topic at hand. They said that many times classmates would just hurry through the pages not caring about correct answers. I had corrected workbook pages for Laurie's second grade teacher and had noticed that myself. Sometimes, Laurie told me, she did her work correctly but still did not understand why she was doing it. In one of her classes workbooks were used both as a form of busywork and as punishment.

Susan did not have excessive workbook experience in school. But her Sunday school teacher started assigning workbook pages as homework. To the teacher's consternation parents came to her asking her not to do this as their youngsters were being swamped with workbook activities at school. I had noticed Susan balking at her assignments even though she loves her Sunday school teacher. Susan complained that she did not like doing these workbook pages. As soon as the teacher let up on workbook pages Susan and her class settled down happily.

When I find an especially attractive and well-done workbook I will try it. We are selective in which pages and which activities we do in the workbook and I am careful to give immediate feedback on pages done. I do have several workbooks just lying around which I thought were great, but the youngsters vigorously disagreed with me. When they themselves choose one, however, I notice that the workbook is almost always well used.

I find it interesting that in one of the supplementary materials catalogs the publisher felt it necessary to devote nine pages to justifying the value of workbooks. There is no substitute for judicial use of workbooks. Used creatively, workbooks can motivate youngsters. But research shows and people experienced with working with children know that you learn to read by reading and to write by writing, not by filling in blanks.

When I use workbooks I have found that they are most effective if you keep several things in mind. Use workbooks that reinforce concepts which you have already introduced. Be certain that students understand what they are to do. Select appropriate workbook pages related to your topic and matched to the student's abilities. Periodically discuss with students how they arrived at their answers. They can surprise you with their depth of thinking! This also gives you an opportunity to discover any misunderstanding of the material. Provide opportunity for cooperative learning with their peers. Use the workbook as a chance to develop related topics or activities.

When our family becomes engrossed with a particular project we continue with it unless something else demands our immediate attention. Our schedule has to be quite flexible in order to allow for this. Sometimes we work on an joint project, but more often projects are individual.

I do not find that working with three different ages at the same time has presented much difficulty. On their cooperative days, they help each other with projects or when one is having difficulty understanding something, the others help. On their uncooperative days, nothing would help anyway. They are constantly having to adjust their own needs to the needs of someone else, and this of itself is an invaluable lesson on life. The more refined their basic skills become, the more independently they learn. All I need to do is stand aside and be ready to provide necessary resources.

Television plays its part in our learning. There are some worthwhile programs. We do limit the amount of time that television is on and many days we do not use it at all. We all like watching three excellent programs on public television. *Square One* clarifies math concepts. Laurie had no problem understanding prime numbers after watching their presentation. For science we watch *Newton's Apple* and *3-2-1 Contact.*

Another fascinating science program, *Mr. Wizard's World,* is only on cable television. Some of the educational programs produced for the school system on public television have been very useful to us. Jim learned useful art techniques from some of the programs on how to draw. Susan likes to watch the wild animal programs on public television and on cable television's Discovery Channel.

It is an advantage to have a VCR. Often we tape a program to watch at a more convenient time. One winter *In The Attic,*

Miep's story of how she hid Anne Frank and her family during World War II, was on late in the evening. We taped it and watched it at an appropriate time as we were studying the effects of war. With a look of disbelief and tears close to falling, Laurie asked me, "Mom, is this a true story? Did people really treat other people like that?"

During the October, 1987 Los Angeles earthquake, we stayed by our television listening to seismologists explain earthquakes and viewing the damage an earthquake can cause. California schools are required to give instruction in earthquake safety. My girls had been given the proper instruction each year, but nothing is more impressive than to have the event occur close to home (we did not feel it) and to see the aftermath graphically presented. We all learned new facts that morning. Laurie was so fascinated that she ordered more earthquake materials to study.

We followed the Presidential primaries, campaign, and election closely using television, newspapers, and a marvelous poster from *Weekly Reader* on which we recorded the results of each primary. As each candidate dropped out of the race, he was crossed off our chart. Even Susan was interested in following the progress of the campaign.

Games are a rich source of learning materials. Part of our interest in the Presidential election was heightened by playing *Hail to the Chief*, produced by Aristoplay. The faces and some facts about each of our Presidents are easier to remember because we play this game. When we play no one loses points for not knowing the answer as long as he or she repeats the answer back. That way mom is not embarrassed because she forgot (or worse yet, did not know) the answer, and the youngsters do not feel bad because they don't know the answer. Since the Presidents are in sequence on the playing board it is simple to get a cohesive feeling for our country's rich history. The map of the states with their capitals which you travel on the campaign trail impresses you with the vastness of the west and the denseness of the population on the east coast.

We have found that the games produced by Aristoplay are of exceptional quality and value. *Hail to the Chief* was the first one I bought. Since then we have purchased several more and I have not been disappointed in any of them. *Made for Trade* acquaints you with early American colonial life as you barter and trade on your journey through town. *Where in the World?* was an instant success with the family as we learn world geography painlessly. You are able to play this game in many different ways by focusing on populations, capitals, major religions, languages, exports, imports, or monetary units. *By Jove* pits us mortals against the Roman and Greek Gods as we try to snatch the Golden Fleece and maneuver the Labyrinth. *Music Maestro* introduced us to old as well as modern musical instruments, and *Art Deck* increases our awareness of master painters.

We even found a game that teaches nutrition. *Super Sandwich*, produced by Teaching Concepts, Inc., is based on planning well balanced dietary habits. You must purchase foods that meet your recommended Dietary Allowance of protein, calcium, iron, Vitamin A, Vitamin B-complex and Vitamin C and yet not exceed the calorie allowance. Trips to the "gym" are often necessary during the game. The girls enjoy this game, and I have noticed that their knowledge of nutrition has changed as a result of playing it.

An old favorite game of mine from childhood was *Authors*. I was not certain how the youngsters would react, but could not resist purchasing it too. It is our most frequently played game. They especially love to ask for a book we have read and they look for opportunities to read those with which they are not familiar. As a child I had to memorize *The Charge of the Light Brigade* by Tennyson. Because this poem is listed on the Authors cards, we read it. Susan now goes around the house reciting it for the sheer joy of hearing the words roll off her tongue.

Games play an important part in our learning experiences. We aim to keep competition at a minimum most of the time. This has worked well as no one is hesitant to play because they might not know the answers. At times something comes up in a game that stimulates exploration of the subject in greater depth.

Games of strategy also have their place in our education. Susan and I often play *Craze*, a challenging math game that includes an element of luck to make it more interesting. You use any possible math operation with the numbers shown on the three dice you have tossed, with the object of being the first to cross off a given square on the grid. There is a rather complex method of computing your score, but Susan quickly mastered that part.

There are so many games from which to choose. I generally make my choices after reading about the games in a review or a catalog which provides greater description. Recommendation from people whose opinion I trust is another determinant. There are some companies that you know from experience provide quality items. *The Presents For The Promising* catalog from *Gifted Children Magazine* is a good source of information about games (second edition update: *Gifted Children Magazine* is no longer published, and the *Presents for the Promising* catalog is no longer available). A local educational toy store has also been an invaluable resource for me as they will let me look at the game before purchase.

We use these games as an integral part of our flexible schedule. Learning takes place during these games. Sometimes there is a noticeable awareness of learning occurring right before my eyes. Most of the time, however, I discover much later how much knowledge they gained in the process of playing a certain game. Why can't learning be fun as well as work?

Marco Meirovitz, author, educator, and inventor of the game *Mastermind*, wrote an article in *Gifted Children Monthly* titled, "What's in a Game?" He says few people realize the full potential of games to develop and strengthen thinking skills. He claims that games prepare us to face school, home, and work situations more easily. According to him, perceptive educators realize that education must provide students with tools for effective thinking, not just more knowledge. Games are the simplest and most pleasurable ways to accomplish this.

Skills learning in game playing include problem solving, creative thinking, memory, visualization, and communication. Other benefits to game playing are coordinating body movements with thinking (psychomotic activity), planning (strategy), discovering rules (inductive logic), and using information (deductive logic).

Game playing is a practical tool for improving thinking skills because students *want* to play and therefore will willingly practice. This practice does not become boring because each time the game is played it is different. Having fun provides motivation for learning.

Games reflect life because all the basic skills can be used such as memory, strategy, logic, creativity, communication, and problem solving, and these thinking skills are utilized in a responsive, dynamic environment. Games build self-confidence as they can be played at different levels according to the participants' abilities. The social process (learning to communicate, cooperate, compete in real life situations) promotes the use of imagination and trying out of new roles. It is possible to develop personality and expand life experiences through games.

When I was reading Meirovitz' article, I thought immediately of Laurie's favorite game, *Clue*. He compares a doctor diagnosing a patient's illness to the process required in many games. The doctor has to eliminate possibilities by testing (asking questions), getting more information, eliminating groups of illnesses, and proceeding through other tests until he determines the illness. The doctor with the best way of grouping possibilities and eliminating them finds the fastest solution. He adds that the same is true for many other professions: car mechanics, appliance repairmen, scientists, chemists, etc. Each must obtain information and find an effective way to keep track of that information. Games provide practice in these skills.

Jim learned to play the bell lyre while in middle school. He had never played a musical instrument before. This class proved to be the one class in middle school that he enjoyed. Between September and the following February he learned the basics of reading music. The girls taught themselves to read music (my own music background is sparse so I could not assist them). We have an electronic keyboard, some recorders, the bell lyre, and a xylophone which they use.

Most of our art activities center on crafts. Susan is teaching herself the art of rug braiding and is learning how to use the sewing machine as a result. Laurie taught herself how to knit and crochet and has recently taken up counted cross-stitch. And we all do needlepoint, including Jim.

An excellent resource for many different art activities which we use is *KidsArt News*. Kim Solga's publication is a bargain that can't be beat. She introduces readers to a wide range of art activities and appreciation, including the fine arts. Her explanations on how to do a project are clear and concise. Susan constantly refers to back issues for ideas when she is ready for a new activity.

Learning is a highly individual matter. It is important to provide the opportunities for learning to occur and be nurtured. With our flexible schedule we strive to enhance learning experiences according to the individual needs of each of our children. When I schedule learning activities spontaneity suffers.

There is so much information available today that was not available twenty years ago. What was taught in science and technology in the fifties is now obsolete, and this period of time has been labelled as the age of the information explosion. With diligent searching I do locate some workbooks that keep us up to date on information. But I find it necessary to use them only when my youngsters regard them as useful.

We prefer to teach our children how to research answers in order to have the latest information. And then we show them how to be able to update that information continually. We prefer to teach them to think for themselves rather than parrot back information that someone else deems important. By allowing Jim, Laurie, and Susan time to reflect on this barrage of information to which they are exposed, I believe their education will have a firm foundation on which to build throughout their lives.

Our youngsters have demonstrated to us that there are learning rhythms which involve advancing in knowledge and then retreating to quietly consider the knowledge gained. This consolidation of assimilated knowledge cannot be predicted or controlled. Every time I have interfered with this rhythm I have broken a fragile phase in their learning. It is not always easy for me to step back to allow the periods of quiet reflection to do their work.

Workbooks sometimes give me a false sense of security until I receive feedback from my youngsters as to a particular workbook's value to them. I can offer information but I cannot force my children to be receptive to that information. People are uncomfortable when they are in a situation where they feel they have no control at all. Being uncomfortable is not conducive to learning. Just because I am an adult does not mean I know what is best for Jim, Laurie, and Susan.

Students rebel, even though they may not show it outwardly, when they do not feel control over a learning situation. This is why I offer my children learning opportunities and then try something else when I meet with resistance in them. As soon as I hear groans from them when I bring out a particular work-book, I know without a shadow of a doubt that use of that work-book will produce questionable results. If the written work is sloppily done, results are unmistakable. The work was done only because I said they HAD to do it. Add a few tears and I'm really in trouble!

We have had success with a few workbooks. In most cases one of the youngsters chose it. Very few times has one I have chosen been received enthusiastically. I am convinced that the success of a workbook depends on the interest of the student. Telling them to do it because "it is for your own good" just does not work in my family. And I am glad of it!

Chapter Four

Trusting Our Children to Lead the Way

Susan often picks up a book to read on a subject in which I have had no clue she has any interest. At the age of seven she chose some high school books on electricity. An experiment in one of the books caught her eye. Following the directions, and with her father's assistance in locating the proper materials, she constructed her own question/answer board that lights up a bulb when you pick the correct answer (a low-cost version of *Questron*). She amazed us with what doing that one project taught her. The next morning she proceeded to tell me why our family room light would come on when we flipped the switch. We had never discussed this, she just figured it out from what happened in her project.

Trusting our children to lead the way depends greatly upon recognition of two basic principles. The first one is that the amount a person can learn at a given moment depends on how she feels about her ability to do the work. The second one is that interest-initiated learning allows the student to utilize her abilities in the optimal manner. The old saying, "You can lead a horse to water, but you can't make him drink," expresses the futility of forcing a student to learn something when she does not think she can succeed and/or she is just not interested in the topic.

My husband is an electrical engineer. Yet whenever he volunteers information about electricity to Susan, she sets her face and no amount of cajoling will induce her to listen. She must freely come to him for the information she seeks. She prefers to search out her own answers in her own way. Of our three youngsters, she is the one most likely to adamantly refuse to proceed unless she feels confident of success and the one who prefers to find her own answers without assistance.

One May we planned to drive to Minnesota to visit grandparents. In March I gave each child a map to plot out the route we'd take. All I specified was that it had to be completed in three weeks, at least five days were to be at their grandparents', and we would travel no more than 450 miles in a given day. Even Dale and I plotted out our plans. Then we compared our maps to come up with a final itinerary.

Once the route was settled upon, each child chose which state tourism office to write for further information. They also wrote to the chambers of commerce in selected cities for motel information. We studied information from the American Automobile Association. Beautiful tourism materials arrived and as they did we started noticing things of historical interest, such as the wagon trails through Nebraska and Wyoming.

With tourism materials in hand we decided where to concentrate our time during this trip. Going to Minnesota, we spent extra time at the Grand Canyon and in the Colorado Rockies. Leaving Minnesota, we stayed five days in the Rapid City area of South Dakota visiting the Badlands, viewing Mount Rushmore and the Crazy Horse Memorial, and exploring the depths of nearby caves.

Because the children were actively involved in the planning, we had a delightful trip. We did not try to see and do everything, so that we could enjoy ourselves. There will be other opportunities to see and do what we missed the first time if it is important enough to us.

Two years after the trip they still mention things learned on that trip. What better way to grasp the enormity of a buffalo than to have to stop the car so one can amble across the road right in front of you in Wind Cave National Park? Going along the Platte River for so many miles we tried to imagine the wagon trains going westward without the benefit of freeways. Visiting Crazy Horse Memorial sparked more than a passing interest in the plight of our American Indians.

The ever changing scenery changed their concept of our American desert through California and Arizona. Finally, leaving relatives in Carson City, Nevada, we travelled Highway 88 over Kit Carson Pass. Jim marvelled, "Mom, I had no idea California had scenery as spectacular as the Rockies."

(Something I took for granted as I have often been to the Sierra Nevada and suddenly realized our youngsters hadn't.)

When Jim won the essay contest that took the family to Washington, D.C., I remember one of the other winners, a high school senior. We were almost done with a tour of the White House when he stood looking in awe at one of the many paintings decorating the White House. He commented, "These are *real* paintings! I've seen them so many times in my history and American Government text books, but I never realized they were anything more than a picture in a book." The next day as we were finishing up our last tour as a group, this young man told me that now U. S. history made sense to him. It really happened. He was standing where it happened. From then on it would mean so much more to him.

Ever since that trip four years ago, Jim and Laurie watch the news with interest when scenes of places they visited on that trip are shown. Susan does not remember as much, although she does remember being in the Washington Monument. Just knowing that she was in those historical places is important to her though. United States history is more interesting because of this trip.

Our youngsters read the newspaper daily. Jim usually reads it while rolling his papers for delivery. They each have their favorite parts and all agree on the comics page. Laurie even wrote a letter of protest when they dropped the cartoon, *Marmaduke*. (I knew nothing about that letter until it appeared in the "Letters to the Editor" along with an apology from the paper with a promise to reinstate *Marmaduke* due to popular outcry.) But sometime during the month they have read each section of the paper.

According to the varying interests of the family, we subscribe to several different magazines. The periodicals change as our interests change. Jim reads *Sports Illustrated* practically from cover to cover. If he could afford to he would subscribe to *The Wall Street Journal* and *USA Today*. Laurie loves *Kid City* (which used to be called *Electric Company*). Susan's favorite is *Ranger Rick*.

Being avid comparison shoppers all three kids love *Zillions*. We also have several computer magazines around. There are many more we like to read, but there are only so many hours a day and so much money available for subscriptions.

The universal favorite magazine in our family is *Reader's Digest*. By far, *Reader's Digest* has stimulated the most learning experiences. One day Susan started discussing viruses, what they are, what they do, what scientists know about them. At first I was puzzled as to where she had come upon that information.

Then she told me she had been in her room reading a back issue of *Reader's Digest*. There is such a broad variety of topics covered in this magazine. The youngsters are exposed to many different subjects while reading it.

The "Spin Off" pages in *Gifted Children Monthly* provide many opportunities for interesting activities. The games and puzzles intrigue the children. Jim has participated in their surveys and obtained several pen pals. Susan won a book and had her Constitutional Bicentennial poster published in "Spin Off." Laurie has been chosen as a Student Advisor for a year because of an essay she wrote.

Dale is an amateur radio operator and involved in local emergency preparedness. His interest in ham radio was sparked as a young teenager and has been a lifelong source of enjoyment for him. For a while Jim showed some interest in being a radio operator also, but that interest has died down. While Dale would love to share his interest with the youngsters, he also recognizes that, at least for now, none of them are likely to take up this hobby.

I have edited many different newsletters. The youngsters have grown up watching me do this and assisting me with the newsletters. How much this has influenced Laurie I do not know as she claims that editing her own newsletter was entirely her own idea.

She started her own newsletter, *Monthly Star,* two years ago and has kept it going despite not receiving the input from other young writers that she expected. In addition, she and her friends Missy and Sabrina co-edited a joint effort called *Kids Monthly.* I do not enter into any part of the editing unless I'm specifically asked. At first I offered suggestions but was told in no uncertain terms that this was her project and when she wanted help, she'd ask for it.

Jim and Susan also tried their hand at editing their own newsletters. Susan's abiding interest is science so she entitled hers *Sleepover Science*. Jim's reflected his interest in baseball. Their endeavors only lasted for two issues but they received a positive reaction from their readers.

In my efforts to encourage their writing skills through actual writing exercises, I quickly learned that unless it is a project in which they have a special interest my urgings are usually ignored. Sometimes they give an outright refusal to participate in a project. Many times they will halfheartedly go along with my project, and it is obvious that they are only doing it to please me. Yet when I least expect it they can produce a high quality piece of writing even if I am in a state of despair of their ever writing anything I consider worthwhile. It comes down to a definition of "worthwhile." Is it worthwhile to me or to them? If it is worthwhile to them they produce a written piece that many times is quite impressive. This often occurs after a lengthy period of writing barrenness.

Herb Hammer introduced Jim, Laurie, and Susan to an interactive public radio program for youngsters called *Kids America*. Since we could not receive the program on our public radio station, he taped the 90 minute program each weekday for us. The live program originated in New York. Youngsters could use an 800 number to call in live responses to the program.

Even though we listened to the program on a delayed basis, Jim and Laurie did call and were on the program several times. Jim introduced the song of the week on his birthday on the air. Laurie stumped the show's spelling wiz and won a book for her efforts. She also received a book from Dr. Book when she suggested an interesting book to listeners. Both youngsters were delighted to hear themselves on the radio thanks to Herb taping the show. They would have participated in other segments of the program such as the geography treasure hunts if we were able to listen to the program live.

Laurie participated in their joint project with Kodak and the publishers of the book Christmas in America. Kodak provided two rolls of 36 exposure 135 film, and the youngsters took pictures of Christmas activities to submit. The publishers selected some of the pictures for inclusion in their book. Laurie learned that when you commit to a project you see it to the end even when the project becomes tedious. She found having to record the event and identifying all the participants in each picture tiresome by the time she was shooting her second roll of film.

Due to lack of adequate funding for *Kids America,* the program is no longer broadcast. But Jim and Laurie worked up a petition to our local public radio station in an effort to save the program. They also wrote letters to various homeschool newsletters and magazines encouraging families to join their effort to save the program. This written project was all of their own doing and I was impressed with their efforts. It had meaning to them, and they produced well-thought-out and grammatically superb letters without much assistance from me.

One nice spring day we noticed electric company linemen changing the configuration of the poles on the hill above us. We knew about the red tail hawk nest on the pole closest to us. Laurie and I watched fascinated while five men carefully brought down the nest with two chicks and three eggs. They built a new platform for the nest about halfway up the pole, then returned the nest to the pole. Acoustics were excellent so we heard everything the men said even though the distance from us was great. In their concern for the nesting parents, the linemen left the site for five hours. Laurie and I rejoiced as the parents circled and finally landed on their new nesting site.

Later in the day Laurie sat down at the typewriter and wrote a report on what we had witnessed. I had no idea at the time what she was typing. She then submitted her story to *Home Education Magazine* and was thrilled when they published it. Had I told her to sit down and write this report, I know without any doubt that she would have resisted. Even if she had done it to please me, I do not think it would have been as well written.

One time Laurie did ask me, in fact begged me, to assign a special report to her about some aspect of American history. We came up with a mutually acceptable topic but that was as far as the report went. She had lost interest in the subject. I could have held her to the report, but it would have become a struggle and no educational advantage would have been attained.

Another time we were doing a joint study of American Indian tribes using a specifically marked U. S. map. Laurie asked me for a blank U. S. map as she wanted to see if she could still identify all the states. Two of the New England states gave her a problem but she found her way using a road atlas. Finding her own answers gave her a sense of satisfaction and helped impress upon her the relationship of our various states.

For this reason I have numerous blank maps of every region of the world which the youngsters are free to use when and how they please. During the Olympics these maps were used almost daily. Susan's favorite maps are those with mileage distances as she loves to calculate distances. At first I could only locate blank maps to copy on spirit duplicators (we had a friend with one available so that was no real problem). We no longer have that resource, but in the meantime I found some excellent blackline maps in the Good Year Education series book, *The Map Corner*, published by Scott, Foresman and Company.

Home Education Magazine and *Growing Without Schooling* contain many first hand stories about how trusting children to learn what is needed when it is needed is rewarded by eagerness to learn even more all the time. Repeatedly you read of incidents that the amount learned was related to how the student felt about her ability to accomplish the work. When the parents allowed the student to use her abilities according to her interests, she learned more and retained this knowledge. *Home Education Magazine* compiled some of these stories in their excellent book, *The Homeschool Reader*.

David and Micki Colfax are well known as parents of the outstanding scholars Grant and Drew. They began homeschooling because they were concerned that their boys would lose a love for learning and exploration. In their book, *Homeschooling for Excellence*, they emphasize the necessity of providing our youngsters with the tools for learning and then letting the student take control of the direction of learning.

John Holt wrote several books in which he constantly emphasized the necessity of trusting our children to choose wisely. He claimed that if we give a student the opportunity, she will make better sense of the world than if she is constantly told what is best for her.

One summer day as I was hanging clothes on the line Susan was nearby studying the local crawling creatures. She dearly loves to be outdoors observing nature closely. She was holding a science textbook in her hands. Looking up at me she said, "I like to learn by teaching myself. I don't like someone else to teach me because I learn better by teaching myself."

Being in a classroom frustrated her because she never felt she had enough time to pursue her studies in her own way and often had to waste time waiting for her classmates to finish up a project so she could go on. She told my husband and me, "School puts too much pressure on me. It makes me feel hot all over and uncomfortable. At school I can't learn what I want to when I want to."

Often Susan will play with her dolls and have lively conversations with them. After one particularly lengthy session during which I overheard her making many remarks about geography, she looked over at me and explained that this is her favorite way to learn something. Acting it out with her dolls impresses it on her mind. She also hastened to add that she liked to have her homeschool friends over for the same reason. With her friends she is able to have interactive learning.

Shortly after I had started homeschooling, I wrote to a friend:

> At first I was puzzled by "motivation" battles I had with Jim and Laurie which always resolved themselves in surprising ways. After one such incident I really had doubts about what was happening to Jim and Laurie. But the last couple of days they have really astounded me with their activities. Jim has been willingly working in his algebra book and Laurie picked up a couple of math booklets I found at the textbook center but did not think either one would be that interested in. She found several projects which she became engrossed in. One was making geometrical shapes and boxes out of paper. Both of them conducted separate crystal garden experiments without any prompting from me yesterday.

With the passage of time this anxiety has eased. I see how many ways there are to indicate a growth in learning. My file cabinet is filled with examples of their creativity and projects. I realize I had unrealistic expectations. My youngsters are ordinary youngsters, yet I was expecting extraordinary feats. When we are relaxed, learning abounds, but when I am anxious about progress very little is accomplished. The biggest lesson has been to accept each child for who she is and myself as I am. Trust is not static. It changes with circumstances so I must also change and allow my students to change. What worked yesterday will not necessarily work today.

There certainly are days when I question what is taking place. While the youngsters are doing very well, I am the one feeling pressured to get them to perform some externally measurable school work. There is that nagging worry about someone demanding to see proof acceptable to them that learning is taking place. I personally see invaluable learning occurring but still worry that it is acceptable to "others," whoever "they" are.

My children need to know that I have confidence in them in their quest for knowledge. In my own efforts to learn to use a computer I quickly retreat whenever I lack confidence in myself. I am influenced by what I perceive others think of me. I have to remind myself that it is okay to feel uncertain of myself. I am the one who has to choose to rise above my current level of ability.

My years of experience with life spans many more years than those of my children. I know from experience that the struggle to master the computer is worthwhile. I consider it my responsibility to inspire similar confidence in my children so that they, too, can expand their horizons.

I will not inspire this confidence if I am their judge and their manipulator. I want to encourage their efforts in problem solving and thinking skills. This includes nurturing their interests and respecting their capability to decide what is of importance to them. They do not need to compare themselves to others. First I want to instill in them a feeling of competence and self-worth.

A remedial reading teacher, Ellen Brandoff Matter, wrote an article in *Learning 88* describing her experience with a wood working class offered at an adult night school. She wanted to make a six-foot cabinet that would fit in her dining room. It was an ambitious undertaking for a beginner. During the construction phase she had to overcome many frustrations and misunderstandings as to how to proceed. The finished product was far from perfect but she was proud of her accomplishment. Because of this experience she began to appreciate what her students face on a daily basis as they are asked to learn new skills. Her comment was, "By becoming a student again, I got a chance to walk in my students' shoes—and ended up with blisters."

As I read her article I mentally compared my experiences in learning how to use this computer and word processing program to how my children learn. At first I doubted I could ever learn to use the computer. It seemed so complicated. I could hardly understand the manuals, and when I asked questions about the computer the answers I received sounded like they were in a foreign language. The demonstration disks did not help me that much as I preferred to start out on a real project.

The books, manuals and instructors I questioned assumed I knew more than I did. For instance, it took me many months to figure out why I could not get my sequential page numbers to print. In the meantime I avoided using page numbers or else used the typewriter to put them in place. This was tedious. One day, quite by accident, I happened to read one vital sentence buried in a place that I did not expect to find it. I had been putting the correct codes in but was also unknowingly cancelling out the codes by one simple keystroke.

We do our youngsters a disservice by introducing them to grades and testing before they are ready. Letter grades on the elementary level are irrelevant and can be detrimental. This is the time to concentrate on learning the basic skills and laying a firm foundation for the future. With sadness I watched some youngsters fall behind in the first grade when I was a classroom volunteer and had the time to closely observe what was taking place. As I followed their progress, several of them became used to receiving low grades and could not catch up to their classmates later on.

Seeing no educational value in giving grades on work accomplished, I do not grade my youngsters. They and I know without any doubt how they are performing. When they experience a problem we work it out. Sometimes it means dropping a project temporarily until that child is ready to proceed. Other times it is apparent the topic was inappropriate for that particular child. I am not placed in the position of a judge and they are not being judged by anyone other than themselves.

What real purpose do letter grades serve? My grades in high school have had little influence on my lifetime activities. Going to several of my high school reunions I noticed that academic success was not recognized. My classmates who excelled in sports or social skills were given recognition during the festivities.

During my studies at junior college I participated in an interesting experiment. Students were expected to do their best but were not told what their final grades were. I felt freer to pursue my interests in my studies without worrying about my grades. Only when I enrolled in the University of San Francisco three years later did I learn of my final grades, which were right where I expected them to be.

This experiment influences me today. I don't grade my youngsters' work unless it is required by an outside agency. When it is necessary, I point out to my youngsters that this is my assessment of their work but they know themselves better than anyone else can, including their mother.

Testing is another matter that requires consideration. Studies show it can be detrimental. What positive value does testing have? Standardized tests do not measure what they claim to measure. They are biased and have long term negative effects on students, especially creative thinkers, minorities, women, and anyone who does not possess the same values or experiences as the testmakers.

Standardized tests are a vote of "no confidence" in the learner. If you are confident that a student knows something, you do not need to test her. She wants to please adults so she takes the tests, then considers herself a failure despite the wrongness of the test for her. Standardized tests interfere with learning by fostering the use of a standardized curriculum or else requiring that hours be spent preparing for and taking these tests.

My youngsters took many standardized tests during their

years in public school. I assisted in administering tests several times so can appreciate the amount of time during the school year devoted to taking these tests that could be more productively spent on interesting projects. Conditions for the testing are not always ideal, either. I've administered some of the tests in a crowded janitor's equipment room and also in the classroom where someone was constantly coming to the door or the intercom was active. James R. Delisle, Ph. D., answered a parent's question on standardized tests and test anxiety in *Gifted Children Monthly* by commenting that all too often these tests are administered under conditions that cause anxiety in even the most relaxed student, yet we expect optimal performance.

Susan was in a school that was part of the Chapter One program to offer slower students personal remedial help. We do not know what happened the day she took the test with all her kindergarten classmates, but the results showed she was in great need of remedial attention. This is a child who excels academically. It turned out to her advantage as she was entitled to independent study projects very much to her liking, but in another school where I also volunteered she would have come away feeling incompetent.

One time I obtained copies of standardized tests. When I showed them to Jim, Laurie, and Susan they let out a collective groan and expressed strong distaste. At my insistence, they did consent to taking them. When we went through the results I found that they were right where I observed from their work that they would be in each academic area. What was particularly fascinating was discussing their reasons for choosing "wrong" answers. In each case they could come up with a valid reason for choosing the answer they did. Their reasons, in my opinion, were more valid than the "right" answers.

I encourage every parent unacquainted with standardized tests to obtain copies of them. This removes the mystery that surrounds testing for parents unacquainted with the content of these tests. Standardized testing has become a fact of life. Until the movement to reduce the status of testing strengthens, it is important for us to become more aware of the facts about standardized testing.

Testing is an effective means of control. If a student is to perform well on a standardized test, the curriculum needs to be geared to the tests. This assumes that a school choses a standardized test and then chooses a curriculum that prepares the student to pass it. The student's interests, aptitudes, abilities, and needs are not taken into account. The goal of learning thus becomes to pass the test, not to acquire lifelong skills and a love for learning.

The Friends of Education from the state of West Virginia announced the results of their survey on standardized testing in newspapers throughout the nation in November, 1987. *Gifted Children Monthly* wrote a review of the article from *The New York Times*. Their finding was that no state is below the average at the elementary level in the six major nationally normed commercially available tests.

How could that be since "average" assumes that someone has to be below and someone has to be above the average, they asked. These 1987 students were compared to out of date norms. Schools were teaching to the test by tailoring curriculum to increase test scores. The Friends of Education group warned that in order to find the time to teach to the test, you have to take away time from enrichment activities, independent projects, and accelerated learning.

Bruce McGill, president of Educational Records Bureau, a Wellesley, Massachusetts-based testing organization used by many top private and public college preparatory schools, praises the Friends of Education analysis and adds another reason for the unrealistically high test results. He states that the tests are geared for all students and all kinds of schools therefore the tests don't have enough difficult questions to challenge 25 to 30% of the students taking the tests.

The reviewer noted that several publishers of the tests were reluctant to revise the tests because of the great expense involved. It would require hours of additional testing of hundreds of thousands of students. Because of the concerns raised by the Friends of Education, the publishers of the Iowa Test, the California Test of Basic Skills, and the California Achievement Test are in the process of updating their norms. The other tests involved in the Friends study are the Stanford Achievement

Test, the Metropolitan Achievement Test, and the Science Research Achievement Test.

Gifted Children Monthly also reviewed *Beyond Standardized Tests: Admission Alternatives That Work,* a publication from the National Center for Fair and Open Testing (FairTest). They provided a list of colleges and graduate schools dropping or de-emphasizing standard admission exams. The reasons given for dropping the exams were unfair biases against women and minorities, distortions due to pre-test coaching, and the impact of tests on curriculum and self-esteem. Among those dropping the exams were Harvard Business School, Johns Hopkins Medical School, and the Massachusetts Institute of Technology.

James Alvino, editor of *Gifted Children Monthly,* states that the Educational Testing Service developed the SAT to measure *developed* abilities rather than innate abilities of high school students. This was to be a tool to predict the student's success in her freshman year of college. The test may measure what he labels "school house smarts" but fails to measure any creative or practical abilities needed for success in life.

There are several books about the harmful effects testing can have upon students. One of these that I have read is *None of the Above: Behind the Myth of Scholastic Aptitude,* by David Owen. The aim of this book is to debunk the mythology surrounding standardized testing. Owen claims that we defer to the tests because we think the tests see what we cannot. We have ascribed power to testing that is out of proportion to the actual content. This allows the sense of insecurity to overcome the test takers. We tend to be better at concocting excuses for giving tests than we are at making sense of the results of the tests. Most of the book is about the SAT, but it does cover test making and test taking in general. Often we hear American children compared to Japanese children. David Owen addresses that issue by showing how testing determines the Japanese educational fate without instilling a lifelong love for learning.

Frank Smith wrote in *Insult to Intelligence* that systematic testing has its roots in Britain during the early years of this century. He claims it was closely linked with the influential eugenics movement seeking to breed an intellectual elite. Cyril Burt, a psychology professor knighted for his service as a designer of mental and scholastic tests, was convinced that the intelligence his tests measured was inherited. Eventually he was discredited when it was learned he had faked his data, but not before the damage was done.

Psychology gained its hold over education through the testing movement. Initially psychologists needed educational data for their own research, but gradually test results were used to make educational decisions. Until recently educational research has been almost entirely a matter of testing children, but some researchers are now probing the classroom environment and the behavior of teachers as well. Standardized tests promise to lead to improvement in educational practices and teaching, yet data gathered from schools suggests otherwise. The Center for the Evaluation of Data at UCLA conducted a five-year survey of test use. The conclusion they arrived at was that school personnel give more weight to teachers' judgements than to information from mandated standardized tests. Teachers felt they had a better feel for students' strengths and weaknesses from their own observations and measures.

I think it is important to consider carefully when deciding the value and goal of testing. There are other means at our disposal for measuring educational progress. One way I use is to establish general learning goals and objectives for each child, keeping records on progress, and assessing the progress by observation and periodic reviews. This takes into account many more of the student's abilities, and does not have the problems associated with standardized testing. It becomes a much more realistic view of the learning that has taken and is taking place. Learning in this manner stays with the student longer. How often we deplore students learning something for a test and then promptly forgetting it when testing is over.

Trust. A small word with an enormous meaning. Learning is based on trust. We are always learning. Learning does not require coercion or irrelevant reward. Our children deserve our trust. A child learns best when she understands what she learns and how it affects her personally. Most learning is incidental because the child learns as she is doing things she finds useful and interesting. Learning is collaborative and it is defeated when instruction is delivered mechanically. A student demonstrates the worthwhile things she has learned by engaging in related activities, and she should not have to rely on grades, scores, or tests. Learning involves feelings. She will remember how she felt when she learned—and when she failed to learn.

Until we can accept that the human mind remains a mystery, we operate under the delusion that it is possible to know, measure, and control what goes on in our children's minds. Possibly "control" is the key to why so many adults have a problem accepting the fact that children learn much more through interest-initiated learning than through other-directed learning.

Chapter Five

Keeping Future Educational Opportunities Open

Friends and acquaintances looked at us with raised eyebrows and puzzled looks on their faces when they saw my husband and me attending the special meeting for incoming freshmen at our public high school. What were we doing there? You could see the thoughts parade across their faces. Maybe we had finally come to our senses regarding schools. Some showed shock that we had changed our minds. Various fleeting emotions flashed in their eyes. Mostly we were just greeted with looks of surprise.

We were singled out because we had chosen to homeschool for awhile. In our town it is assumed that students will attend public school. A few attend small private schools. Many parents are unaware of the varied educational opportunities that are available.

Jim personally chose to enter the public high school. He now feels that he has control over his education and is making some wise choices. During Back to School Night, his teachers told us how much they enjoyed having Jim in their classes because he is so interested in learning and because of his meaningful participation in the classroom.

He has a good relationship with his peers and his teachers. He wants to be in his classes so there is now no struggle to get up in the morning as there used to be. The pressures he had been under in earlier years no longer are there so he can now develop healthy peer relationships. Homework is promptly completed. He was even able to tolerate a boring social studies teacher. Jim no longer feels trapped because he realized that he does have other options open. He has the freedom of choice.

Every year the high school anticipates difficulties with the incoming freshmen who had been at the local middle school. The majority of students come to high school from a closed campus where all the gates lock them in for the school day with the exception of an open gate by the administrative office. There are very strict rules on campus to curb violence that occurs. Their day is regimented. They cannot leave campus without compelling reason. Then they go to the high school which is a completely open campus and have an hour long lunch period. They may leave campus at any time during the day (assuming they do not have a class that period). Many students have problems with their relative freedom of choice for the first several weeks. This year there were more problems than usual. Jim had no difficulty adjusting to his schedule since he had just come from an environment of choice.

Enrolling Jim proved to have unexpected advantages. Incoming students not from local public or private schools must register just a few days before the start of school. Most incoming students do not get to personally meet their counselor prior to some problem. Jim and I had to see his assigned counselor for the enrollment process. We discussed what subjects Jim had studied at home.

On the strength of our discussion his counselor placed him with excellent teachers (with one exception, but according to Jim the other teacher was worse). The counselor signed him up for advanced computers and for geometry. These courses had a prerequisite of algebra I so most freshmen are ineligible. The counselor looked at Jim's algebra book and was satisfied. Later on Jim was placed in Honors geometry.

What Jim's future holds now depends on him. He knows he has choices. It is up to him to research these choices to find the ones which will equip him with the skills he wants. His father and I are here to provide him with information and insight when he wishes. He needs to discover on his own what contributions he wants to make to society. We have tried to provide the atmosphere that promotes excitement in him for learning all he can.

To address this issue, the editors of *Home Education Magazine*, Mark and Helen Hegener, published a book, *Alternatives in Education*. The editors of *Gifted Children Monthly* considered this such a valuable book that they have included it in their highly selective catalog, *Presents for the Promising*. Topics include the meaning of alternative education and many of the options available to parents and students. Various alternative educators' philosophies are succinctly discussed. A chapter is devoted to homeschooling but most of the book reminds the reader that we do have many educational options available to us. It is up to the individuals involved to explore these possibilities for the most suitable program.

Thomas Kane homeschooled until he entered the University of Maine where he maintained a triple major of science, foreign policy, and writing. He entered the University at the age of 14 and encountered no difficulties because of his age. However, he noticed a girl his age did encounter problems because she looked more her age than he did. His experience with his professors was positive because they were delighted to have a student more interested in learning than in grades. He voices a common complaint among high school students when he notes that many students are capable of graduating long before traditional schools let them.

The major consideration in looking at educational alternatives is to find the option in which the student will succeed. The learning style as well as the interests of the student is important. It is not that a student fails, but that a student is placed in a situation that is not right for her.

Christopher Hurn, from the University of Massachusetts, devotes his sociology textbook, *The Limits and Possibilities of Schooling*: *An Introduction to the Sociology of Education*, to the premise that American schooling cannot change until people are willing to let go of the status quo. Competition for the top jobs and status makes it difficult to risk losing a person's spot on the social scale to someone perceived as an inferior.

Shortly after we brought Jim home for his studies, I attended PTA council meetings as an officer of the board. The outgoing president remained on the board and never hesitated to speak forcefully on any issue that came up. Someone mentioned the local continuation high school for troubled teenagers. She thought the very idea of a continuation school alternative was abhorrent. Her main concern was that it was unfair to her own youngsters because they had to go all four years to high school while these youngsters could obtain their high school diploma in less time and with less work. She cited cases where some able students had deliberately misbehaved so that they would be sent to Maple High School to finish their high school early. She successfully did all she could to dissuade the school district in attempts to begin an Independent Study Program. In this she had allies among some of the district administrators and teachers as well as other parents.

Tyra Seymour, a fifteen year veteran teacher/coordinator for the School Within a School at J.F.K. High School in Los Angeles, wrote of her increasing frustration with the educational community's inability to accept any differences in schooling practices. She asked support from the National Coalition of Alternative Community Schools in her article for their newsletter. Recent California reforms have moved school districts toward greater uniformity and conformity. We live in a country that professes freedom of choice and uniqueness. The program salvaged students who could have otherwise been lost to society. Graduates continually write or personally return to thank their teachers for turning them back on to learning and even on to themselves.

The College of Creative Studies at the University of California Santa Barbara has its share of critics who constantly attempt to undermine it because it does not conform to preconceived ideas of education and control over students. Colleges and universities offering Independent Study Programs also face this opposition.

Columbia Pacific University sends a reprint of an article that appeared in *The Chronicle of Higher Education* to prospective students in their Independent Study Program. Michael Beaudoin, dean of continuing education and external degree programs at Saint Joseph's College in Maine, agrees that there is much prejudice against academic programs not conforming precisely to the curriculum for full-time students. Skepticism remains despite the fact that home study has successfully existed for hundreds of years. He notes that some of the most ardent opponents to alternative education through independent study often have vested interests in classroom instruction.

Educational options exist. Opposition to many of these options also exists. Knowledge about the opposition and the reasons behind opposition forces us to be more aware of our own educational goals for ourselves and our students.

We chose the educational option of homeschooling our three youngsters primarily because we want them to have a lifelong love of learning and to feel good about their ability to learn. We recognized that each of them had their own approach to learning. Each youngster has rewarded our faith in them to choose wisely what is of importance to them. At no time do we want to close any other educational options, though. We continually reassess their progress and their needs. And we expect to make mistakes, but we also expect to learn from these errors in judgement.

Brian Ray, Ph. D. presented a paper, *A Comparison of Homeschooling and Conventional Schooling: With a Focus on Learner Outcomes* in 1987 in which he reviewed relevant literature. Summarizing what other researchers had found, he concluded that homeschooled students benefit enormously from the low student-teacher ratio and the high involvement of the parents in the learning process. The extra attention afforded by the parents may raise the child's self concept which in turn is associated with improved learning.

Because the parents tend to have higher expectations of their children than teachers, greater academic performance may result. Homeschooling is frequently involved in learning within the frame work of daily living activities. This promotes active involvement in learning by discovery. In terms of curriculum, homeschooling lends itself to a high degree of individualization and flexibility. Dr. Ray notes that parents who homeschool frequently exhibit the behaviors consistent with teacher effectiveness such as flexibility, enthusiasm, task orientation, and clarity of organization.

As we have homeschooled, I have personally witnessed the benefits as outlined by Brian Ray not only in our family but also in other homeschooling families. We have the time to offer our students that no teacher in a conventional classroom situation has. Due to financing I have watched the teacher/student ratio climb in our school district despite efforts to lower it. I watched teacher enthusiasm wane in our neighborhood school when an inept principal was appointed. I felt I had something better to offer my youngsters for as long as they desired and needed it. This is the option we choose for now.

Besides his dissertation on learner outcomes of homeschooling, Brian Ray has produced a lengthy home-centered learning annotated bibliography with over 350 entries covering relevant research. He also edits a quarterly publication, *Homeschool Researcher*, as a means of sharing the latest research available pertaining to homeschooling. The June, 1988, issue contained two articles relating to research into the amount of structure used in homeschooling and the effect on achievement.

Sonia Gustafson is at the Woodrow Wilson School of Public and International Affairs in Princeton University. Her project involved exploring the motivation and goals of homeschooling parents through a survey of families listed in the publication *Growing Without Schooling*. Of the 143 respondents she found that 65% of the families used highly informal or flexible structures. Only 30% indicated formal instruction. Most families stated that flexibility was more important to them than formal lessons or schedules. They placed more value on "teachable moments" no matter when or where they occur than on a required number of academic exercises in a given day.

She adds that parents who responded to her survey exhibited a fierce devotion to providing an educational environment which offer their children the opportunity to develop freely and fully in more than academic areas. They consider it important to develop all areas of being. She also noted that the parents whose children had taken standardized tests reported the students had scored above average.

Jon Wartes, Project Leader for the Washington Homeschool Research Project, reported on the results of homeschool testing using the Stanford Achievement Test. His finding was that the test data suggested there is virtually no relationship between the level of structure used and the academic outcome. The level of structure used had no value in predicting the outcome of test scores. There seems to be no support for imposing curriculum for the sake of structure nor for imposing minimum hours per week of formal schooling.

It is interesting to note that Jon Wartes, a public school administrator in the state of Washington, readily admits that at first he was opposed to homeschooling because he was convinced quality education requires highly trained teachers. He wanted to protect teachers, funding, and the imposition of a particular philosophy on students. Once he was convinced that homeschooling is a viable option, he became a proponent of the movement.

In an article in *Growing Without Schooling*, he cautions homeschoolers not to claim academic superiority when dealing with school administrators. While there is evidence that supports the claim, too many important variables have not yet been controlled in the research conducted to date. This is one of the reasons he is working so closely with the project in the state of Washington where similar groups of public school students and homeschool students in the same locality are being studied.

The question of teacher certification is of importance to parents who choose to homeschool their youngsters. Teacher certification is supposed to be a guarantee of educational quality and the capability of the person to teach students. If teacher certification is the means to assure quality education, why can't the various states agree on a nationally uniform course of study and standard means of evaluation of who is qualified to teach?

My cousin cannot teach in California public schools because her certification is from Oregon and my sister-in-law cannot teach in Oregon because her certification is from the state of Washington. We probably all know someone who is eminently qualified to teach but unable to in the state where he or she now resides because that state does not recognize their teaching credentials.

Dr. Sam Peavey, Professor Emeritus of Education at the University of Louisville, was actively involved for years in training new teachers. Yet he admits that half a century of research has failed to prove there is significant relationship between teacher certification and student achievement. He considers the only valid measure of teacher effectiveness is learner achievement.

Another concern for some parents who believe in student-initiated learning is: will their children be able to handle post secondary studies? Depending on the individual student, there seems to be no particular problem with higher studies. In fact, some students have reported that their college and university experiences were enriched because they were more interested in learning than in their grades. College admission seems to pose no more problems for homeschooled youngsters than those entering out of public schools. There may be a variation in the manner of applying for admission to the college or university of choice, though.

Brian Ray reviewed a study made of university admissions requirements for homeschooled applicants. The researcher was Leslie Barnebey who did her doctoral dissertation on this topic. The study showed that private universities were more likely to accept homeschooled applicants than the public universities were. homeschoolers are more often required to submit letters of reference, essays, and Achievement Test scores. Almost 84% of the accepting colleges and universities accepted the GED in lieu of high school transcripts. Many of the colleges and universities encouraged prior attendance at junior or community colleges. Three quarters of the accepting colleges believed that homeschooled applicants would be successful as other applicants. Nearly all of the colleges and universities surveyed (91%) do not have a formal policy regarding homeschool applicants. In conclusion, homeschooled students are accepted into a wide range of four year universities and colleges, especially the large, private, research oriented universities.

As homeschooling parents, we wonder whether our children will be penalized when seeking college admission if their high school program is not accredited. My research into the question reveals that accreditation is not an indication of the legal status of the school, but of its acceptability to the standards of a recognized accrediting agency. These are independent accrediting organizations who usually charge for this service and have varying standards. Schools can be perfectly legal and the work of their students can be accepted by other schools and colleges without ever being accredited.

The significance of accreditation depends on the student's plans for the immediate future. Accreditation has no meaning at all if the student's plans do not include college, but rather getting a job after graduation. If the student wants to attend a college or university immediately after graduation, accreditation can enter the picture. At times it does play a part in the selection process at competitive four-year universities. On the other hand, hundreds of colleges throughout the nation accept diplomas from non-accredited high schools without any difficulty at all. If a student has a particular career goal in mind, it is wise to investigate the requirements early. Entering college after several years in the work force seems to pose little problem.

Generally, college and university admission standards are becoming more flexible. The key element which they often rely upon at present seems to be the SAT scores. With favorable test scores even competitive four-year colleges and universities will often accept a student, regardless of attendance at an accredited school, a non-accredited school, or even no school at all.

A high school diploma or its equivalent is almost a necessity in the job market. There are some jobs available where it is not required but usually these are low-paying and there is no advancement without the diploma. California provides the California High School Proficiency Examination which is accepted in the state as the equivalent to a high school diploma.

The General Educational Development Test, or GED, is a more widely accepted high school diploma equivalent. Originally designed during World War II to allow veterans to go to college without returning to high school to finish secondary courses, the GED is used for purposes of higher education, employment, promotion, and licensing. The age and residence requirements vary from the state, territory, district, or Canadian province, in which the test is taken. The purpose is to measure the skills mastered and general knowledge that would be acquired in a four year high school education. There are many books available in libraries and bookstores to assist in preparation for the test.

National attention has been focused in recent years on the academic achievements of the Colfax family. They are examples of the educational heights that can be achieved by home-schooled youngsters. During an interview on the Phil Donahue program the parents emphasized that most of the boys' learning took place without parental assistance. While the boys were encouraged to spend at least twenty minutes a day on basic subjects, there was no pressure to do so. Never were they forced to spend several hours a day on studies.

Another former homeschooler, John Wesley Taylor V, based his doctoral dissertation on the self-concept of homeschooled children. His findings showed that the self-concept of the home-schooled children studied was significantly higher than that of conventionally schooled children. He concludes that this may be due to higher achievement and mastery levels. Other factors are the independent study characteristics and tutoring situations found in the homeschool environment. Higher levels of parental involvement, independence from peers, a sense of responsibility and lower anxiety levels are other factors he considers important.

John Wesley Taylor began his homeschooling at the age of eight. His family was in Latin America at the time he began homeschooling. During the ninth to twelfth grade he studied on his own using Home Study International courses. He remembers this as a time to follow his own interests and for community service. At the age of eighteen he entered college where he became interested in the field of education. He currently is on the faculty of Andrews University, having obtained his Ph.D. in Curriculum and Instruction.

As I described in Chapter Two, John Boston is the administrator for Home Centered Learning. His philosophy is one which he calls "invited teaching" which he defines as helping someone else when they ask for help. As word has spread of his encouragement of student initiated learning, his enrollment has doubled in one year's time to nearly 300 students by the end of 1988. In his homeschooling program he encourages parents to communicate with their students so that the student's needs are accurately assessed. A former public high school teacher himself, he no longer believes that the best situation for learning can be guessed at by a curriculum developer. The educational needs of his own son compelled him to found the School of Home Learning as he discovered other parents with similar experiences.

Sean Boston was one of the first graduates from the School of Home Learning. Since then twenty-one other students have joined the ranks of School of Home Learning alumni. I wrote to several of them explaining my book on the value of allowing students to follow their interests during the learning process. Then I asked them to share their comments.

Heather finished high school at home after getting into trouble at the public high school. Her highlights in homeschooling were time to read and other quiet "productive" times. She began to understand balancing a checkbook. She planned to take courses on becoming a medical or dental receptionist until she eloped and became pregnant. She cherishes her time to write fiction and even had a book accepted for publication at the age of 15. When asked what she would tell teachers about effective teaching, she mentioned she'd stress individual attention, praise for a job well done and to let students do it at their own pace.

Diana wrote a lengthy reply to my letter. She homeschooled for six years (from the fourth grade) then took the CHSPE. Now she is enrolled at a community college

> The decision to homeschool (my parents' at the time, though my brother and I readily agreed) was based mainly on a dissatisfaction with the schools available to us (both public and private). My parents didn't feel our needs were being met, and looking back I certainly agree. I had been to various different public and private schools during my short career as an elementary school student, and none were satisfactory to myself or my parents. I'm not sure any school could have been. Children aren't meant to sit at desks for six to seven hours a day, and I can remember hating it.
>
> Highlights? There have been so many. My parents' way of teaching us was very unstructured, so we had a lot of time to play. That play time is so important for children, I wouldn't trade it for anything.
>
> I don't feel that homeschooling has in any way hampered any of my goals. I don't really see how it could, at least not any goals I might have. Perhaps that would differ for someone else, I don't know. I am presently a student at both Grossmont and

Cuyamaca community colleges, and if anything my educational background has helped, not hindered me. I haven't had 12 years during which to get burned out on school. I'm here by my own choice.

Besides asking in general about her homeschool experiences and how they have affected her educational opportunities, I also asked Diana what effect her learning experience has had on her life. Diana replied,

One definite factor for me has been time. My more liberal time schedule enabled me to get a job at age 14, something I really wanted to do. This past January marked my third year at the health food store. I don't think it is bragging or exaggerating to say I'm one of the more valued employees. I also feel as if homeschooling helped to enable me to relate to people on a more adult level at an earlier age. This, however, was also affected by the way I was treated by my parents—as an equal. I trust my parents completely, and I was never made to feel afraid of them. I suppose that's a difference between me and a lot of public schooled friends I have. I get along with my parents, I enjoy their company and I think we have a mutual respect for each other that isn't an every day thing.

Accomplishments? Well I'm not up for any Nobel prizes or anything. I guess my job is something I'm proud of. I think I work pretty hard—when I do something I try to do it well. Another thing I could mention is my grades. I began college at age 16. This month marks the beginning of my third semester, and so far I've kept up a 4.0 GPA. To me that's an accomplishment because I really went into school cold turkey—at home we never really had a set curriculum—we did 'school work' whenever we felt like it—which wasn't very often at all (almost never). So for me to go into college with no study skills and little formal schooling at

all and do as well as I did is something of an
accomplishment.

Diana presented her ideas on how teachers can most
effectively teach and how parents can be effective in their
children's learning experiences.

First and foremost, I stress that teachers have
to like kids a lot. Someone who doesn't can't really
interact effectively with them. Also, they have to
be teaching for the right reasons—not because
they like the schedule (summers off)... And they
should enjoy what they're teaching. It isn't fun to
learn from someone who's not interested in what
they're teaching. I've had teachers like that.

Every child is an individual and has varied
needs, so what each family does will be different.
It's hard to recommend anything without knowing
the situation. What I would stress is that children
be allowed to learn (or not learn) at their own pace.
I don't think it's necessary to be constantly providing entertainment for children, or to provide
sources of educational material. There's a lot to do
in your own backyard, and children will discover
that if given the opportunity.

...A final note of advice to parents is not to
worry. Parents worry that they aren't giving children enough mental stimulation or that they aren't
providing the necessary educational background
for them to attend college. I'm living proof that the
case is otherwise, so don't worry! Just enjoy!

One respondent, Felice, struggled with her studies in both
the formal school setting and the unstructured setting of the
School of Home Learning. She homeschooled for two high school
years because "my interests were not learning; at the time they
were more on playing around." She lamented that her public
high school classes were so crowded that the teachers did not
realize, "that I needed special attention, because lots of the time
I didn't understand them and then they would just go on to the

next thing." She thought the highlights of her homeschool experience were that she could make her own time and not get up so early.

When discussing what she would do differently, Felice said,

> I think if I was in a better homeschooling program, that I would have stayed with it regularly—because of that I do sort of regret not finishing regular school—because I think I would have grown to appreciate it. Yes, I do need someone to tell me 'This is due tomorrow, you have to do it now." I didn't have that with my homeschool program.

By the time she was 18, Felice had several work experiences. She worked in a store and was manager for some time. While working for a year in a Century 21 realty office, she programmed their computer. And she has worked at a medical billing office where, she says, she learned a lot.

Felice had family problems including her father's death and mother's divorce. Because of her mother's job, Felice did not see her very often. She says,

> One thing, I have had to grow up a lot faster and my parents have taught me to be real responsible. When I see my old school mates I feel like I am five years older than them—they're still stupid as ever.

As to what she would advise teachers and parents, Felice pointed out that it is important to be aware of problems students may be facing. Also, it is important to keep things simple and to the point: "So many teachers try to explain five things at one time." She points out that it was her mother who burned out during the homeschooling and feels that a lot depends on the program chosen. "Be very selective!!" Felice cautions.

The advice Felice would give to a friend who was having problems is to give it your all. Don't quit when the going gets hard, but explore all your possibilities.

> And if they are still having a hard time, try

home studies. It takes a lot of discipline on the student's part, though. So be prepared and if it does-
n't work out, don't quit, it may be your attitude.

Originally I had written to Meshawn, but her younger sister
saw the letter and was intrigued so she responded instead.
Cheannie started homeschooling as a high school freshman.

I had no choice in this situation. My parents did-
n't like my attitude, my friends, or the whole
school system. I loved school, did very well with my
grades, and had no problem being liked.

Local drug abuse at the high school motivated her parents to
remove Cheannie from school.

Once in the homeschool program, Cheannie began to realize
the benefits of studying at her own pace. She now has set her
sights on going into the fields of psychology and nutrition.

I plan on combining the two and becoming very
successful in it. One thing about home study that
was always on my good side was working at your
own pace. That's real helpful if you plan on going
to college because, if you wish you can start your
college training earlier.

As for advice she would give a friend having difficulties in
school, Cheannie would tell them to

consider home study if they have the initiative
to learn and work hard. If a student hates school
and is struggling to keep their head above water,
the chance of them actually learning and enjoying
something is small. And that, to me, is a waste of
a precious mind.

Earlier I told of Laurie Struble's experiences with her son,
Sam, and how unstructured homeschooling filled his education-

al needs. She shared her story of her daughter Krishanda, which illustrates the varied needs of our children.

> On to Krishanda… she's so different, as I mentioned before. She was a "late bloomer". I was so glad I knew about homeschooling with her, because it would have been traumatic to have had to make her go to school when she was only 5 or 6. She was very needful and was my constant companion for years. When she was 7, she started taking dance class one day a week for one hour. And I was always right outside the room. Scholastically, she just wasn't interested. She never really liked books when she was little, and wasn't must interested in learning to read. I'd read about the theories that thought early reading was detrimental. And sure enough, when she was ready, she caught up with no problem.

Laurie noticed that when Krishanda was nine she got serious about wanting to go to school. Laurie was busy with a new baby so she put her off for about six months. Finally Laurie gave in and signed her up for a Montessori school.

> I really didn't want her going to school, but I knew I couldn't, in good conscience, hold her back. It turned out beautifully. She was ready.

After a year and a half Krishanda begged to try public school. Despite strong misgivings Laurie felt it was important to let her "follow her own path." That worked out well.

After Sam's terrible experience at high school, Laurie again had misgivings as Krishanda entered junior high. But once again it was right for Krishanda.

> She's so mature and we have a close relationship and I just couldn't ask for more. Academically she's doing great, her teachers love her… .I can see

that as much as I love homeschooling, she is where she belongs.

Chapter Six

Coping With Parent-Teacher Wear and Tear

"I could never teach my youngsters at home. I could not stand being around them all day every day. Most of all, I do not have all the time necessary to teach my own youngsters. How in the world do you manage it?" Every home schooling parent has probably heard these comments many times. Some could truthfully respond that it does indeed take a great deal of preparation time besides time necessary for lesson presentation.

However, I find that I actually spend just about as much time as I did when Jim, Laurie, and Susan were in school because I was so actively involved in each of their schools. My preparation time is minimal since all three youngsters know what they want to learn and how to find their own materials. Often they inform me that they do not want my interference in the learning process.

But this does not mean that every day runs smoothly nor that there are never days I anxiously hover over them checking progress. Some days it is impossible for them to get along with each other. There are days when learning is actively resisted. Other days are spent in nothingness. The house is in greater chaos than usual. Chores are undone because "It's not MY job!" A skateboard goes through a sliding glass door—"I didn't mean to do it! It wasn't going that fast." I am preparing a salad so reach for the vinegar only to discover just in time that the vinegar also contains baking soda because of an experiment constructing volcanoes performed without my knowledge.

There are days when I wonder if anything works. One youngster is in tears because she does not want to do her math and another has stubbornly set her face in refusal to do a writing assignment. I have reverted to my teacher role and everything seems to be wrong. Maybe I am not giving them enough or not teaching something their peers already have learned. I am not as clever as the teacher who lives down the street who does marvels in her classroom. Doubts assail me from all sides. Will they survive in college, in the world of work? Am I hurting their futures?

One day Pat tells me how happy she is when my youngsters come over to her house because they help her own youngsters' study efforts. She loves to observe them at play because my youngsters are teaching hers so much about geography and proper word usage during their play. Suddenly I realize everything is working out. I can truthfully tell Pat that I have observed the very same characteristics in her youngsters when they are at our house. Both of us gain perspective.

Pat has struggled with first using a highly structured learning program with her youngsters and nearly burning out because of her lack of confidence in herself. She has relatives who are public school administrators and very critical of home schooling. Each year Pat gains confidence and gradually gives her youngsters greater freedom in their studies. She readily admits that had she continued with the strict study schedule she started with she could not have worked very long with her youngsters. Her youngsters are much happier now and progressing rapidly from the love they have of learning.

Coping with parent-teacher wear and tear involves knowing deep down that the children will learn despite your worry and efforts. As Diana Scheck reminds parents,

> Don't worry—just enjoy. Trust your children.
> When they feel the need to know something, they
> will learn it much easier and faster when they
> have the freedom of choice and self-confidence.

A Canadian friend once reminded me in a moment of doubt that even when children go off to school some place, parental responsibility does not cease. She said to look at my children and listen to them. Most of all I should listen to my heart. Professionals don't have all the answers in education any more than doctors know all about illness or health. It is so important to explore alternatives and to step in to change a situation that is not suitable for a given child. Beth ended by saying that no one loves my children as I do, nor understands their specialness as I do. I am their protector, spokesperson, and defender until each is able to take on the task for herself.

To prevent my own burn out I find I need to replace my self-doubt with trusting myself. Whenever I start setting too high expectations on myself and my children, I notice lessening ability to cope in myself. Even though I have had the advantage of extensive volunteer work in the classroom as well as my own experiences of teaching other youngsters, there are times I catch myself with an unrealistic view of what takes place in the nation's classrooms. This teacher is doing a fantastic unit on the space shuttle with her first graders, why can't I?

Susan's kindergarten teacher stressed math manipulatives while another terrific kindergarten teacher in the same school presented an in-depth study of flowers to her students. A third teacher emphasized dinosaurs and used a lot of music with her kindergarten class. There is no way in the world that every kindergarten class in the country is going to learn exactly the same things. Why should I expect myself to be all things to my students? Even on the high school level teachers will present their subjects differently from each other even if both teach social studies, science, or whatever.

My youngsters want me to be a facilitator not a dictator. They are freer to let me know what they think about something I want them to do than they are with another teacher. When they do not want to write, or whatever I want them to do, tears will flow if I pressure them too much. Learning will not take place even if my will prevails. Yet they did not do this in school because it would have been useless. Instead they did the assignment resenting every moment of it. Learning did not take place then, either.

Sometimes it requires skillful questioning to find the source of the resistance. Usually it is a result of lack of interest in the project and seeing no sense in completing it. The projects that they want to pursue by far present the best results—and often surprising ones at that.

"I'm bored!" is sometimes heard around here. But not all that often since I usually hand their boredom right back to them. I tell them that they are the only ones who can do something about the problem. There are times they really do want some suggestions from me, though, so when I sense this I offer ideas. Other times I realize that they are only saying they are bored to obtain a reaction from me. I tell them that I have yet to read of a documented case where someone actually died from boredom. At times I do scrutinize our activities to see if the boredom is a result of unsuitable activities. Boredom can be beneficial when it leads to new explorations.

I find the use of a year round flexible schedule has its advantages in warding off burnout. It affects me more than it does the youngsters as we don't change our daily activities much all year around. However, for record keeping purposes I only need to be concerned about a nine-week stretch at a time with a four-week break from record keeping. My records are minimal but there is a psychological relief every so often. A flexible learning schedule prevents cramming studies into specified days or hours because activities taking place outside the Monday through Friday nine to three time frames are considered of value to the learning process. So if nothing seems to happen between nine and one on Monday, all is not lost.

I do not have to always be present for learning to take place. Depending on the ages of your children, you do not have to be present at all times either. I find it necessary to take breaks away from the children. When the children are older it is possible to go off shopping or running errands while they remain at home. My youngsters are also a big help with shopping and running errands. They have become skilled comparison shoppers and can handle financial affairs with ease.

Every morning while they are preparing their breakfasts and doing their few morning chores, I take a brisk twenty- minute walk to a nearby park. This is my time of peace. Sometime I use it to plan the day's activities and other times I just quietly enjoy my surroundings without much thought in particular. I call this time my sanity saver.

Because my youngsters are older, other homeschooling families ask them to baby-sit. Mothers of young children and preschoolers appreciate having Laurie or Jim around their youngsters. When the mother remains at home while Jim or

Laurie is present, she feels the relief of having the youngsters occupied by someone else. Other times the mothers welcome the opportunity to run errands, etc., without small helpers.

Jim, Laurie, and Susan sometimes help their friends with their studies. This works out very well for all concerned. Mothers have free moments to themselves, students learn more readily, and student/tutors clarify their own skills.

Many areas have homeschool support groups. Our support group is very informal. We meet in local parks once a month to plan field trips and discuss items of interest. We also make arrangements for rental of our municipal swimming pool each week. It is important to have someone with whom you can exchange ideas. Our group serves this purpose. Some people do not seem to have as great a need for outside support. Or maybe they have other sources of support. Burnout seems to occur more often among those lacking some kind of support.

Besides our local support group, I have subscriptions to *Growing Without Schooling*, *Home Education Magazine*, *Northern California Homeschoolers Association News*, and the newsletters put out by John Boston for the *California Coalition-People for Alternative Learning Situations* and his Home Centered Learning. Another publication I find useful is *Learning 89*. These magazines and newsletters reinforce my belief in the value of student interest-initiated learning. I am always searching for appropriate books to add to my already extensive library.

Occasionally I do begin to show signs of parent-teacher wear and tear. My first signs usually are the sensation that I am working harder, accomplishing less and feeling very tired. Then disappointment in myself and the children begins to set in along with irritability. Making one phone call or writing a letter becomes harder to do. There is less joy and I start to regard events and people negatively. The question about whether it is worth the effort begins to nag at me. This is when I need to seriously examine what is occurring in my life.

I discovered that Dr. Wayne Dyer's book, *What Do You Really Want For Your Children?*, helps me to reassess what I am doing and why. It is almost as if he looked over my shoulder the day I put down on paper my educational goals for my children. He reaffirms my desire to impart to Jim, Laurie, and Susan the ability to enjoy life, to be risk takers, to value themselves, to handle stress, to be creative, to have a sense of purpose, and most of all to value themselves. His aim in writing his book was to offer specific suggestions to parents for assisting their youngsters to realize their full potential based on his experiences in working with troubled youngsters and families.

When preparing to present a series of classes on parenting, I found another book that I use in moments of doubt and stress. Dolores Curran wrote *Stress and the Healthy Family* because in her research into what differentiates functional families from dysfunctional families most, she found, was the ability to handle the every- day stresses that occur. She listed the top family stresses as economics, behavior of children, lack of shared family responsibilities, insufficient family and individual time, lack of communication, and guilt for not accomplishing more. The two important stresses most overlooked are insufficient family playtime and over-scheduled family calendars.

Her book shares the dramatic turnarounds some families have made in eliminating pressures and increasing pleasures in family life. One conclusion to her study that helps me resolve my own doubts is that functional families seek solutions while dysfunctional families seek blame.

A third book that I find beneficial is Adele Faber and Elaine Mazlish's *How to Talk So Kids Will Listen and Listen So Kids Will Talk*. The authors continually remind me that my youngsters are people, too. They have feelings. They have reasons for doing what they do. I must truly listen to them. And I need to help them express their own feelings in a positive and accepting manner. I have had this book for so many years and read it so often that I now only need to glance at its cover on a prominent bookshelf during a time of frustration to remind myself that I want them to control and be responsible for their own actions. Every now and then I have to open the book to one of the graphic cartoons to bring perspective back into my reactions to something the youngsters have done or failed to do.

Sometimes my concerns center more on whether I am taking the correct educational approach for my children. When this is the case, I retreat to certain favorite books and magazines which reinforce and renew my sagging spirits. I am committed to providing Jim, Laurie, and Susan with the opportunities to pursue interest-initiated learning in the manner most suitable for them as individuals.

There are times I feel overwhelmed by people and literature that warn me I must control my children's learning because they are incapable of choosing wisely for themselves. Then I seek out other opinions with the realization that no one has yet discovered any definitive answers as to what constitutes learning and how to most effectively enhance it. The workings of the human mind are still a mystery to mankind. Therefore I have to discover the philosophy of education with which I am most comfortable and then act accordingly.

My teacher training background emphasized classroom management more than it did subject content or how learning occurs. When Jim had his problems in middle school I became more acutely aware of the learning environment. I had already read David Elkind's excellent books, *The Hurried Child*, and *All Grown Up and No Place to Go*. He deplored the pressures to succeed our young people are put under in the educational system and from parents. In his more recent book, *Miseducation*, he is even more worried about the harmful effects of the move to push academics on preschoolers.

In *Miseducation* Dr. Elkind cites a study of 120 gifted and talented people conducted by Benjamin Bloom and his colleagues. The parents of these eminent people did not impose their own priorities on their children but chose to follow each child's lead. The most important factor was the excitement and enthusiasm for learning. Skills were easily learned when there was motivation.

Dr. Helen K. Billings planted the seeds of doubt in my mind as to the effectiveness of most schooling. At a conference on parenting in 1976, I had the privilege of introducing Dr. Billings during the session she was to present on giving your child an educational advantage. In preparation for my introduction she and I had a lively conversation. She impressed me with the importance of following a child's interests. Because at the time I only had preschoolers I only applied what she said to preschoolers. Now I realize she meant all children, regardless of age.

Her professional career went from teaching in a one room country school to head of the Department of Education at the college level. She founded the Montessori Institute of America. While Advisor on Academic Affairs for Southeastern University she developed a masters program in child development designed to apply the philosophy of independent study to higher education.

Dr. Billings believed that student-initiated learning is the basis for true education. In her books she insisted that learning cannot be carried on solely within the walls of a classroom. The child best learns about life by living it within the community. The student needs the freedom to learn on her own with the adult standing by to answer questions or to guide when asked.

I read a reprint of a 1952 article by Carl Rogers entitled "Personal Thoughts on Teaching and Learning" in which he laments ever telling someone how to teach. He had come to the conclusion that only a self-discovered, self-appropriated learning influences behavior. He found that the results of his teaching seemed to cause the student to distrust her own experience and stifled significant learning. He was relieved when he discovered that the Danish philosopher, Soren Kierkegaard, had come to a similar conclusion.

The many books written by John Holt as well as his bimonthly newsletter *Growing Without Schooling* were the catalyst that caused me to find out as much information as I could about the effectiveness of interest-initiated learning. I find myself referring constantly to one of his books or back issues of his newsletter. He insisted that most of what he knew he did not learn in school and was not even "taught." Between 1964 and 1983 he wrote eleven books on how people learn most effectively. In one of his last articles before his death, he observes that the fewer unasked-for corrections the student experiences, the better the results of the learning process. Children need time to find their own way.

In *Teach Your Own* John Holt warns against parents trying to make the home more of a school than school itself is. He argues that this is the fastest way to burn out. Many home-schooling parents start out trying to know too much, do too much, and control too much. My own youngsters do not hesitate to let me know when I fall into that trap. Thank goodness, because it is when I am inappropriately trying too hard that I am most susceptible to burnout.

Dr. Raymond Moore is a developmental psychologist whose research on the family and school has appeared in nearly every academic journal in the field of education in the United States. He is the founder and director of The Moore Foundation. Along with his wife, Dorothy, who is a reading specialist, Dr. Moore has co-authored several books on the benefits of homeschooling.

In their book, *Home Grown Kids*, they introduce parents to the idea that they can provide a first-class education in the home environment that enhances creativity and character development. The focus of the book is from birth to about the age of nine. *Home Spun Schools* presents case histories of homeschooling parents. They demonstrate that one-on-one teaching is more effective for learning than crowded classrooms. In their third book in this series, *Home Style Teaching*, the Moores present practical insights into the art and science of teaching.

Addressing the issue of socialization, they assert that while learning at home the youngsters experience relative quiet and simplicity in schedule, thereby attaining a sense of personal worth. Then when the child does interact socially with greater numbers of people, she is already confident and independent in thinking and values. There is not the negative peer pressure to affect actions.

During a homeschool conference, I listened as Raymond Moore gave a presentation where he stressed the necessity of letting youngsters learn according to their particular interests. He cited numbers of instances where he knew parents had given up working with their children at home because of burn out caused by "schooling at home" rather than "homeschooling." He referred to families that expected far more than the school systems expect of their students. The families most prone to burnout are those who cram learning down their children without regard for the abilities and interests of the students.

Dr. Moore says that the more formally the parents approach homeschooling the higher the rate of burnout. Those families who persevere are the ones who come to recognize the true educational need of their children to pursue learning in a more relaxed manner according to their interests.

In order to concentrate on working with my youngsters, my husband and I have chosen to be part of John Boston's Home Centered Learning because he emphasizes the benefits of student interest-initiated learning. This psychologically frees me to focus on my educational goals without unnecessary worry over administrative details. However, I consider it my responsibility to keep abreast of legal concerns for homeschoolers.

Other parents choose to participate in their public school district's Independent Study Program (where available) for the same reason. However, in some cases the local Independent Study programs have not worked in the children's best interests. Many other parents I know choose to file their own private school affidavits according to California's present educational code. Different, acceptable, alternatives exist. Each family can choose what works best for them.

How each family reacts to parent-teacher wear and tear determines how successful they will be in homeschooling. For me it has been necessary to reassess my firm belief in the value of interest-initiated learning and the goals I have for myself and my family.

Sometimes I do this by reviewing how I have struggled this past year to learn how to use a computer and a word processor. This has given me renewed appreciation of how important it is to be interested in a subject to learn it effectively. Laurie has quickly mastered using a desktop publishing program because she uses it to put out her monthly newsletter. I've struggled to use it the few times I've wanted to do work on a newsletter.

I have recognized the value of my claiming personal time for myself to pursue my interests. And I know that I need the periodic support that my friends provide. Most of all my youngsters have taught me that they indeed can be trusted to select what is of importance for them to learn. They will learn when they are ready and when they see a purpose to knowing something. These are my ways of coping with parent-teacher wear and tear.

Conclusion

Interest-initiated learning is that learning which the learner herself controls and initiates according to her interests. When it is interest-initiated, learning is guided by internal personal priorities not imposed from the outside. The learner herself chooses when and how to learn about a given topic or skill. It is entirely self-directed. The teacher only enters into the learning process when invited to do so.

Most learning is unmeasurable. Close observers of how learning takes place in students who are self-directed note that ideas will gestate for some time, even months, and then reappear in more mature form than when first introduced. Standardized tests are unable to measure the learning that has taken place during periods of seemingly unproductive periods of daydreaming.

John Holt stated that it is better for a child to figure out something on her own than to be told what to do. She will then remember better and she will gain confidence in her ability to figure things out. When we try to measure the knowledge gained we undermine the learner's self-confidence. To John Holt, testing was detrimental to the success of interest-initiated learning.

He felt that too often teachers and parents believe that learning only happens in children when the adults make it happen. Because children have to be in school and have to do what they're told, many teachers rarely get reliable feedback from the students they are teaching. People who teach their own children at home are likely to quickly become effective teachers because they receive unmistakable feedback from the children that tells them when the teaching is helpful and when it is not.

Because many American educators did not listen to what he had to say about the value of interest-initiated learning, John Holt turned to the first teachers of children, parents. He devoted his later years to developing the theory of the importance of interest-initiated learning. He firmly believed that the amount a person can learn at a given moment depends on how she feels about her ability to do the task. Most of all, he emphasized, adults must overcome distrust of the learning capacity of children and the desire to control children.

It was largely because of the influence John Holt had on me when I decided to homeschool my children that I become interested in the concept of interest-initiated learning. Friends pointed out to me that I already had been practicing interest-initiated learning with my own children from the time of birth.

My mentor, Dr. Joanne Deaton, in my Master's program with Columbia Pacific University prompted my writing this book when she suggested that others could profit from my experiences with implementing interest-initiated learning. I thought that the experiences of other families who practice student interest-initiated learning would enhance the book.

There are many theories relating to education prevalent today. The more popular ones seem to emphasize adult control and the necessity for an "expert" to direct learning activities. We have a nation that believes in freedom of choice and equality in differences. Yet there are those in power who prefer conformity and uniformity that disregards the needs of the individual.

Christopher Hurn devotes his entire textbook, *The Limits and Possibilities of Schooling: An Introduction to the Sociology of Education*, to the conflicting theories on the purpose of our schools and how learning should be implemented in them. In his conclusion he comments that the compulsory character of schooling, crowded conditions, and lack of incentive to learn are all constraints not likely to be easily removed. Because of a loss of faith in schooling as a panacea for social ills many see formal education as nothing more than a rationing of jobs or a credentialing device. If we wish to make our schools better, we must first learn more about how learning takes place and how to implement this knowledge in our schools.

California's Legislature mandated the establishment of a Self-Esteem Task Force to come up with a working definition of self-esteem. The Task Force is to seek ways to promote self-esteem with personal and social responsibility among the citizens of the state. In their publication *Esteem* they reprinted an article from *For Instructors Only*, published by Performance

Learning Systems in New Jersey. The article, "School: Builder or Destroyer of Esteem?", reported that eighty percent of students entering school feel good about themselves. By fifth grade only twenty percent of the students feel good about themselves. They claim that by twelfth grade the student has received only 4,000 positive statements and about 15,000 negative statements. In all, this comes to the equivalent of sixty days each year of reprimands, nagging, and punishment. The teachers control the environment in which the student spends more than 1,000 hours a year.

One of my goals in the education of my children is that each of them will have a healthy self-esteem. After lengthy deliberation, the California Task Force to Promote Self-Esteem, and Personal and Social Responsibility, decided on a definition of self-esteem that clearly states my own understanding of self-esteem: "Appreciating my own worth and importance, and having the character to be accountable for myself, and to act responsibly toward others."

Practicing interest-initiated learning can only enhance the student's self-esteem. She is in control of the learning process and thereby recognizes her individual worth. She is not subjected to countless negative reactions to what she is accomplishing.

I watched my own son restore his self-esteem when he experienced interest-initiated learning. Although he has chosen to return to the school system, I see him controlling his own life and studies because he values his own judgement.

I am watching a daughter who was beginning to lose her sense of self-worth while in first grade. She was in a classroom that allowed more student initiative than most classrooms in our school district. She is now showing me daily that she does understand her capabilities and how to put them to the best use. I have no doubts that she is a much better judge of when she is ready to proceed in her learning experiences than I am. At the age of nine she has an understanding of math that I will never attain.

Our other daughter delights in being around people. She knows characteristics of every subscriber on her newspaper route and receives generous tips from her appreciative customers. Her contacts reach over the Pacific Ocean with a long time pen pal in Australia and another one in Japan. Her Campfire leader relies on her to organize many of their activities. Because of her our family rarely has dull moments. She flourishes when she directs her learning activities.

Not every person is suited to interest-initiated learning as a means of education. In my observation, the longer a student is exposed to other-directed and controlled learning, the harder it is to adapt to interest-initiated learning. John Boston, Raymond Moore, and John Holt have also made this observation. Many students (adult students included) depend upon being told what to do and how to do it.

When I told a neighbor I was completing my college degree work through independent study projects she asked to borrow my brochures on the program because she is completing college requirements after raising her family. A week later she returned the materials ruefully commenting that she could never do it as she needs someone to tell her what to study.

In talking with other homeschooling families locally and at conferences, it is evident that the older the student is when starting home study, the more difficult it is for her to adjust. Of the alumni from the Home Centered Learning who answered my letter, those who began the program earlier were more likely to continue through high school.

Entering school after homeschooling does not seem to present many problems. There may be a few problems with daily routine at first, but most youngsters quickly master them. My cousin's husband teaches fifth grade. A girl enrolled in his class after homeschooling for all her academic life. To his delight he found that he wished he had more students like her because she was so enthusiastic about learning and was self-directed.

My friend, Laurie Struble, commented, "As to the question of entering school after homeschooling, I can't see that it's any problem. If the kids WANT to go, they'll do fine. Sam is finally getting serious about starting college, but it took him awhile after passing the CHSPE. I think most people assume homeschooled kids will be eager to go to college as soon as they're old enough, but I don't see why. Sam learns so well at home and enjoys it so much, there's really no hurry." Her daughter,

Krishanda certainly had no problems with entering school when she chose to after completely interest-initiated learning at home.

In summary, interest-initiated learning is that learning which the learner herself initiates according to her interests. She is guided by her own priorities, not by those imposed from outside. The teacher only enters into the learning process when invited to do so by the student. In choosing our learning materials, my youngsters prove to me that it is possible for children to make better sense of the world on their own than adults can through curricula produced by adults.

The student needs both time and opportunity to reflect on the barrage of information to which she is exposed. Her learning rhythms of advance and retreat, exploration and consolidation cannot be predicted or controlled.

Trust is the key to success in interest-initiated learning. interest-initiated learning allows the student to use her abilities in the optimal manner. The amount she can learn at a given moment depends on how she feels about her ability to do the task. "Control" seems to be the reason that some adults have problems with accepting the idea that children learn much more through interest-initiated learning rather than through other-directed learning. Until we accept that the human mind remains a mystery, we operate under the delusion that it is possible to measure and control what goes on in students' minds.

A student needs to discover on her own what contributions she wants to make to society in an atmosphere that promotes excitement for learning all that she can. Long term enthusiasm for learning is a result of allowing the student to set her own learning priorities and pace in a supportive, non-pressured environment.

Still Teaching Ourselves

Agnes Leistico

Lovingly dedicated to the memory of my mother, Lorene Rapp, and to the memory of my father-in-law, Everett Leistico, both of whom inspired us to constantly pursue our quest for learning.

Foreword

When we published Agnes' first book, *I Learn Better by Teaching Myself*, we were testing the homeschooling waters, so to speak. We had already published two other books, but Agnes' was something different: the story of how her family discovered, and then embraced, homeschooling.

There was nothing especially newsworthy or unique about Agnes' story. Her kids hadn't achieved academic acclaim, her family hadn't trekked across the Australian continent — they had simply chosen to learn together at home, like hundreds of thousands of other families. And yet Agnes' story had a familiar, comfortable and reassuring quality. It answered all the basic questions about homeschooling while offering a look at how her family moved toward a student-led, interest-initiated approach to learning. It promised to be a very reassuring book for anyone trying to move away from a highly structured approach to homeschooling.

I Learn Better by Teaching Myself struck a chord with the homeschooling community almost immediately, primarily because of the common-sense approach to homeschooling which Agnes advocated. She repeatedly questioned the popular and accepted ways of education, for example:

> A child can make better sense of the world on her own than we can do for her through adult produced curricula. My own children had to teach me the truth of this statement. I had been schooled to believe that certain trained adults were the only ones qualified to choose what is important to learn.
>
> Why do we allow adults greater freedom to learn according to individual learning styles than our children? More importantly, why don't we adults trust children to learn according to their

personal interests? Could it be we turn many of today's American children away from learning long before they attain adulthood because we do not allow our children the freedom of choice in utilizing their personal learning styles? These questions have puzzled me. I realize there can be no easy answer. I take comfort in the knowledge that many noted educators also ask these questions and seek answers.

The first edition went through three printings in two years. We revised it slightly (updating resource addresses) for a fourth printing in the Spring of 1994. The warm response from readers who wanted to know "What happened next?" convinced us (and Agnes) that a sequel to her book was in order.

Still Teaching Ourselves continues the story of the Leistico family's adventures in learning. As Agnes admits in her introduction, most of this story is about her struggle to learn to really trust her children's educational choices. But she rightly points out that it is also about her family's changing approach to education, and how their ideas and perceptions grew and developed into a program that works for them.

The author and the publishers hope that this book will be a helpful guide as your family travels the homeschool trail.

Mark and Helen Hegener
Publishers, Home Education Magazine

Introduction

One of the most valuable pieces of parenting advice anyone ever gave me was: "Follow your own parenting instincts no matter what anyone else says, as you know your child better than anyone else can ever hope to." I've found that when I don't follow my "mother's instinct" I often regret it.

Trust yourself. Forget about looking for experts to show you what you must do; do what is comfortable and right for your family. You can turn any mistakes you make into an important learning experience—the choice is yours. Our family is an ordinary family. Things do not always work out the way we want them to. We have our bad days as well as our good days. Mistakes happen, but we live through them. So take from this book what applies to your family, adapting it to meet your own needs and educational goals.

I face a personally uncomfortable challenge in writing this book because of the danger that some readers will seek answers in it as to how they should approach homeschooling and what results to expect. In my first book, *I Learn Better By Teaching Myself*, I asked readers to take it for what it was—simply the story of how our family learned at home five years ago. What I wrote about in that book worked for us at that time, but we do things very differently now. Each year, in fact, has been different because the educational needs of individual family members have changed.

Responses to my first book came from around the world. A mother in Micronesia wrote that she treasures the book.

Another mother from the Virgin Islands was visiting relatives near us and asked if she could stop in to visit and see firsthand how we homeschooled. People wrote from Europe and Africa. Reassurance poured in that other families also believed in trusting their children's educational choices, and that parents *can* know what is best for an individual student. It has been a wonderful experience to have strangers—many who have become friends—share their stories with me.

When *I Learn Better By Teaching Myself* was first published I received the following note from a Michigan mother:

> After I opened the package, the book sat on the couch. When my 7 year old homeschooled son noticed it, he read the title and said, "Hey, Mom! You see this? This is what I am trying to tell you!"

I wrote *I Learn Better By Teaching Myself* because I saw the need for a book that encourages parents to follow their own instincts and to trust their children. Numerous readers have written and visited with our family, expressing appreciation and asking specific questions about our approach. Many other readers inquired about an update on our family's activities. Helen and Mark Hegener asked me to consider another book, and this is why I have written *Still Teaching Ourselves*.

Still Teaching Ourselves reaffirms my strong belief that parents need to follow their personal parenting instincts and to trust their students to know what is best for them. Sometimes what we read in homeschooling publications gives an unrealistic view of what actually occurs in families. I hope you discover in this book that our family is not perfect; what we have done, you can do also. Over the years I have met numerous families whose stories are very similar to ours, and it is comforting to know we are not alone!

It seems to me that if we don't constantly question ourselves about what we are doing, we miss out on opportunities to expand our horizons. I constantly search for elusive answers concerning how we learn. In the process I learned the valuable lesson that copying what someone else does is not always satisfactory. It is all right to have doubts and to muddle your way through. Many people expect our school administrators and teachers to know what they are doing, but the reality is that often they know no more (sometimes even less) than we do as parents of our students.

I personally fought the idea of homeschooling because I could not imagine children learning any other way than within public or private schools. But my youngsters taught me a marvelous lesson. This is my story about my struggle to learn to trust my youngsters to make wise educational choices. I learned that it is possible to educate children without following strict schedules or guidelines. As a parent I am in the ideal position to fit the learning experience to each child as an individual student.

I have become much more aware that it is the "ordinary" part of life that is much more inspiring to me than the "outstanding accomplishments," because life consists primarily of ordinary happenings and accomplishments. It is important to accept myself, leading a personally satisfying life that is not built on someone else's standards.

Our family struggles within ourselves and with others, just as your family does. We face the challenge of serious health problems as well as the challenges our world presents to us. One of our family's current challenges is that our son Jim had to return home from college due to lack of finances and is not able to find a job. We are meeting this challenge and will come out better for it. Our challenges are more from today's world than from the educational choices we have made.

One caution: resources mentioned in this book may no longer be available when you read the book. Some of them had already become obsolete even before I wrote the book, but new resources are constantly becoming available. This can become an overwhelming challenge unless you keep in mind what your learning goals are and keep to them. Having lots of materials handy is not necessarily helpful—we found that having too many materials on hand was often distracting as well as a waste of money.

This book will provide an update on our family activities. You will also peek into some more specifics as to how we practiced interest initiated learning during our homeschooling years. Not everything was roses—there were thorns along the way. Nevertheless, no one in the family regrets our home-schooling adventure. In fact we grew from having experienced it.

Friends have allowed me to relate parts of their stories. There are so many other families experiencing similar events in their lives, whether homeschooling or not. To protect anonymity for these friends I refrained from giving identifying details. One friend, Chris, graciously allowed me to share her thoughts about homeschooling with you throughout this book, but there are many more friends who have shared their lives with me whom I have not mentioned. Thank you, every one of you, for offering our family your support and encouragement. Particular thanks go to John Boston and to Mark and Helen Hegener for making publication possible for both *I Learn Better By Teaching Myself* and *Still Teaching Ourselves*. Both books are about our family, but they each contain entirely different information.

Agnes Leistico
Lompoc, California

Chapter One

Our Family

Jim, Laurie, and Susan are eager students, and in the mid 1980s I thought things were going well for them in our local public schools. When Jim started refusing to go to his sixth grade classes even though he was doing quite well academically, I was forced to change my opinion about homeschooling. At that time I did not consider homeschooling a valid educational alternative, but seeing the depths of his misery, we decided to try it. My husband had grave doubts about the wisdom of doing this.

We took him out of the middle school in March, but the healing of his hurt spirit required many months. Even though previously he loved to read, now he could not stand to look at a book. Gradually he began to read for pleasure again; I tried not to pressure. I had to unlearn the mistaken ideas I had acquired over the years as to how people learn, and it required great patience for all of us in the family. The journey was not easy though we grew from this experience.

I had what I thought were terrific ideas of what and how Jim should learn, but he adamantly refused to cooperate with my schemes. In the process he taught me the wisdom of allowing students to learn in the manner that feels natural to them, according to their interests. Jim broke the ground for his sisters as they gradually joined him in homeschooling. The truth is that I still am learning from, with, and through them. After two and a half years of learning at home, Jim chose to go to the local public high school, where he eventually graduated eighth in a class of 250. A typical comment from his teachers was that they appreciated having a student in class who was there to learn. Indeed, Jim and Laurie's biggest complaint about high school is that very few of the students want to learn.

Jim had his own reasons for attending high school. He once

commented to a mother inquiring about homeschooling her high school-age son that he was grateful for his homeschooling experience because it taught him that he does indeed have a choice in his education. When in high school he saw what he had to do to work in and with the school system, and he freely chose to do so. This attitude enabled him to make it a positive experience for himself. When he went to high school he no longer refused to do the assigned homework because he realized it was part of the cost of choosing to go to school.

He got himself up to go to school in the morning. Previously, when he was going to elementary and middle school, I had a real struggle each morning to get him ready for school, and the struggle resumed in the evenings to get his assigned homework completed. (Interestingly, while homeschooling, getting up in the morning was not a problem, even though I expected him to get up at the same time he would have had to go to elementary or middle school. Of course, assigned homework while home-schooling was no problem because there was none!)

Laurie joined Jim at home six weeks after she started fourth grade. At Back-to-School Night Dale and I discovered that Laurie's teacher wanted every student to work on the same thing at the same time as all others in the class, even when this meant students had to be held back to the level of the slowest student. The teacher appointed class tattletales (whom she called "captains") to report the activities of classmates whenever her back was turned, and she chose Laurie to be one of her "captains." Now Dale and I understood why Laurie complained so much about being a class captain. Since I was actively involved in the school, I knew the principal well. He would have made the situation worse if I complained, so we had no recourse but to remove her from the campus. Dale told me as we left the classroom that we had to homeschool Laurie. This was particu-larly significant as he still was not convinced about home-schooling at that point.

Susan was in a good situation in a public modified Montessori magnet school. However, she wanted to join her brother and sister at home. So when school began the next fall we brought her home, too. Her biggest complaints about school were that there were too many interruptions, and she was not free to pursue her own interests.

One specific incident involved Susan wanting to learn to write in cursive. That was not in the curriculum, so she had not been allowed to pursue it, and as a result she lost interest in it completely. No amount of encouragement to practice her cursive while she was homeschooling had any effect. She simply refused. It was wasted effort to insist she improve her handwriting because she attached no importance to doing so. To this day she avoids writing in cursive when she can get away with it. Her handwriting is barely legible and she still has no desire to improve it. This has not hindered other aspects of her education, so I've decided it isn't worth worrying about.

No wonder each year we homeschooled was different! Not only did the youngsters have changing interests, but we also varied who was homeschooling. Jim was the only one at first; from March through September. He quickly taught me the basics: allow time for healing, you can't teach what the student does not want to learn, the student learns best when allowed to pursue personally chosen interests, and (most important) trust yourself as a parent while you trust the student to choose what is best for him or her.

After Jim began my education about learning, Laurie joined us to continue my education. The second year I had a seventh and a fourth grader at home. We still were fairly structured in approach, though I had already relaxed considerably. The following school year I had an eighth, fifth, and third grader at home. Susan had completed kindergarten and first grade in public school (we had delayed her entrance into kindergarten a year). I felt that she could easily handle third grade (and beyond) work so we considered her a third grader.

This was a wonderful year for me! Having all three youngsters home was so much easier than having them in three separate public schools. It definitely was less time-consuming for me to have them all at home.

I noticed many positive benefits in their relationships with each other that year. They got along better and were very cooperative during joint projects. There was considerably less conflict among them and they enjoyed being in each other's company. I also learned that sometimes the squabbling was done just for the fun of it - and sometimes it was done solely to get a rise out of me.

Providing meaningful learning experiences for them was no problem for me, although now I find out from them that sometimes I provided too much for their liking. A few activities which I thought they really enjoyed they now tell me they only did to make me happy and to keep me from bugging them! (They hasten to add that they are so glad they were home-schooled that they forgive me for my misplaced enthusiasm.)

Jim, Laurie, and Susan read extensively. One activity they still refer to with fondness and gratitude was my reading aloud to them in the evenings, and I have to admit it was my favorite activity, too. I read a wide variety of books covering many topics. Selections included fiction, historical novels, fantasies, myths, Shakespeare, classics, and "just for the fun of it" books. Jim tells me he used some of that reading background for his college classes.

As I became more comfortable with trusting them to make their own learning decisions, I relaxed more. In a letter to a friend, I wrote:

> Every now and then I get a little nervous about what they are learning since I don't do anything formal with them (they won't allow that anyway!). Then they do something that makes me wonder why I bother to worry. The other day Jim was talking about his high school American Literature class. He mentioned they had just finished Emerson and Thoreau, so he and I got into a discussion about Walden Pond. We agreed Thoreau did not greatly appeal to either of us (Jim loved Emerson, though, saying that he was his kind of guy). We were only using their surnames. Laurie did not want to be left out so she piped up that Henry David Thoreau did ... (I forget what she said because I was in shock that she knew his name, let alone that he was an author!). She insists she does

not remember how she knew him, but she obviously did. And I was worried....

Enrollment in high school turned out to be a very simple
process. I purposely waited until close to the beginning of classes because by then most of the teachers' schedules were settled,
thus assuring us of the possibility of better class schedules.
With Jim, I took along samples of books we used, including the
impressive algebra book from the University of California
Young Scholars math tutoring program (he had participated in
it during seventh grade, and continued using it on his own in
eighth grade).

I was apprehensive because I didn't know what to expect, but
what I learned was that the school was eager to enroll anyone.
The counselor was more interested in setting up a class schedule than in the materials I brought along. Because I appeared
more confident than I felt, he listened to my brief description of
Jim's abilities, then assigned him to several outstanding teachers. At Back-to-School Night I made a point of introducing Dale
to the counselor and thanking him for his assistance. We wanted him to be aware of our presence and interest.

This has paid off over the years. When I enrolled the girls in
high school, the counselor already knew me, and this made it
much easier. I gave him a copy of *I Learn Better By Teaching
Myself* when I became more comfortable with him. He read it
and asked if I would consider coming and talking with the
teachers on campus. I smiled, asking him if he really thought it
would make a difference, to which he ruefully admitted that he
did not think it would. With this counselor, at least, it has been
easier for other homeschoolers to enroll at that high school.

Homeschooling is not a guarantee that all students will succeed in the school system. Unfortunately, there was a case when
Laurie enrolled in high school of another homeschooled girl who
chose friends who were into drugs and truancy, and she ended
up in lots of trouble at school. This girl had been in our homeschool group for a year and had been to our house several times,
so we were surprised by her choice of lifestyle. Her parents
placed her in another high school the next year. We do not know
what has become of her since then.

Homeschooling Jim, Laurie, and Susan was the catalyst that spurred me into gathering together all the college credits I had accumulated over the years into a college degree. The year Jim chose to enter the local high school, I decided to pursue a degree in the field of education. Because I had no focus or compelling reason for having a college degree I could see no purpose to it, even though I had sufficient credits for a bachelor's degree spread over several colleges and universities. It was just a matter of doing it. Through homeschooling contacts I learned of the alternative, or independent study, route to a college degree. This suited me well because I resisted having to take classes in which I had no interest. I decided to also go on for a Master's in Educational Services.

In this independent college study program I was assigned a mentor who guided my degree work according to the requirements of that institution. She recognized my desire to make a meaningful contribution rather than to write a thesis which would probably gather dust on the school's library shelves. My first book, *I Learn Better By Teaching Myself*, was the result.

After Jim went to high school, Laurie and Susan continued homeschooling for two years. Then Laurie decided to join Jim at high school. As in Jim's case, I had no problem whatsoever enrolling Laurie in high school. By now the counselor knew and respected Jim so he was helpful in seeing that Laurie, too, received a good schedule of classes and teachers.

Laurie did not care for math so she had done very little at home, yet she quickly caught up with algebra class. It helped that she needed algebra if she was to stay in one of her favorite classes, a pre-chemistry/pre-physics class. The teacher made science live. He was so popular that his class was quickly filled. Before he came, the physics class barely got the minimum number of students, but after he arrived, there were several full physics classes. Laurie was determined she would do whatever it took to succeed in his pre-chem/pre-physics class. The algebra teacher made this a real challenge for her because of his teaching methods, yet this made her more determined than ever to master algebra.

Two years later Susan also chose to go to high school because of the activities and classes offered. Some teens seem to need more than can be offered at home. I cherish the year Susan and I had together before she made the choice to try high school. She is a very quiet person with deep feelings; when she is determined to do something she follows through with tenacity. Of the three students, Susan seems to have the greatest need to pursue her own interests.

The high school counselor was delighted to see Susan and me come in for enrollment. Several teachers have stated they wish there were more Leisticos coming because they were students in their classes eager to learn. I point out to any one who will listen to me that this is because as students they know they have a choice and because they have not lost the desire to learn as so many of their peers have.

It has not been an easy year for Susan due to severe health problems, but they have not deterred her in the least. I have had to face many frustrations working with the system because both girls have been quite ill this year. As long as they choose to remain at high school they have our full support. They know they can return home if necessary, and both of them have said that knowledge has helped them the most to cope with the school bureaucracy.

The transition Jim, Laurie, and Susan made into high school after homeschooling went very smoothly. In fact they experienced fewer adjustment problems than their friends who entered high school from the middle school. The middle school is a closed campus with strict controls on student activity, but the high school has an open campus where the students suddenly become responsible for getting themselves to classes on time and have an hour for lunch. The freedom to leave the campus any time of the day overwhelms many of the incoming freshmen, causing many problems of adjustment, but Jim, Laurie, and Susan were used to being responsible for themselves.

One thing in particular that I noticed was that even though Jim, Laurie, and Susan did not have specific math or science classes at home, they readily adapted to their science and math classes at high school. They did better than many of their classmates who had already covered most of the material in middle school and then found it repeated in their high school classes.

Articles in homeschooling publications sharing experiences of families whose children have gone to school after a period of homeschooling encouraged me to accept Jim, Laurie, and Susan's decisions to go to high school. We found that while this is primarily a personal choice, it involves the whole family.

The experiences of returning to a traditional school can differ even within the same family. One family I know has a daughter who chose enter the school system for the first time in sixth grade. She never regretted that decision even though her parents would have chosen differently for her.

Her brother had been in the school system through the third grade before his parents discovered homeschooling. He decided to try high school and it was a disaster. His mother said he became very mean spirited and ran around with the wrong crowd. After one year he came back home, where he was much happier. Later he took the California High School Proficiency Exam (the equivalent to a high school diploma in California that exempted him from compulsory education laws), and when he was ready he entered college quite successfully.

Several families in our support group report that local public school teachers usually cite the advanced thinking skills most youngsters have when entering their classrooms from homeschooling. In some cases the students were behind in one or more subjects, but in every case of which I am aware, the students caught up to their peers within a few months. Teachers remarked that their eager desire to learn was refreshing.

Going from the homeschool setting to the public school classroom has not been detrimental for any of the students I've known personally. My friend in Indiana proudly announced in 1991 that her son who had homeschooled from fourth grade through high school was granted a full scholarship to Purdue. He is still doing well, encouraging his younger brothers and sisters to continue their homeschooling.

At long last there are several other older homeschoolers in our area. This was one of the harder parts of homeschooling Jim and Laurie. We were the family with the oldest homeschooling students, and I often wished they could have homeschooling friends. During Susan's eighth grade there were several older homeschoolers though Susan could not find friends among them. Being homeschoolers does not automatically provide friendships any more than does the traditional schooling setup. Personal interests and interrelationships are the key to finding friends, not the educational setting.

While homeschooling, I was primarily guided by the youngsters' interests. I found it easy to cover all the subjects required by the state of California, while making them as interesting as possible. Our homeschool support group rented the municipal swimming pool once a week, helping to fulfill state physical education requirements in a fun way. We also organized several fascinating field trips.

I have found having a support group invaluable and enriching, but those of us homeschooling for primarily non-religious reasons seem to be in the minority. And in that we practiced "natural learning," "interest-initiated learning" or whatever you want to call it, we definitely were in the minority. We knew we were doing the best for our own children, but it was difficult to find people who understood.

Finding like-thinking parents helped us tremendously, although our belief was firm enough that we could do it by ourselves if that had been necessary. Feeling the need for further support when we removed Jim from the middle school, our family chose to join John Boston's California private school administrative unit, the School of Home Learning (later renamed Home Centered Learning). In 1992 John turned Home Centered Learning over to Susan Jordan and her husband David Zimmerman.

When we brought Jim home from the middle school we first chose another private school independent study program. This bought him time to begin the healing process while we struggled to become comfortable with the idea of homeschooling. However, the program's written assignments were too much like the schooling from which he needed to be released. When we encountered a problem with local school authorities, this particular program did not give us the support or information we needed.

Thanks to a homeschooling exhibitor at a parenting conference we attended, Dale and I met John Boston and were impressed by his low-key approach to homeschooling. He guided us through the unfortunate encounter with the district official, and further problems were avoided, even though we still were associated with the other independent study program. Three months later we decided to enroll in John's School of Home Learning, forfeiting the enrollment costs for the other program. This turned out to be a good decision for our family. Because I was a long-time active volunteer in the local school district and thus well known in several of the district's schools, I felt it was wiser not to file the California private school affidavit, which is publicly recorded. In our situation it was more comfortable to have the anonymity of filing under a private school administrative unit until school officials had forgotten about us.

I liked the freedom from handling administrative details (even though they are minimal in California) as I concentrated on my family's education. John has a calming effect with his quiet approach to handling problems as they arise, and as time went on our whole family enjoyed John's friendship and encouragement so much that we continued with his program until Susan entered high school. (And this friendship is still important to us.)

Home Centered Learning allows each family to choose its own course of studies according to the needs of the students. John provided us with a role model by always being ready to provide information when asked. The key was offering suggestions *only* when asked. Like some families, we did not fully appreciate this concept because we still were too used to being told what to do when directing learning activities. At first this was scary to us as we were so new to homeschooling and we lacked confidence in ourselves, but John's confidence in our ability to direct our own studies soon made us realize we *could* do it. We also realized we could do it on our own without joining Home Centered Learning.

Home Centered Learning provided us with a support group that extended much farther than our community. It was exciting to belong to a statewide organization where other families shared their learning adventures. While most families were choosing less structured, interest learning education, none of us were doing it in exactly the same manner. Freely sharing ideas with each other through the newsletter and through small informal conferences helped all of us discover the varied ways we learn. A key factor in this sharing was acceptance of each other and our choices even when they differed. There was recognition that there is no "right way" to learn.

Through John we also came into contact with the National Coalition of Alternative Community Schools (NCACS). We attended one of their conferences along with about 400 others, some from France and Japan. Laurie became good friends with one of the Japanese girls. They have continued to write to each other ever since meeting in 1986. In 1992 Dale and I attended the National Homeschool Association conference, where we renewed friendships made during the 1986 NCACS conference.

Some local school authorities and teachers want homeschool students to return to the public school system. However, other than sending letters focused on the tutoring section of the California Education Code to claim homeschooling is illegal in California, little action has been taken against local homeschoolers. This misrepresentation of the Education Code seems to be up to the discretion of individual principals. There are principals who just look the other way or, in a few cases, encourage individual parents to homeschool, offering assistance if desired.

One principal followed through on his threat to engage child protective services in a case I know about personally. The mother (brand new to homeschooling) had filed a private school affidavit but under pressure from the principal tried to re-enroll her son in the public school. The principal then refused to accept the child because he was "a disruptive influence" on the other students and had excessive absences. The mother then enrolled him in another district school because she was still under threat of a visit from child protective services. The principal and staff there welcomed her son, placing him in a much better situation than he had at his neighborhood school. Ironically, the principal and several of the teachers at the new school were favorable to homeschooling.

Later the mother discovered that her son was interviewed by a child protection agent at his new school. The agent later told the mother that she could tell immediately that there had been no "psychological abuse"—the charge made by the first principal about the parent. The agent further told the mother that she had not expected to find any signs of abuse when she learned that the reason for the complaint was homeschooling. She told the mother that people in her office tend to look the other way when the complaint involves homeschooling. The agent added she was aware of only one other "homeschooling" complaint in our whole county, but neither case of abuse was founded in fact.

Our community has been a good one in which to homeschool. Most of the time our family has encountered positive reactions from people when told what we were doing. When Jim first came home from the middle school, our district superintendent knew what we were doing because I was so visibly active in the district and personally acquainted with him due to my activity. While he did not see the wisdom of choosing to homeschool, he told me that as long as he was superintendent, homeschooling families would be left alone. Since then the district has had two other superintendents. I do not know their views on homeschooling, other than they wish we would go away, but neither one pursued ending homeschooling in the community.

While some local authorities have made efforts to make homeschooling uncomfortable, very few families in our community ever have any contact with them, and the few incidents which occurred have been resolved. Parents who seek our local support groups find the information they need to homeschool if they so choose.

During the last two years I have been asked to speak to a group composed of community leaders who devote a year to getting to know the community resources in depth. Different people are selected for this intense training each year, and they are expected to give back to the community a more knowledgeable leadership. A typical group can include representatives from the local Air Force Base, health-care professionals, members of the local media, city council members, and various business people. One month of the year-long program they focus on local education alternatives. Someone suggested having someone speak to them about homeschooling as an educational alternative.

Because the day's schedule is so full, they can only allot a short time to each presentation. The day's format varies. One year I spoke about homeschooling after the director of adult education, and before the representative for the public school nurses. The next year I was on a panel with a district official, a representative from the local teacher's union, and a representative for the school voucher movement.

The response both times was warm and positive, although very few participants on either occasion had ever heard of homeschooling. I noticed several men nodding their heads when I mentioned that not everyone's learning styles are addressed within the school system. Afterwards the event coordinators sent me a copy of the wrap-up evaluation saying that participants agreed that homeschooling is a topic to have in future training sessions.

Not everyone has the opportunity to present homeschooling to community leaders in this manner, but every family does have the opportunity to share homeschooling information within their community. I have had a positive response from most of my encounters, but there have been numerous times I was afraid of what response I'd get so I said nothing. Speaking to these community leaders was scary, but I'm glad now that I said yes.

In my experience, it is the mother who is most often the parent who is actively involved in homeschooling. Fathers are just as concerned about their children's education, but have fewer opportunities to explore the homeschooling alternative. The parent who is most actively involved in the education of their children is aquiring more information about educational alternatives, sometimes without even realizing the growing gap of information between the two parents, so open communication between both parents is essential.

One reader of my first book wrote in a letter to me:

> I'm eager for my husband to read your book, too. He's really left me alone this year in terms of what I'm doing. I hope that means he has faith that I know what I'm doing. He's so busy at work and working such long hours that he doesn't take a

very active role. I'm grateful that he can help the older boys (who go to public high school) with their math homework because it's sure out of my league! The other day he and I were talking, and I mentioned that I thought I'd like to go on a year-round 'schedule' so we can take more frequent breaks for record-keeping. He immediately said that it would never work because the little ones would never learn anything with the older boys home for the summer. It reminded me a lot of his old 'socialization' arguments that only died away when he saw how destructive the schools were to our younger boys. I realized then that he doesn't understand or trust interest-initiated learning yet. I've been here with the boys and seen exciting things happening that he's missed. I'll need to share these triumphs with him.

Chapter Two

Our Goals and Course of Study

Contrary to popular opinion, even among some of my closest friends, I am not a very organized person! Goal setting and writing out objectives are just *not* my favorite pastimes—if I can get out of either of these activities I will. It just goes against my nature to have to do this type of detail planning.

Over the years I have successfully managed my life, my family, and my activities with a minimum of organization. Friends see all I have accomplished and marvel at my organizational skills, but they only see what I want them to see. I function best when I focus on one project at a time. Everything on the fringes of a particular activity has to wait (sometimes in chaos) until I can refocus my attention to another project.

It requires great energy and determination on my part to prepare even a rudimentary outline for a talk or article, let alone for writing a book. Setting objectives for students in a specific learning situation is even more difficult for me to do because I do not believe I can command a student to learn. I can provide opportunities and resources for learning but I cannot force someone to learn what they don't want to learn.

Reading certain articles in homeschool publications and some books about homeschooling, you can get the impression that to successfully homeschool you have to spend hours setting up a course of study, formulating learning objectives, and writing lesson outlines. My college teacher training classes said I had to do that to be a good teacher, but I found out that I can't do that. If that works for you, fine. I can accept your approach as one that works for you. But I suspect that I have plenty of company and I want to reassure those of you like me that we are OK, too.

Despite how I feel about writing goals and objectives, I have found that there are times when it is valuable to write down the reasons why we are homeschooling. By writing our homeschool philosophy and goals we clarify what we are doing and why we are homeschooling. I've found it very reassuring to occasionally reread our family's educational goals as written when we first started homeschooling. Amazingly they have not changed over the years; our approach to learning specific subjects may have changed, but not the underlying reasons for choosing to home-school.

Another advantage to keeping a printed copy of our educational philosophy and goals was the comforting thought that should we be challenged I could produce a written document. There would not be a panicky race to prepare such a document as it was already there. We were never challenged, so I never had to produce it, but knowing it was there was a freeing thought.

I have also found it extremely helpful to review our goals and philosophy once in a while. Sometimes reviewing them encouraged me to keep going when I was assailed by frustration or doubts, and many times it reaffirmed me to reread them.

Following is a copy of our family's documentation of our educational goals and philosophy. If you are considering developing such a document, feel free to borrow what you want as long as it reflects your own family's goals. This is not an original document as we, too, borrowed phrases from many different sources, putting it together in a way that expressed our beliefs.

What We Want
For Our Children's Education
Dale and Agnes Leistico

We want our children to enjoy learning. We want them to become well adjusted adults who can function capably, have a good self-image, be sensitive and caring, and ever wanting to learn more. We want them to know and accept their strong points as well as their weak points. We want them to be able to enjoy their environment.

To us true education is not knowing all the answers but knowing where and how to find answers when applicable. We recognize our children have great intellectual capacity and want them to be able to reach their potential through being allowed to think creatively without undue stress.

We want our children to be allowed to learn at their individual pace with their self-esteem intact. We believe that a home learning situation can foster a warm, loving environment where acceptance and security to possible in a greater degree than in a large classroom setting.

Our country was founded on a strong value system which had its source in a strong family life. Our country's greatness depends on integrity, honesty, respect for others as well as for ourselves. A deep faith in a Supreme Being plays an important role in our country's history, which is today being eroded. Parents can best develop positive values such as religious belief, self-reliance, initiative, kindness, resourcefulness, creativity, and responsibility.

We feel social development is important. We have three children, which provides daily group experiences within the family. We believe that family cooperation should be the model and basis for broader relationships. In addition to family relationships, friends are important. Our children continue to interact with their friends in and out of the neighborhood. And there is a greater age range which is an enriching experience. We are more concerned about the quality of relationships than the quantity. We have observed that homeschooled children tend to be more outgoing, friendlier, and more self-confident. They usually are better conversationalists and tend to become stronger leaders than children who have attended schools. They are better able to withstand peer pressures to conform because their value systems are stronger and are not daily exposed to negative influences until maturity has been attained.

Our Goals

1. To promote good health practices: good nutrition, ample rest, exercise.

2. To provide a pleasant learning environment.

3. To maintain consistent, loving discipline.

4. To foster motivation—by providing a wide variety of opportunities for study, within and without a basic framework of fundamental areas and to encourage learning by doing.

5. To evaluate readiness for various tasks according to knowledge of changing physical, social, mental and moral development of each child.

6. To learn WITH them and enjoy their discoveries and achievements.

7. To provide a schooling experience compatible with our religious values and philosophy of education.

8. To provide the time for our children to develop their special interests without a harried lifestyle.

9. To meet the need for active learning from real life situations and to provide a place where learning is not separate from the rest of life.

10. To measure progress and achieve a competence level without grade competition and to provide a solid base for future learning.

We gave ourselves a name—Somerset Academy. Not exactly a very creative name, but it worked well for us. Our street name is Somerset. I did not want the word "school," so "academy" indicated an alternative education facility to me. Having a school name opened a lot of doors for us with school suppliers. Since we were part of John Boston's Home Centered Learning we were not inundated with the junk mail sent to homeschoolers who were listed in the California Private School Directory (because of filing the private school affidavit). Still, Somerset Academy received its share of advertisements, some of which we even benefited from.

Another document which I prepared and kept on file at all times was a listing of our courses of study. Home Centered Learning provided us with a basic course of study in case of a challenge, but I felt it would be wise to supplement it with one of our own. After doing a lot of research on this, I developed one that covers all the courses outlined by the state for California students. It helped me greatly to find a model when I wrote up our course of study. My primary model was the publication *California Modern Curriculum Standards*. Again no one ever challenged us, but it was comforting to know I was prepared. I might have had to expand on it if challenged, but at least I have a basic document on which to build. Again, you are free to adapt this for your circumstances, if you choose.

Somerset Academy
Courses of Study Offered

English

Students will be encouraged to enhance their speaking, reading, listening, spelling, handwriting, and composition skills, using methods consistent with their learning styles and capabilities. There will be emphasis on a knowledge of and an appreciation for many different types of literature and uses of language skills.

Mathematics

Students will be encouraged to increase their knowledge of mathematical concepts, operational skills, and problem solving. There will be emphasis on every day applications of mathematics. Student learning styles will govern the approach to mathematics.

Science

Students will be encouraged to learn about the biological and physical aspects of our world and the process of experimental inquiry. This includes basic concepts, theories, and processes of scientific investigation as well as the interrelation and interdependence of the sciences. They will be encouraged to explore further their particular interests in the field of science. Emphasis will be placed upon humanity's place in the ecological system, in particular, wise use of natural resources. Methods of learning will be consistent with each student's learning style and capabilities.

Fine Arts

Students will develop their aesthetic appreciation and their skills of creative expression according to their learning styles and interests. The instruction in art, drama, and music will reflect these interests and learning styles.

Physical Education

Recognizing the need for a healthy body in order that students may optimally learn, students will be offered the opportunity for regular physical exercises, according to their interests and capabilities, of a minimum of 200 minutes for each ten schooldays.

Health

Students will learn the principles and practices of individual, family and community health. Included in these studies will be the effects of alcohol, narcotics, drugs, and tobacco; personal protection and public safety; accident prevention, emergency first aid, hemorrhage control, treatment for poisoning, resuscitation, and fire prevention; AIDS education.

Social Sciences

Students will be encouraged to explore more deeply, consistent with their learning styles and capabilities, the fields of anthropology, economics, geography, history, political science, psychology, and sociology. They will be encouraged to build on their understanding of the history, resources, development, and government of California and the United States. They will explore the American economic system, man's relation to human and natural environment, world wide cultures and civilizations, and contemporary issues. This includes the historical roles of men and women as well as the ethnic groups particularly involved in American history such as black American, American Indians, Mexicans, Asians, and Pacific Island people. Students will study the American legal system—such as the operation of juvenile and adult criminal justice systems, rights and duties of citizens under the criminal and civil law and the Federal and State constitutions. Human rights issues will be emphasized, especially the inhumanity of genocide.

Foreign Language

Students will be encouraged to study a foreign language according to their interests and capabilities with a view to understanding and appreciating the foreign language. Enhancement of speaking, reading, and writing skills in a foreign language will be encouraged.

Applied Arts

According to student interest, the study of the following applied arts will be offered: consumer and homemaking education, industrial arts, or general business education.

Vocational-Technical Education

All students will be prepared for gainful employment, according to their interests and capabilities.

With these documents safely stored in our file cabinet along with our enrollment forms for Home Centered Learning, we proceeded to homeschool in our own way. Your way will be different than ours. As I describe what happened during our learning adventures, you may find something you can use or maybe something you want to avoid. Most of all, my hope is that you will keep in mind this is what happened to us. I am not saying it is something you should or should not do. Do what works for you, whether you use a more or less structured approach is your business. I respect you for your choice.

Memories came flooding back as I reread what I wrote to John Boston shortly after Jim decided to try the local high school:

> The girls and I sat down to plan this quarter on Monday (I should say "I" sat down to plan as they weren't at all interested in planning—they were too busy with their own plans and I was so wrapped up in "my" ideas I hadn't noticed until I met with unmistakable resistance). Actually, we are so busy living life to the fullest as it confronts us, that when I take the time to study what has happened I realize we have magnificently covered all "subjects"!

Interfering or planning too much was my biggest problem. Thank goodness they would not let me get away with it. Now that both girls are in high school I can observe how adults deceive themselves when they think that because they are the teachers they know exactly what should be learned.

Laurie is getting high school work education credit by being a fifth grade teacher's assistant at a local elementary school. The other day the teacher asked her to help a student with math phobia. Laurie could relate to the girl's difficulty, so she told her that when she was her age she felt the same way but had now discovered how much she needs to know these math basics if she wants to succeed in life. Laurie helped that girl in a way no adult could; Laurie had learned her lesson well. I can remember when I thought she would not realize how important basic math skills are. I continued in my letter to John:

> For example, September was our break time since we are on year round schedule. During the month the girls took the Parks and Recreation swimming lessons. Susan is suddenly swimming where just a few months ago she would not leave the side of the pool. Laurie is diving off the diving board where before she, too, did not venture very far from the edge or into any great depth of water. They were finally ready to take these steps. Laurie planned a special "Back to School Party" at a local park for homeschoolers. She handled all the details and planning and everyone thoroughly enjoyed the event. We attended a six part series on the role of cults in American society today. We again provided an inexpensive book ordering service for families through Scholastic Book Clubs. We spent three long days preparing for and assisting at a huge rummage sale for Laurie's youth group at church. Laurie began her special Confirmation classes at church. Both girls are active in their Campfire groups. And both read, read, read, and read some more. All of this on "break"! So why do I worry about the times I am recording their "attendance" at class for the state? The girls keep me in line— when I listen to them.

Each year had its share of surprises. We would start out doing one thing and end up doing something we never even dreamed of at the start of the year. It was rather exciting! Our documented goals and philosophy were fleshed out. Some things worked for us and others were dismal failures, but we weren't committed to doing specific things because of our generalized goals. We were simply committed to providing the best learning circumstances we could.

Flexibility allowed us to experience learning naturally. I had to have great patience, which was not always easy as I like to see results. For instance I once wrote to a friend about Susan:

> Right now she is not in one of her writing periods. She is in her dreaming stage. I never know what to expect out of her when this stage comes to fruition. Sometimes there is a quiet advance that can easily not be noticed unless I am specifically observing. Other times she outwardly starts producing some activity on which there is no doubt whatsoever that it came from the dreaming stage. I honestly do not think she is even aware of what the end result of her period of dreaming will be. The few times I question her as to what she is thinking about I almost never receive a concrete answer. Usually it is something like, "Nothing in particular." And my impression at that time is that she is being totally honest with me—even to her nothing seems to be happening.

Most homeschoolers are so busy with their learning activities that they do not realize how eager others are to find out what they are doing and how. This sharing is invaluable, it gives fresh perspectives, encouraging creative adaptations for other families. The challenge is to get people to share their experiences. "I'm not doing anything special, glamorous, stupendous, or even exciting. Who would be interested in how our family approaches learning?" is a common response. Knowing this, I share our experiences. Talking with a variety of homeschoolers, I quickly realize that our story is not unique; many other families have similar experiences. We are not alone.

Sometimes I feel a subtle pressure to produce articulate students who (seemingly) should be eager to tell the world about their experiences so they can be analyzed to death. It is the impression that we have to prove homeschooling works by producing extraordinary students. My own youngsters don't feel they are doing anything extraordinary and don't really want to share anything with others concerning their thoughts and feelings. Yet when they feel like they have something to share, they freely do it. Laurie's biggest hangup in high school is being told what to write about. Left to her own devices she writes letters and notes prolifically and expresses a depth of meaning in them.

What are our goals? Looking over our family's goals, I see no mention of college. Yet I get caught up in the pressure society places on parents to put their children through college. Some of us feel a lot of this pressure. At those times I have to ask myself how necessary college will be for their happiness.

Homeschoolers are not at a disadvantage when it comes to college. Individual colleges may have specific entrance requirements which pose a challenge, but the enormous choices for a college program make it possible to find a suitable one for any student. I do not find that there is that much difference concerning college entrance for students, no matter what their high school background. Homeschoolers who direct their own studies seem to have no more problems entering college than other students. The college entrance maze is just as perplexing for families with school counselors who supposedly offer guidance as it is for homeschool families. In our case, we found out most of our information on our own. School counselors often do not have adequate training and almost none have the time to skillfully guide most students into colleges.

So, if college is part of your student's goals, there are resources readily available to guide you. Consider this: is this your goal, or is it his or her goal? That is an important question to ask yourself honestly.

Writing my first book, *I Learn Better By Teaching Myself*, I interviewed several homeschoolers who had chosen to either go into college or into the work force after completing their high school experiences. What struck me was their sense of confidence in their decisions. Those who chose college were often told by their professors that it was refreshing to have a student in class who was there to learn, not just to do what everyone else was doing. The respondents who had chosen to enter the work force also felt they had made the right decision (some commented that college was still an option for later on).

College is no guarantee for a career in today's fast-paced,

fast-changing society. Career counselors are increasingly telling those who come to them faced with a forced career change (due to lay-offs, company take-overs, and   business failures) not to consider going to college unless they have a specific career goal in mind that requires college courses or degrees. Counselors caution clients to find out exactly what is required for job advancement or procurement.

It is important to carefully consider all aspects before encouraging our youngsters to go into college; it is no disgrace to be without a college degree. We do not prove to anyone that homeschooling works by sending our students to college. A college education is most valuable when there is a specific goal in mind or it is a requirement of a chosen profession. I certainly will encourage my teens to obtain a college education when this is evident, but college only has value when it provides useful and meaningful experiences voluntarily chosen by the student.

Planning for the years after high school is more a question of helping youngsters decide what they want to do with their lives than choosing the best college to get into. The best use of our teens' high school years is to allow them to explore their interests and talents. Homeschools are an excellent place for this to happen as our institutional schools do not usually have this as a part of their curriculum. This is the time teens should use to discover who they are and what they would like to do with their lives. This demands patience on our part as we allow our teens the space and time to explore the many possibilities that exist around them for creative, useful lives.

There is wisdom in letting children proceed at their own pace. When they are ready to move on, they will do so with greater confidence if they've been allowed to do it their way. I've watched one friend's girl change from a young child that would go into hysterics if she lost sight of mom for even a second, to a ten-year-old who looks forward to activities away from home and mom, even for days at a time. Her mother met her needs when she was young.

Another friend was very concerned because her son was not the least bit interested in reading until he was nine. Under pressure from her husband, she placed him in a public school when he was ten years old. His teacher was impressed by his reading ability and in particular his reading comprehension skills. His mother was so grateful he had been able to start reading when he was ready. She admits that it was difficult on her because she wondered if he would *ever* be able to read. Her husband thought she was not pushing him hard enough!

Homeschoolers have the opportunity to do something that is difficult, or that they don't particularly want to do, in order to reach some larger goal. Neither Susan nor Laurie feel they have faced particularly difficult things to reach their goals, yet by our adult standards, they have indeed done just that—except for Laurie and Susan it was "easy" not "difficult."

A good example is the ease with which they have learned to use the computer. I have had to struggle hard just to get to the point I am in using the computer—and I have lots more to learn. It was a big deal when I got comfortable enough to use the tape recorder with our Radio Shack 64K TRS-80 computer. I used that method to produce several newsletters. First, though, I had to spend weeks (more like months!) learning to use the word processing program for that computer.

Then when we got our first IBM clone I was forced to learn how to use a floppy disk if I wanted to continue using a computer. Besides that, I had to relearn using a word processor program that was much more advanced than the basic one I had used. When we installed a hard disk in the computer I had to learn all over how to start the computer. (I've never regretted any of this learning—just wished it could have been easier!) Almost everything I know about a computer, I have taught myself, and this experience reminds me why Jim, Laurie, and Susan react the way they do to certain educational situations.

Just after we got our IBM clone, Laurie wanted a program to produce newsletters so we bought PFS *First Publisher*. I sat down for two days with it, finally succeeding in producing a fair flyer for Laurie to give the customers on her newspaper route. It took her less than three hours to produce her first newsletter, and she quickly learned how to make clever cards for friends. It was no big deal to her, but to me it was a great accomplishment to get out one simple, no frills flyer in two days.

Susan went through the tutor manual for the *Alpha Four* database program. I had spent four long, intense, days on that manual, yet in less than an hour she was competently breezing through the first few chapters.

Dale has become very knowledgeable about computers, even to the point of doing most of the troubleshooting necessary when our computer has a problem. This knowledge is a direct result of his own interest in learning all he can about computers. Jim, Laurie, and Susan have varying interest in using the computer, with Susan being the least interested. They use it as a tool to accomplish what their present interests direct them to.

Jim was the first one to become interested in a local computer bulletin board through a good friend at high school. We had a modem for our Radio Shack TRS-80 (which we have kept and still use on occasion) but because the TRS-80 only has 64K he could only operate on 300 baud. Besides, the screen added letters to what you typed when using the modem, making use a challenge. But he persisted. All three youngsters now appreciate using the more powerful IBM clone computer.

We purchased a better modem which did not work properly at first. One afternoon I came home to find Jim and a friend surrounded by a dismantled computer—they had decided to track down the problem on their own. Jim had learned so much more about the workings of a computer through this experience than he would have in a year in his high school computer classes. (Of course my husband, Dale, was still not thrilled to see the computer dismantled!)

Dale is a self-taught computer person and has more knowledge about computers than I ever will. He learned about them because as an electrical engineer—and a ham radio operator—he sees the necessity for knowledge about computers. I have to give him great credit for restraining himself when he learned what Jim was doing, as Dale's first instinct was to protect the computer investment. It was not easy for him to let Jim learn about the working of the computer in his own way.

Shortly after Jim got on line with the bulletin board, Laurie also started using it. It took them very little time to learn how to operate the modem, they just did it. Shortly after that, Susan decided to join them online, and she quickly mastered using the modem, although Susan still is not that comfortable using the computer. But she knows it is available for when she chooses to use it.

A challenge the youngsters encountered with using the modem was getting correctly connected between the modem and the bulletin board. One day, quite by accident, they discovered that if you lift the telephone receiver at a certain point in the attempt you will connect. (This is a unique situation with our equipment so it won't necessarily work for anybody else.)

They knew they had a problem, spent a lot of time experimenting with solving it, and eventually found the solution by accident—sounds like a familiar story in science, doesn't it? They creatively attacked their problem from many different angles—some of which Dale and I, had we been asked our opinion (luckily we weren't!), would have discredited or discouraged.

Over the years, Chris and I have become good friends, often sharing our joys and questions about how our children are learning. Her children are younger so I appreciate her insights. One time she wrote an article for our support group newsletter about who homeschoolers are:

> When people ask me about homeschooling, I'm happy to talk to them about my experiences and their options. The qualifier in all these conversations, however, is that my experiences are unique. So are every other homeschooler's.
>
> I know people who started homeschooling very loosely and gradually developed more structure as their children grew or as they recognized that it worked for them better that way.
>
> I also know homeschoolers who started out very structured and found that things went much better when they relaxed more.
>
> I know people who withdrew their children from school and found that the healthiest thing to do for their child the first year was to take a break and allow that child time to re-focus and discover some reasons of their own for learning or pursuing an activity.

> Some people have had a different experience. They withdrew their children from public school, expecting to embark on a very relaxed, unstructured, "unschooling" experience and found that their children wanted some class-like activities every day. And, it worked out best to provide that.

There are innumerable versions on the homeschooling theme, all of which can work for the family that practices them. There are also some underlying principles which tie all successful homeschooling families together.

The first truth about homeschooling is that it's based on relationship. Relationship is the curriculum upon which everything else is based. Relationship is a day-to-day awareness, an honest looking at oneself and others and an honest dealing with oneself and others.

Successful education, including home education, is based on reason, not absurdity. That sounds obvious, but much conventional school is unreasonable. Random facts are taught to cover state mandated curriculum requirements.

The mind needs a reason to learn. When it doesn't have one, learning becomes divorced from life and thought and therefore absurd. The parent who wants a child to learn something may have some very good reasons for thinking the child should learn it, but the child needs to be infected with those reasons—and reason needs to be expected if learning is to occur.

Education that empowers children, gives them a lifelong skill or strengthens the mind has its own reasons for compelling a child to learn. Interest-initiated learning is particularly successful because the reasons are built into the process by the child.

Another principle of education is that it starts and ends with the child. It's individual. Every child has his or her own particular time-table and special qualities. The mind of a child, or anyone else, cannot be controlled. The mind can't even be taught, really. Not in any significant way. But, it can learn. That's where relationship and reasoning play their part.

These all—relationship, reason, individuality—require an atmosphere of freedom to thrive. Freedom is a necessary requirement for the development of an active, intelligent mind. This isn't freedom to do anything you want, to pursue any whim, but freedom based on reason, good relationships and individuality.

Education isn't so much about the superficial things we remember from our school days, math problems or textbooks, as it is about these essentials. Focus on the essentials and find the peripherals that align with them. This focus might lead to some of the traditional things of school, a good textbook or math problems. But it will be in a way that works for you and your child, and for reasons that fit.

Let's give our children the opportunity to be secure at home. Let them stretch out when they are ready, not when others think they should. My own children have surprised me with their choices and timing—and the directions they have then taken. Having written down our learning goals and educational philosophy was well worth doing. They freed us to learn our own way.

Chapter Three

Activities and Resources

This is a scary chapter to write. I am so afraid a reader will see all the activities mentioned and think: "How can I ever come up with that many activities?" However, these took place over a period of seven years, and thanks to the Quarterly Reports which I wrote up, many forgotten activities are included. Memory plays many tricks on me—thank goodness I noted at least some of our activities, though now I wish I had written down more.

At first I only wrote up Quarterly Reports because I wanted to be ready just in case someone challenged our homeschool activities. But as time went on and no one inquired, I did not write as many details. Now I wish I had continued in greater detail so I could have preserved many more precious memories. When I reread the Quarterly Reports I marvel at just how much we did do, even though at times I wondered what we were accomplishing.

No matter where you live, there are numerous opportunities for activities that promote learning. Look around your community; rural and urban opportunities vary. Make the most of what you have. We live in a large town that is surrounded by rural areas that stretch for miles; our surroundings probably are different than yours. Read about our activities, then creatively consider what is available to you. I remember reading an article shortly after beginning to homeschool about a family living in the San Francisco Bay Area. I was envious of their location until I read another article about a family living far from any neighbors, yet they had equally enriching activities. Then I began to appreciate what was available to *us*.

During the summer, our church sponsors a Vacation Bible School, and Jim, Laurie, and Susan enjoyed going to this. As they got older they became active in planning and supervising some of the games and classes. Seventh and eighth grade students had a shortened class and then helped in the younger classes for the rest of the morning. Jim preferred working with the Games Director. Laurie became the first grade teacher when she was an eighth grader, and handled the experience very well. Until this year our family was the only homeschooling family in the congregation. We are making our presence known in a positive way to the community.

Jim and Laurie often babysat and tutored for several local homeschoolers. Susan was not interested in doing either, although she would on rare occasions. Laurie was a very popular babysitter; she has a special knack with children. When Laurie was only ten years old one mother had her come watch her two younger children while the mother taught her older son. The boys also regarded Jim as their hero and would follow him around when they could.

The mother was very pleased with this arrangement. On Fridays her son began spending time with Jim doing activities involving reading and math based on their mutual interest: baseball card collecting. Another mother asked Jim to teach her older daughter and son one morning a week so she could devote time to her two little ones.

One quarter I wanted all three youngsters to learn typing skills on the computer. It was a boring activity, but Dale and I tried to motivate them; we considered it an invaluable skill. I can laugh about this attempt now, but at the time I was frustrated; no matter how hard I insisted it was "good" for them, the results were always the same—a big fight which I could not win. Jim did take a semester of typing in high school because he was motivated to increase his speed on the keyboard, but neither Susan or Laurie yet see a need for increasing their typing skills.

Another time I planned to devote a large block of time to use some resource materials to discuss the problem of AIDS (a California requirement). As a service to all of their customers, Scholastic Magazines sent resources to assist in AIDS education. As usual the youngsters amazed me with their accurate information concerning AIDS; in twenty short minutes we had covered all the suggested material. Often the youngsters gave

me the information before I could give it to them, yet I had not
"officially" presented this material to them previously. They had
no misinformation needing clarification. Who needs teachers?

I did not find it difficult to work with all three at the same
time despite their age differences (8, 10, and 14). For instance,.
when we were devoting time to health issues we used both the
Visible Man and Visible Woman models, as well as several
interesting anatomy books. Together we briefly covered body
systems and functions. Then I let them know what resources we
had available. They took it from there, but none of them were
particularly interested. I figured they at least know where to
find any information they need when they need it. I had
obtained copies of the appropriate grade level health textbooks
used by the school district—which they mostly ignored.

Our support group planned many field trips, and the field
trips we went on with homeschoolers were usually more interesting and fun than most of the field trips I assisted with in the
school district, even though they were similar: the fire station,
museum, library, mission, grocery store and post office.

Our homeschool support group also planned field trips to
many places the local schools did not. One trip was to an underground missile silo on the nearby military base. Another one
was an all day tour of an airport facility that included a
National Weather Service station and a chance to go up into the
airport control tower. We visited a fancy restaurant and were
treated to lunch by the staff afterwards. Visiting a bakery and
a store where fresh fudge is made by hand also ended with eating some of the goodies!

Our field trip to City Hall was a highlight in our family's
homeschool experience. We were graciously treated. Since our
group was small enough, every City administrator whose office
we entered explained what their responsibilities were to the
local citizens. The youngsters afterwards mentioned how they
had not realized before that as citizens, we should be involved
in local government.

For about three years we visited a local wilderness beach
monthly, observing first hand the seasonal effects on the beach
habitat while getting healthful exercise. This was a popular
activity with most of the members of our original support group.

Nothing special was planned; we just met at the beach, relaxed, and enjoyed ourselves. One day we were treated to the sight of dolphins swimming near the shore. We parents were careful to avoid making this excursion a "learning" experience, although at times we were tempted to become "teacherish." The looks on the youngsters' faces quickly let us know we were starting to spoil what had become a learning experience in the best sense.

I noticed a big difference between the attitudes of the students on field trips with the school district and the trips I took with our homeschool group. The homeschool groups were smaller, with a wide variety of ages among the children. Going to a pumpkin farm in October was much more fun for everyone with the homeschool group than it was when I went with two busloads of public school youngsters.

Someone I happened to know was our tour guide for a field trip to the post office. When I saw him a few days later he said that when we left the post office his supervisor called him over to ask why he had spent so much more time with our group than with the other school groups who were touring the post office. He replied that this was the most interested group of youngsters he had ever encountered. They asked more questions than he had had from other groups, so he took the time to answer all their questions. He wondered why the attitude of these youngsters was so different from most of the school tour youngsters he had encountered.

Only a few adults went on the school field trips whereas at least one parent from each family was almost always present for our homeschool trips. Seeing how interested their parents were made an impression on the youngsters. They were doing this together and could, if they chose, discuss the trip later. We found that we could take our homeschool youngsters on any field trip the school district could, plus a wide variety of other tours the district could not. This year, due to budget woes, our school district has eliminated almost all field trips, but our homeschool group continues offering a wide variety of field trips.

I did nothing special in preparation for field trips as far as Jim, Laurie, and Susan were concerned; they chose which field trips they wanted to go on because of their interests. Whenever

I did try to give a pep talk beforehand to prepare for what they would see, do, or hear on the field trip, I found I unwittingly spoiled the effects of the excursion for them. With them it was preferable to let them make whatever preparations they chose (or none). Afterwards we usually discussed what they had seen and done on an informal basis. This seemed to be the most effective approach for us.

As Jim, Laurie, and Susan got older, field trips appealed less to them. They had gone to the fire station, the grocery store, and the museum with both the school district and the home-school group. But these tours were aimed for younger students anyway. Gradually we stopped going on the field trips for two reasons: their interests had changed, and, for a while, the time field trips were offered had changed to afternoons instead of mornings. We preferred morning trips because we were already committed to some afternoon activities as well as having an early supper.

To fulfill California requirements concerning first aid, I arranged with the Red Cross to present BAT (Basic Aid Training) classes for our homeschoolers. Another time I shared videos of damage caused by the 1989 Loma Prieta earthquake. Some of the video was a personal look at damage done to my parents' house and to their neighbors who were at the epicenter. Some of the video was taped from news broadcasts containing scientific information and earthquake preparedness suggestions. This also meaningfully fulfilled the California requirement on teaching earthquake safety.

Other activities which I organized for several homeschooling families included three different ones related to the Constitutional Bicentennial. The events were planned with student participation in mind, and during most of them the youngsters willingly participated. It was quickly evident when the activity was not interesting, but some parents tried to force participation in the event. I did put a lot of time and effort into preparation but could see no point in proceeding if the youngsters were not interested.

One September Autumnal Equinox was at noon time. The TV weatherman on a local station told listeners about an ancient custom of standing eggs on end during the Equinox. Knowing he regularly visited schools to talk about weather and weather forecasting, I wrote asking him to join us at a park to share weather information and for standing eggs on end during the Equinox. He called asking if he could also bring a cameraman to record the event. Parents in our group gave their permission to do this. The youngsters were delighted to see themselves on the evening news that night, but because some parents were uneasy about possible repercussions, we were only identified as a group of school children, not as homeschoolers.

As a result of this encounter, another reporter from the television station came to our house for a story about homeschooling. The reporter did some research before coming, as homeschooling was new to him. We had such a good time with him as he filmed Laurie and Susan that he stayed almost three hours instead of the one hour he had originally planned. His news piece was sensitively done. He had caught the spirit of homeschooling as opposed to schooling at home.

Parents have asked me how they can find out what their children are interested in so they can tailor the learning experiences accordingly. Remembering my own initial concern and how I had had to realize for myself that I already knew my own youngsters best (although I did not think I did at the time), I usually suggest they unobtrusively observe their children's current activities.

It's easy to take these activities for granted; they may be so obvious that you don't see the clues they give you. Are they interested in 4-H, Campfire, Scouts, community or church groups? These can often give you unexpected clues. Which activities keep them engrossed? What are their favorite topics of conversation? How do they spend their free time?

Most homeschooled youngsters who enter into the school system encounter few problems adjusting. For many, the adjustment is similar to students who adjust to a new school in a new district or state where procedures vary from the previous school.

An advantage for most homeschooled students is that they approach the new school experience with a more intact desire to learn than their counterparts. This can be a detriment in some instances if the enhanced thinking skills are not desired by certain teachers—who want to teach "cookie press" classes. It comes down to what you as a parent expect from your student. Homeschooling encourages enhanced thinking skills and a love for learning, and parents should have some say in who teaches their child.

Of course there are homeschooled students who encounter problems, sometimes large problems, when going into the school system, private or public. However, I wonder if these problems are not because the child homeschooled, but because of other reasons. Being homeschooled did not necessarily cause the problem, just as being homeschooled does not necessarily mean that the child will smoothly enter into or excel in the system. When a child encounters problems on entrance into the school system, I wonder if the problems are not as severe as they would have been had the child been in the system all along. Homeschooling may have provided a safe place for a child with problems—an opportunity to lessen the severity of whatever problem is involved.

Because of increasing pressure from influential members of their church congregation, a friend of mine, whose husband was the church's pastor, had to place her three children into a local school after homeschooling for several years. The oldest son adjusted well to his new school immediately, but the younger two had problems so they switched schools.

During all of this the parents learned that in homeschooling they had adjusted to the different learning styles of each child. The two younger ones had learning styles not well addressed in a classroom setting, and one child also had an eyesight problem which they were not aware of until the child had severe adjustment problems in her new school. The parents and children in this family are grateful they homeschooled for as long as possible.

Our family's homeschooling approach of interest initiated learning was different from the more structured approach taken by most of the other local homeschooling families, but now there are many more families with a more relaxed approach to learning. We joined John Boston's Home Centered Learning program because we appreciated the support and encouragement he offered us; it cut the feeling of isolation due to our interest initiated learning approach. Fortunately our local support group was at that time tolerant of differing educational philosophies, but it helped to be in contact with other families with a similar philosophy.

Once someone wrote to Susan and Laurie asking them to write an article for publication about if and how they learn something from other children. Neither girl responded to the query. As I pondered why they did not respond, I began to realize that because they were learning from others constantly (from both children and adults), they didn't consider what was happening extraordinary enough to write about. They just took it for granted, and did not question from whom they learned. I still observe them constantly learning from people of all ages and, in turn, helping others learn.

For over a year we cared for a neighbor's four-year-old daughter several days a week, and both girls, each in her own way, interacted with Cathy all day long. Laurie helped Cathy with reading and writing because Cathy showed a natural readiness, while Susan imparted her appreciation for nature. Our yard is a typical small California backyard, but it teems with life. We have three fish ponds, literally thousands of polliwogs, a wide seasonal variety of birds (because we are on a migration path), as well as all sorts of bugs, lizards, spiders, plants and trees. Cathy insistently asked, "Why?" and Susan would patiently explain. One day I overheard Susan explaining contrasting and complementary colors to Cathy after our issue of *KidsArt News* (devoted to the topic of color) had come.

A science resource we enjoyed using as a family was learning modules from TOPS Learning Systems. All three youngsters worked with the Pendulums and the Magnetism units. Jim worked some with the Probability task cards. This year Susan is using materials from the Oxidation module in preparation for her high school science fair project. A feature I especially appreciate about these modules is that each one is complete in itself. All the experiments are clearly explained using materials that are readily available. An added advantage is that they are not expensive. Jim, Laurie, and Susan found the experiments fun to do, and so did I.

In the magnetism unit, we covered what is magnetic and

what isn't, using objects around the house. We learned about the meaning of magnetic poles, made pin magnets that really worked, made magnetic gears, learned to predict what could disturb magnetic fields, built a hairline compass, built an electromagnet, mapped magnetic fields, and worked with Morse Code.

Not all of our homeschool projects worked so well. Susan (at the age of nine) became very interested in chemistry as a result of working with some of the TOPS units. She had also become interested in electricity. So we bought one of the larger Radio Shack Electronic Lab kits which she used for hours on end and from which she learned a great deal. With that background, I looked around for a good chemistry set and bought one with a wide range of experiments and clear directions. She used this set just one afternoon; all the safety precautions discouraged her from further use. While she remained interested in chemistry, she would not use this set any more. Now she is having no problems with her biology class in high school where she does extensive chemical lab work.

Jim and Laurie were introduced to keeping financial records at an early age because of their newspaper routes. Our credit union allowed them to open checking accounts so they quickly became comfortable with handling a check book. We encouraged them to balance their check books monthly and to keep careful financial records. This does not mean that they keep their finances in as straight a manner Dale and I had hoped. But we do have the satisfaction of having shown our youngsters how to do it.

Their least favorite time of the year was tax time because they made just enough money from their paper routes (and later babysitting) that they had to file with the IRS. At least tax filing is no longer a mystery for them, an advantage they have over many of their peers as they get older. Because Susan did not have a paper route and has not made enough money to have to file, she has yet to file with the IRS. She does have her own checking account, though.

Early in the 1980s Dale saw the need to become computer literate as a means of keeping or advancing in his job. We started with a 64K Tandy TRS-80 Color computer, progressed to an

IBM clone 8088, 286, and now 486 computers. Over the years Dale has basically taught himself, with help from a few computer classes, many mentors, lots of reading, and plenty of hands-on experiences. He even taught himself programming. In the process he is now someone people come to for help or information about computers.

I, on the other hand, have progressed very slowly through each step; each progression for me is a major triumph. Every change in computer meant I was forced to relearn how to use the computer, building on what I had previously known. On the TRS-80 I would only use tapes for recording and retrieving data. When we bought the 8088, I had to learn how to use disks. Each new computer brought me the opportunity to learn new skills.

For my purposes I have only used word processing features. There are so few times I would use a spreadsheet, so that is a skill I have not yet learned. However, I suspect now that I am going to be using WordPerfect 6.0 I will be using the spreadsheet capabilities in that program. First I have to learn to become comfortable using Windows. As I said earlier, it takes me an enormous amount of effort and time to learn each program so I am selective about which programs will be most useful. It is a major triumph for me to learn something new on the computer.

My struggle with learning to use the computer is a graphic example for me of how people learn. I can better appreciate what my own youngsters go through in their learning adventures. More importantly, it emphasizes the validity of interest initiated learning. I want to learn what I can about word processing, so I do what it takes to improve my skills using the computer. On the other hand, using a spreadsheet is not as important to me, so I do not waste my efforts unless it becomes a useful skill to me. Isn't that what our students are trying to tell us?

When Susan was ten she read about an experiment that caught her interest. She cut a plastic soda bottle in two, placed water in the lower section, stuffed paper toweling in the upper section so that it came through the narrow neck, and inverted the upper section into the lower section. The paper toweling formed a wick to draw water into the upper section. She placed several kinds of seeds in the paper toweling. It was fascinating to watch the different seeds sprout and send trailing roots downward towards the water. As two of her bean seeds became stronger, they dominated Susan's "germinator" (as she called it). The germinator sat on Susan's desk where she could easily watch its progress. The two beans produced long plants that eventually grabbed a nearby peacock feather for support for further growth, which Susan found amusing.

For a few years we went to the open house held at the University of California, Santa Barbara because of the wonderful activities and experiences offered during the occasion. Our favorite spot was the marine biology lab. One year we watched baby sharks hatch from shark eggs. There is at least one "touch and feel" tank, and Susan usually headed straight for that tank.

In the geology building we once talked with someone in the "thin slice lab." He showed us a rock specimen under a microscope, and the colors in the rocks surprised us. The rocks need to be very thinly sliced to see these colors, and the technician demonstrated how rocks are sliced for microscope slides—a delicate, painstaking process. In a computer lab we looked at microscopic fossils and living sea creatures on a hookup between the microscope and the computer. There were many other equally fascinating exhibits throughout the campus.

Word puzzle magazines are very popular in our house. At first I thought the youngsters would like the ones meant for children, but this was another of my many wrong assumptions. Jim, Laurie, and Susan quickly convinced me that if the word puzzle was intended for children it was boring and "stupid" (their word to describe how they felt). At the grocery store I had bought a Penny Press magazine for myself. Before I knew what was happening they were doing the puzzles in *my* copy. No more "children's" puzzles for us!

Jim discovered the logic puzzle magazines and I found it difficult keeping him supplied. I sent away for their bargain bag offer and that led to even better offers. These puzzle magazines were quite inexpensive, thank goodness, as we went through a lot of them in short order. All of us still work on them for relaxation. I did notice improvement in vocabulary and spelling over time because of these puzzle magazines.

Laurie has always loved to work with children. While homeschooling she published a newsletter for homeschooling friends for three years. Seeing her success stimulated other homeschool youngsters to also try their hand at publishing newsletters, and they attempted joint newsletters at times with varying success.

Her biggest project, all on her own, was what she called "Dynamite Club." She organized regular Dynamite Club meetings to which all homeschoolers who wanted to join were invited each month. She had to learn how to plan the event and then how to adapt it to the ages and interests of the youngsters who came. A hard lesson she learned was that people who say they are coming don't always show up and people she did not expect to come would sometimes come without advance notice.

My suggestions were not welcome—she wanted to do all the planning and organizing. For one January meeting she had each child design a page for a calendar on which she had put everyone's birthdays and other special days. After the meeting she assembled the pages, copied them, and distributed them to the families involved. This activity was a hit. Mothers were so pleased to have the personalized calendars and the youngsters were proud of their handiwork.

Often Laurie planned her Dynamite Club activities according to the season. In February she had a Valentine's party, during which they designed valentines for their families and had a valentine's exchange among themselves. Once she planned an Easter "craft afternoon," ordering supplies from a discount craft catalog. Her order took six weeks to arrive. To her dismay she discovered that all the things she had ordered for the Easter basket making were on back order and would be delivered in May! We did not have time to recover so she cancelled that meeting, but as it turned out, many of her regular club members were out of town that week anyway.

One Dynamite Club meeting she planned on teaching them how to marbleize paper. This turned out to be quite a challenge for her. The younsters' enthusiasm for the project was so intense that they used too much paint. The results were not quite as lovely as the samples we had made ahead of time. Our patio was covered with paint drippings; nevertheless everyone had a good time doing this project.

Susan became engrossed with the Nancy Drew book series. Before that interest waned, she had read most of the Nancy Drew books available. A friend lent us her books from years ago; there must have been a least 30 of the early books in that box. We picked up many more books in the series from garage sales and the library. Susan commented on how the characters changed (even in hair color) over the years. She read these books by the hour and could tell just from a glance at the cover what the title was and what the plot of that book was.

Shortly after this, Susan began writing a book of her own, filling page after page of a notebook and then the blank pages of one of those "write your own" journal books. I suggested putting her story on the computer but she was not interested because she was not satisfied with what she had written. She expected to make revisions. However, those revisions were never written because she gradually lost interest in that project.

How well I know about going out to get nifty "educational" resources only to have the children turn their noses up at them—you should see our house full of such items! Over the years I have discarded many untouched "learning aids." When I started homeschooling I had visions of sitting down with Jim and learning or re-learning all kinds of neat things, but he would have none of that. Nor would Laurie when she came home. I had pretty well (but not completely) learned my lesson by the time Susan came home for her studies.

So our house became a library. We acquired books from many different sources, including garage sales. The Scholastic Book Club was one source of books which worked well primarily because they chose the books themselves (instead of Mom choosing what she thought was good for them to read). We were used to ordering inexpensively from Scholastic through the public school. Shortly after Laurie started homeschooling I wrote to Scholastic asking if homeschool groups could order. They welcomed the orders we collected from members of our support group, often giving us bonus offers because we ordered so many books from them.

Jim, Laurie, and Susan would assemble the orders. Making out the monthly orders became a routine activity for us. They were rewarded by receiving free books (used as an incentive for school orders). Sometimes we would also order from Troll Book Clubs for variety. Our family handled the orders for several years. As time passed there were repetitions of books offered and fewer books appealed to them so we turned over the book ordering to another family. Our support group still offers the ordering service with many satisfied families.

I hesitate to recommend resources because what worked for our family may not work for another. Resources that I thought were great, my youngsters didn't. Jim liked Almaniac contests; the girls wouldn't even consider entering them. All three youngsters still eagerly read *Zillions*, the magazine published by Consumer Reports for young people, but some families do not find this magazine acceptable. (Some resources are no longer available, or may not be when you read this book.)

A resource which still endures in our family is *Reader's Digest*. The variety of topics each month means that everyone can find something they are interested in. Articles in this magazine have been the occasion of many discussions as well as for new interests. Articles in back issues sometimes are the basis for a study assignment even for Jim's college classes.

At various stages we used *Weekly Reader* and *Scholastic* magazines (particularly the math and science magazines). These worked well when the children were younger, but they quickly outgrew them because they tended to talk down to students. The teacher's editions were much more interesting. We did receive some outstanding charts and posters along with the magazines.

Provoking Thoughts was a magazine which Susan thoroughly enjoyed. She read it as soon as it arrived, doing many of the projects suggested. Unfortunately it ceased publication before the end of our subscription. This same thing happened with another magazine very popular in our household, *Gifted Children Monthly*.

One year I thought I would use a wide variety of publications instead of textbooks. What a disaster that was! I ordered magazines for adult readers because many magazines aimed for youngsters are boring. Included were news magazines, a science newsletter, historical magazines, and a natural history magazine from a museum. Susan and I read the natural history magazine every month. That was the only magazine subscription I renewed.

We accumulated numerous craft items for projects. Changing interests added to the variety of "stuff" needed for projects. Laurie decided she wanted to design with colored sands. Susan thought it would be fun to work with mosaics. A friend gave us an S & S Craft Supplies catalog. We went overboard ordering supplies for these projects because S & S is a bulk supplier; many local homeschool families benefited from our overabundance.

With the urging of a good friend the girls and I became Usborne Books At Home Consultants. Part of the consideration was trying to find some way for Susan to earn her own spending money as she definitely won't deliver newspapers and she only reluctantly will babysit. I thought she could earn some money this way. Besides, the books are excellent. Once again, though, I realized the girls had already outgrown the reading material in most of the Usborne books offered under this plan. This project lasted for six months. Susan learned many marketable skills but little money. Some of our customers objected to the subject matter in some of the books thus limiting our customer base. These books are very high quality for a reasonable price. You can frequently find them in quality museum gift shops or bookstores.

Both girls were active in Campfire (open to both girls and boys). Their project books were filled with fascinating activities. It was easy for them to earn their beads because we often did the activities required as part of our homeschooling. Most of the time we did the activity unaware until later that they earned a bead or patch just for doing it. Sometimes, though, we went through their Campfire books looking for ideas for interesting homeschooling activities. Several families in our support group use also use 4-H, Scout, and homeschool projects interchangeably.

Resourcefulness was our greatest resource. Most of the homeschooling materials we acquired were either free (from the school district book depository or hand-me-downs from various sources) or low cost (garage sales or thrift shops). We did have a tendency to over-accumulate. Much of what we gathered was barely used or never used. I read Don Aslett's "de-junking" books and still did not succeed in removing excess clutter. When I clean out, someone in the family fills up the vacant space!

In an effort to de-clutter I suggested that our support group have a homeschool swap meet in which we could exchange out-grown or no longer used learning materials. The idea was enthusiastically embraced so I organized our first swap meet. It was such a great success that families wanted to do it again the next year.

For four years I organized well received swap meets. People expressed gratitude for the opportunity to obtain new materials and to shed old materials. This was how we acquired the Saxon math books for a fraction of their new cost. No one else has stepped forward to organize another one so we have not had a swap meet for a couple of years. (People do ask when the next one will be, but don't want to organize it.)

Actually it was easy to put on: I placed a notice in our support group newsletter announcing the date and time. The first two years it was held in our side patio. We outgrew that, so we moved the one day event into our garage, which made early set-up easier. Hours were between 10 am and 2 pm. Any home-schooler was welcome to bring items labeled with name and price to be sold. Usually those who wanted to sell items arranged to stay around at least part of the time to help run the swap meet.

The best part of the swap meets was getting to know local homeschoolers who did not come to our support group meetings. They had heard about it from homeschooling friends. Some came from as far as twenty-five miles away. Not very many of our local people came to the first meet because they thought they would not find anything useful. Word quickly spread that they had missed out on something very worthwhile. With the second swap meet we had a wider variety of items and many more participants.

The swap meet was only open to homeschoolers, not to the general public. Experienced homeschoolers were the most eager to make purchases. Newer homeschoolers were amazed at the great variety of resources available. The last year we held it the garaged was crammed full of items. We took in over $400, which gives a good indication of how much material was sold. Prices were very low for most items. There were many unsold items left, but many, many more were sold.

Another valuable resource for us, and sometimes a source of new pursuits, is going to family-oriented and homeschooling conferences. It is an opportunity to share our joys and our challenges with people who understand what we are talking about. It is an opportunity for renewal and refreshment.

Due to finances and timing, we have only attended a few homeschooling conferences. Our family organized one of them. Each conference proved to be an opportunity for renewal of purpose and for making new friendships as well as enhancing existing friendships. Conference structure varied from highly organized to almost no structure and variations in between, but each structure served a purpose. We came to appreciate the unstructured approach, though it took some getting used to.

The first state-wide homeschool conference we attended was highly structured with little time for interaction with other attendees. The day was a series of presentations. Raymond Moore was the featured speaker, followed by leaders of various homeschool organizations in California and a principal of a public high school. I liked getting to meet people who were only names to me and our youngsters enjoyed the activities planned just for them. We came to know one gentleman leading some of the children's activities who quickly became a family friend.

Two years later we attended a four day camp-out for the National Coalition of Alternative Community Schools which had very little structure. While not strictly a homeschool conference, it was an opportunity to meet administrators from alternative schools around the nation. Over four hundred people attended this conference. We each had a turn in preparing meals for the attendees. Sessions were very informal. There were no formal presentations because everyone was expected to participate in the discussions. Everyone's opinions were respected, and children, especially the teenagers, were encouraged to join in the discussions.

Attendees came from all over the United States. One man came from France to observe alternative schools in the United States. A delegation of Japanese students attended. Laurie has kept up correspondence with one of the Japanese girls for the last eight years. Jim made some good friends who unfortunately lived over a thousand miles away and, like him, were not letter writers, although they did make a few attempts at being pen pals. The friendships we made during this conference have been meaningful although we are all too busy with other things to correspond.

It was pure delight for me to be reunited with people I had met during the alternative school conference at a National Homeschool Association meeting in 1991. The intervening years seemed to evaporate as we quickly picked up where we left off so many years before. Once again we were surrounded by people who wanted the best of educational experiences for our students. We learned from each other.

The theme of this conference was that people learn best when they are interested. Discussions abounded as to how to encourage pursuing personal interests and how this is educationally sound. Our family flourished because we were surrounded by this atmosphere. We came home with renewed determination and the sense that there were many others who shared our philosophy. It is good to be at least occasionally surrounded by like-thinking people!

John Boston wanted to hold a California Coalition of People for Alternative Learning Situations (CC PALS) state-wide conference in the central part of California. There had so far been none in the central coastal area where we live, so I volunteered to organize it for April, 1987. Time was short because he asked me to do this in January. We were able to keep it simple and low cost. Thank goodness the weather cooperated as we had to hold it in a park that had no shelter. There were about 150 participants. It was a rewarding experience.

We planned several informal discussions for each session period. People brought their own lunches. At the end of the day, those who wished to came to our house to continue discussions over a pizza supper. Many participants commented they did not realize how much they could get out of informal discussions because they were used to structured presentations. They also commented how this reaffirmed their commitment and realized that they had something worth sharing with others. The underlying theme of the sessions was that we are our own "experts." People in our support group later asked me when another conference like that would come up again, but since no one was willing to organize it, it did not happen. Many local homeschoolers still look for someone else to guide them because they lack confidence in themselves.

The day was simple in structure. Since I know that sometimes it helps to have a sample schedule when planning an event, I am including our program. This is meant only to give you an idea, not to tell you how it should be done. What works in one situation may not be suitable in another. No two CC-PALS gatherings have been the same; some have been campouts, one utilized the buildings and grounds of a military installation and another used a church retreat facility. Maybe after reading the program I organized, you will say, "I can do that!" I hope you will—the participants will benefit and so will you.

CC PALS ANNUAL MEETING
LOMPOC, CALIFORNIA
Monday, April 11, 1987

Pre-registration—$5 (by April 1)
Registration at door—$7

9:30–10:00 Registration and Welcome

10:00 –10:45 Workshops:
1. Non-Traditional Learning Resources: Using games, magazines, field trips, and other creative ideas for enhancing learning.
2. What Records Do I Keep? Suggestions and ideas on how participants keep their records.

10:45 - 11:30 Workshops:
1. Testing—When? How? Why?: The purposes of testing—how effective is testing? Must I test?
2. Math Learning Aids: How to approach math in the most effective manner for the individual child.

11:30 - 12:00 LUNCH: Bring your own brown bag lunch. Please bring a dessert to share.

12:00 - 1:00 Let Our Children Shine! Open to any child who wishes to share their learning projects with the rest of us. It can be musical, magical, nonsensical, artistic, scientific— whatever. In order that every child who wants to may participate we request that families observe a five minute time limit. If there is still free time after everyone has shared, additional sharings will be welcome!

1:00 to 1:45 Workshops
1. What About Our Older Students? Providing meaningful learning experiences for our teens. High school diplomas in an alternative setting. Advantages of homeschooling teens.
2. Reading Readiness: How to recognize reading readiness. Practical hints for teaching reading.

1:45–2:30 Workshops
1. Storytelling: Why storytelling is important. Storytelling techniques.
2. Simple And Fun Art Projects

2:30–3:00 Break

3:00–4:00 Unfinished Business: An opportunity to ask your unanswered questions about homeschooling.

4:00–5:30 Clean up the park and visiting.

5:30 Pizza Supper (Dutch treat) at the Leisticos' house for those not heading home tonight. After supper we will continue our day of sharing. Come join the fun!

General Information

Please bring with you any materials you use that you want to show other participants. This includes learning materials, games, books, newsletters, etc. Something you use may be just the thing someone else wishes they could find.

The whole day is meant to be a day for sharing. YOU are the expert. Each session is intended to generate discussion. We learn from each other.

We are keeping costs for organizing this homeschool conference to the bare minimum. Anything you can donate—particularly in the way of beverages, fruit or other snacks during the day—will be appreciated by all. The organizers hope that some of their costs (such as phone, postage, and printing) can also be covered.

If you have access to appropriate brochures, pens, pencils, or other items, please bring them to distribute to participants.

We expect your children to actively participate in any of the workshops they wish. We encourage older students to share their viewpoints on their education. Each family is responsible for their own children. Plan to bring something to occupy them if they choose not to participate in the planned activities.

Our gatherings will be in informal groups around picnic tables or sitting on the grass. You might want to bring a blanket and/or folding chair.

I asked individuals whom I knew were comfortable in leading discussions to be co-panelists for each session. By asking for co-panelists I lessened the risk of having no discussion leaders for a session because a family emergency prevented them from coming to the conference at the last minute. The role of the panelists was to start the discussion and keep it on topic.

I have found it is not difficult to keep the discussion going once participants realize they have something to share with the other participants. Experienced homeschoolers love the opportunity to share with people who are just starting to consider homeschooling. I knew there would be no problem having mixed levels of experience in any of the sessions. We had a few teenagers and they readily sat in on sessions. That night one discussion leader told me that Jim sat in on her session and entered into the discussion. Normally he would just sit back and say nothing in a group of adults, but he felt comfortable enough with this group to express his opinions.

Everyone in our family assisted in the organization and activities of this conference. The girls especially helped with pre-registration and with welcoming participants as they arrived. Laurie assisted with the children's activities. Jim and Dale did most of the physical set-up and take-down at the park.

It was exciting as the first pre-registrations arrived. People I asked to be panelists responded enthusiastically, though at first some needed me to bolster their confidence. The only refusals came from people unable to come. As an experiment and because of a scheduling conflict, we chose to hold the conference on a Monday instead of a weekend, which precluded some participants. Interestingly, we did not notice a difference in size of attendance from what we would have anticipated for having it on a weekend.

When I sent a friend her registration materials, I asked her to consider being a panelist. She wrote in reply,

> I'd be happy to speak at the 'Older Students' session, BUT I want to be clear I'm very much a 'natural learner' participant and don't have a bunch of materials to share. Zarn is a voracious reader and my biggest contribution as far as 'educational supplies' goes is seeing he gets to the library! We're VERY casual and unstructured.

Though I did not tell her, this was exactly why I asked her to be a panelist. I already knew she was skilled in leading discussions.

One attendee drove over 200 miles to the conference. She wanted to share her excitement because her ten-year-old daughter had suddenly started reading like crazy that week. Ellen was getting a lot of pressure from relatives; the girl was obviously intelligent but not reading well. Relatives were blaming the mother for homeschooling her daughter.

A few days before the conference she and her daughter were at a neighbor's house (they were close friends). The neighbor's son, a chiropractor, happened to be home that day. While the

two mothers were talking he looked at the little girl. He startled
Ellen by asking if the girl had trouble reading. When she asked
how he knew this, he explained he had recently treated an
adult for a spinal condition and after treatment the patient
could focus his eyes properly. Before that, reading had been a
problem for the patient but he no longer had difficulty reading.
Research indicated some people have a slight misalignment of
the skull that affects the ability to focus the eyes properly. They
can pass vision tests but no one detects the focus problem. With
the mother's permission the chiropractor readjusted the girl's
spine, and the girl could now read with little difficulty.

The physical layout of one facility used for another homeschool conference did not allow for much interaction between
participants. The sessions were scattered throughout several
buildings on a community college campus, with numerous
empty classrooms. We also had to travel to scattered motels several miles from the campus. Nevertheless, Dale and I felt
renewed even with less than ideal conditions. Susan was the
only one still at home then so she went with us and enjoyed participating in some of the children's activities as well as sitting
in on some of the sessions. I was discussion leader for four of the
sessions. We had really great discussions. The groups were
small enough that the discussions kept moving, with everyone
having the chance to air their opinions. There was acceptance
of each other's opinions; people agreed it was okay to disagree
with the opinions expressed.

It was hard coming back to our support group and explaining
how valuable the conference was because most of the group at
that time thought it was more valuable to attend sessions that
had an "expert" lecturer. They lacked confidence in themselves
and had not experienced how invigorating and reaffirming it
can be to attend a less structured conference. It was shortly
after this that our original support group disintegrated.

Opportunities and resources surround us—there is no lack.
Sometimes you just need to look more closely at your surroundings to discover what you have readily available. There is no
need to spend a lot of money on homeschooling activities. The
most successful resources and actitivities are those that appeal
to the interests of the learners. Support groups and gatherings

of like-minded people can give us the encouragement and ideas that lead to enhanced learning experiences for the entire family, for homeschooling is indeed a family affair.

Chapter Four

Support Groups
and Friends

For us, having friends and belonging to local, statewide, and national homeschool support groups made a big difference. Sharing ideas, joys, and doubts enriched our family, offering us stimulation to make the most possible out of our homeschooling experiences. I am very much a people-oriented person. Our friends did not have to necessarily be homeschoolers, but they did have to be supportive of our choice of educational alternatives. In this we were very fortunate. Even friends who at first were skeptical eventually began to accept what we were doing as they saw our children were not being ruined by learning at home. Probably we could have been just as successful without the acceptance of friends and relatives, but it was much nicer to have their support.

Jim, Laurie, and Susan did make friends among other homeschooling youngsters. Most of these friends, however, lived at a distance, so contact was infrequent at best. When we began homeschooling, our youngsters were the oldest homeschoolers. Dale and I looked for older students as far away as thirty miles without success; there were no other homeschooling fourth through eighth graders around. Instead Jim and Laurie became "big brother" and "big sister" to many younger children in our support group.

By the time Susan and Laurie were in their last years of homeschooling there were several older students. However, most of these students had far more structured schedules than we did so there was little opportunity for friendships to develop.

I had to learn the lesson that my youngsters didn't necessarily find friends among the other homeschoolers. There was a wide variety of interests that did not always mesh. Just because they were homeschooling did not mean they would automatically become friends. I found solace when I read in Nancy Wallace's *Child's Work* about her disappointing search for friends for her son Ishmael and daughter Vita among homeschoolers. I've been there! Jim, Laurie, and Susan have found their own very good friends, in their own ways.

Jim had very few friends when he was in elementary school, but those friends he had were good friends. At first when he entered high school without seeming to have any friends, I wondered if I had hurt him socially by homeschooling. As the high school years went by, I realized that he was quietly accumulating a few very close, deep, friendships. It took time for me to accept that this was his pattern and his choice. He may never have lots of friends at one time, but he does have a few very good friends.

Laurie, on the other hand, has no problem finding friends; she loves to be surrounded by people and to have fun with them. She seemed to be the most affected by the lack of homeschoolers her age at first. The last year she was at home more of her age group began to homeschool. However, she did not have any lasting friendships develop with local homeschoolers. She does have a lasting friendship with a former homeschooler who lives about seventy miles from us. This friendship started because they were both homeschooling at the same time and we mothers were already good friends through La Leche League.

Adult friendships among homeschooling parents have had greater effect on our homeschool adventures than peer friendships among our homeschooling children. The common bond we parents share because we chose an alternative education for our children enhances our friendship with other homeschooling families as well as our determination to do what we consider best in our own circumstances.

Acceptance of each other is key. This involves a trust in our youngsters to learn in the manner best suited to them. It also involves acknowledgement that each family is best able to determine the optimal educational approach for their situation. For some families this means having a very structured approach to learning, while other families, such as ours, are much more comfortable with loose structure. We recognize that even within the same family youngsters may have a different learning pattern which works to their advantage. What worked for my family may not work for your family. Some families do not need support groups in the same way we did. Our family found support—and many dear friendships as a side benefit to belonging to support groups.

For a period of time I found it difficult to keep going when it seemed I was surrounded by people who thought homeschooling had to be highly structured. Some religious differences also crept in which made me very uncomfortable. Our family joined Home Centered Learning partly because by doing so, we associated with a statewide group who advocated interest-initiated learning. This cut the feeling of isolation for me.

Our original small local support group was tolerant of many different approaches to learning, from quite structured to the opposite. Over time this attitude changed, eventually spinning off different support groups to fill different needs as the number of homeschooling families grew. We found that support groups that become too large become less effective. Now people have a choice in local support groups and this is healthy, but the process of forming new groups brought turmoil and some hurt. Transition and growth was not easy; new vigor and life are now evident, though.

For several years I put an enormous amount of time into our local support group. That became a tremendous drain on me as our group struggled with increasing members, each of whom had their own visions of the homeschool movement. I decided it was time for me to step aside, though I remained available to provide information and support as needed. Support group activities had become a big time drain on me since most of the activities did not interest Laurie or Susan anymore.

The exciting part of my stepping back from being so active with the support group was that parents who had previously remained in the background now stepped forward, bringing new spirit and fresh ideas into the group. I began to once again enjoy myself at support group meetings. I began to participate in the group in a new capacity.

Our local support group began in the middle of 1986 when six families started meeting at a local park for mutual support and encouragement. The local public library had a children's librarian who was constantly encouraging us. She would tell interested library patrons about our group. Thanks to her efforts, we gradually added more families to our support group. Some of our first meetings were on the lawn outside the library.

Field trips were fun experiences. I planned several other activities that came up in connection with our country's constitutional bicentennial or other interests within the group, inviting homeschoolers from other towns to also participate. The response was great, with some families coming as far as seventy miles to frequently join in our activities.

The enduring activity, which we began shortly after forming Kings Academy support group, has been to rent the municipal swimming pool for an hour each week. At first it was a struggle to reach the required number of participants in order to rent the pool, but we managed. This has become such a popular activity that local homeschoolers now have five different swim times a week. By keeping the maximum size for swimming to 30 participants per session, we have an uncrowded swimming time. For one year some swim groups also chose to have swimming instruction at the same time. However, most participants preferred having no planned swimming activity during the rental period. Many children who were afraid of water were gradually introduced to the fun of swimming this way. At least one parent is expected to be present (and in the water if possible) during the rental period so it becomes a family activity.

We wanted a group that accepted everyone, no matter what their race, creed, lifestyle, or educational philosophy. We chose the name Kings Academy for the group when we discovered that having a name made arranging field trips simpler. Kings Academy was an informal group with no desire to have officers. Our main purpose was to support each other without any of us looked up to as "the expert," since we felt each family was its own expert.

For the first few years our support group stayed around ten to fifteen families although we would occasionally hear of a few other local families homeschooling on their own. Word spread about the advantages of homeschooling as our youngsters were visible in the community and as more information about homeschooling became available. Kings Academy became known as the source of information concerning homeschooling. People in the group freely and knowledgeably shared their insights with inquirers.

Shortly after Kings Academy formed, two families wanted a Christian emphasis and much more structure so they formed a group at a local church. A number of families in that church became homeschoolers, but that group eventually folded due to exclusivity. Many of those families subsequently joined Kings Academy.

Suddenly, because of growing community awareness, we were faced with many new families who were interested in homeschooling. It was no longer so easy to keep families in the group informed so I started a newsletter late in 1989. Our primary concern was the need for the dissemination of accurate information. I started by sending it to 25 families; one year later the newsletter was going to 40 families. A year after that, I was sending it to 65 families!

Feeling that it was time for a new editor, I stepped down. The new editor discovered she was not up to the time and tact needed, so the newsletter floundered. In the meantime the support group had become large and unwieldy, and we went through a painful transition period. The value of having a newsletter for keeping members accurately informed did not get lost; as the dust settled, our newly emerging smaller support group once again provided connection with families through a highly popular newsletter. Some members of other local support groups eagerly read our newsletter because of the information and encouragement provided, even though their activities were not in it.

My purpose as editor of the newsletter was not only to tell when activities were, but also to give the youngsters a chance to contribute (which they did), to explain activities (so everyone had the same facts), to bring us closer to each other, and to provide additional supportive information. The first issues contained copies of the educational code as it applies to California homeschoolers. Later, with a new editor, the newsletter simply became a calendar of events as that was what certain members preferred. Eventually our current editor returned the newsletter to its orignional intent.

The 1990-1991 school year was a bumpy year for Kings Academy because we had grown so much. People had differing ideas of what they expected from a support group. There were several families with strong religious affiliations who preferred a very structured approach to education. They formed a support group which met their needs, setting up many different types of activities each week.

It was an emotional time for long-time members of Kings Academy. Those who chose to go with the new group were torn in their loyalty as much as those who chose to stay with Kings Academy. Great effort was made by many people to keep the good will between groups open and to try for caring and harmony. I believe that this happened because of the genuine concern of those families involved.

Kings Academy had grown much too large to maintain closeness and personal support. Other smaller groups began forming to meet the various needs of individual families. It was a good, healthy thing in the long run. People worked hard to keep an openness to each other and to the other groups.

Kings Academy continued temporarily. Those who were long-time members looked back on the early days of closeness and "being in this together" nostalgically. We knew that we could not recapture this time. We recognized that growth can at times be painful, and with time the pain of separation diminished. It was time to relinquish the past.

Kings Academy served its purpose. Those of us who started Kings Academy look back with gratitude, but the time had come to move forward. Some of us determined that we wanted to accept all homeschoolers, to make homeschooling our focus with each family free to choose their own educational philosophy, and to support and encourage each other in our homeschooling adventures. Because of the experience, we were enriched with a greater understanding of the meaning of acceptance. We realized that if we want the freedom to decide about our own children's education, we have to also support other parents to have the same freedom, even when we disagree with their decisions.

We decided to form an informal get-together for those who are interested in interest initiated learning. We were amazed when twelve people came to our first meeting at my house. At first we were just thinking of meeting every couple of months or so, but everyone was so eager to continue that we began meeting monthly at local parks (our weather allows outdoor meetings most of the year).

We did not want structured meetings. The year before, due to pressures from certain people and the sheer numbers of people coming, our support meetings no longer provided much support because they became structured. We did not want to feel obligated to attend meetings as had been happening; our families were content with our weekly swim at the local municipal pool and an occasional field trip.

The girls and I had not gone on a field trip for over a year because too many parents refused to use morning hours for field trips. All field trips were scheduled for after two in the afternoons. Our youngsters had paper routes so afternoon field trips were out for us. Our dinner time was also early as Dale gets home from work around four and this frees the rest of the evening for family activities. We had enjoyed our support group morning field trips. While many of the field trips were geared for younger children, there were several we would have enjoyed going on with the group had they been during the morning. Now our support group is once again scheduling morning field trips.

One aspect that makes me uncomfortable is when families start considering someone a homeschool leader or expert. I watched this happen in our town. This discomfort is shared within our present homeschool support group. *All* homeschoolers are leaders, otherwise they would not be homeschooling. Each of us contributes to the whole homeschooling community in some manner. Have you ever met a more independent bunch of people? I certainly haven't! I do not consider myself a homeschool "expert" or "leader." I am a parent deeply concerned about my children's education, and I know my family better than any one else. My children know themselves better than even I do; I trust them to make their own decisions

I'm so pleased with the support group to which I now belong. We have so many people with varied backgrounds. It is wonderful to be once again in a support group where each one is accepted as a homeschooler, period. The marvelous part is that the newest members find that they already are contributing to the group through their personally refreshing insights. People don't seem to hesitate to present to the group their doubts, frustrations, or challenges because they know they will receive support, encouragement, and information instead of advice, a sense of subordination, or condemnation. The underlying attitude within the group is that each family knows what is best in their particular situation. Each family is encouraged to trust their instincts as to what is best for them. For many people who first come to our meetings this is a revolutionary idea, but once they realize that we mean it, they become empowered.

As Kings Academy began to grow too quickly, and before it disbanded, some of our field trips were less than ideal. We were no longer automatically welcomed by facilities for field trips. Three of our field trips were too overcrowded. For the first time we had rowdy children, too much talking to hear the guide, and damage to the property—thank goodness it was minor damage. We quickly adopted strict field trip guidelines, insisting that parents had to be present and responsible for their children's behavior on each field trip. Field trip sizes were severely limited. Rapid growth of the support group forced us to reconsider our support group activities.

Most of our field trips were wonderful opportunities. One for which the girls and I are particularly grateful involved a trip to our local California mission—a lesser known mission in the California chain. Juanita Centano, a local Chumash Indian who has since died, spent an entire morning explaining the California coastal Indian culture. She encouraged us to participate with hands-on activities as she told her story of growing up in California as an Indian. She wanted to pass on Indian crafts and lore along with a respect for the contributions of the Indians. Her own tribe was angry with her for doing this, but she chided them with the fact that they are doing nothing to preserve their culture; if she did not spread it to non-Indians it would be lost forever. We spent almost three hours with her and could have spent many more hours. She taught all of us (she would not allow the adults to be idle) to make Indian clappers, necklaces, and hair brushes. During the activities she told stories of growing up as an Indian. Her grandfather raised her and taught her until authorities forced the Indians to go to local public schools. The white children did not want them at first; outhouses were provided for the Indian children while the white children used indoor restrooms. A water trough was set up in the school yard for the Indian children to wash their hands. She told of some of the pranks the Indian children played until the white children came to realize they weren't going to be scalped and started to be more friendly towards the Indian children.

Juanita was thrilled we were homeschooling, telling us at length about how sorry she feels for the school groups who tour the mission. She said it was hard for her to work with many of these children as they often don't know how to learn. She was all for hands-on learning. As far as she was concerned, no youngsters were to participate in any activity she led in which they were not interested. She especially loved all the different age levels in our group, from babies to teens to adults. Numerous times during the morning she would comment whenever she saw one child helping another with a project.

Support groups function best when the members respect each other's choices, offer mutual encouragement, and keep members informed. To be effective, support groups need to recognize that each member has something to offer to the other members. We have been fortunate to have such an opportunity in our community. Our support group newsletter contained the following article about the role of homeschool support groups:

> One of the better impulses we human beings have is to be left free to achieve our own happiness or success in life, however we define it, through the use of our own energies and talents. This impulse is strongly evident in homeschoolers. We express it in many different ways: our children; growing up in homes which practice freedom, self-authority, reason, responsibility, and self trust; receive the tools they'll need to bring out the best in themselves and make their own happiness, joy, success, or possibilities. These can only be self-defined and self-made.

This is the fuel which fires my commitment to homeschool my children. This is also what ties us all together, regardless of our reasons, methods, philosophy, religion or other differences. We want the freedom to do what is best for ourselves and our children.

There is, however, another human impulse, which undermines the first and that is a desire in people to exercise force over other people. Because of this tendency we need to be vigilant, not only with state and school "authorities," but sometimes even with other homeschoolers. We need to be careful that homeschooling is represented as and remains an individual option, as diverse as the number of people practicing it, and not become subject to the intrusion of anyone's idea or system or political efforts.

Stressing the common principle of independent free action is really stressing the right to diversity, with the important limitation of not allowing one's actions to intrude on another.

It is important that we make and keep connections with various homeschool groups, including religious ones, as we will need each other's support and perspective if we need to defend our freedoms.

In support groups and statewide organizations we need to question any tendencies we recognize as intrusive to individual families. We need to keep steering the focus toward our common concern and support the differences.

There is one important exception, and that is in the right that groups have to limit to behavior that hurts people or property, or is verbally abusive. These are defensive measures against intrusion by others.

Accepting the challenge of differences keeps us honest. It forces a person to think about why they do what they do and either strengthens one's position or alters it. Differences are part of creating a healthy environment with self-checks, flexibility, and responsiveness to new needs.

Our goal is to foster the development of educated human beings. Isn't part of being educated the capacity to handle differences intelligently, to be able to disagree with consideration, to be disagreed with without getting our feelings hurt, to be comfortable and civilized with people who are different without losing a sense of your unique self?

Isn't that a major challenge right now, not just in homeschooling, but wherever there are people? We can help our children meet that challenge when they grow up by meeting it ourselves.

I feel fortunate in belonging to a support group that is handling these issues well. We are a diverse group in many ways and we respect each other. Conflicts between children are handled responsibly by the adults, or sometimes smoothed over through the efforts of the older children. I hope we can maintain and build on the start we've begun in our homeschool group.

Chapter Five

Achieving Balance

At a recent support group meeting a mother, new to home-schooling, quietly listened to the conversation among the rest of us. Finally she looked at Chris and me and asked, "But how do you schedule your day?" Chris beautifully summed up exactly how I feel about our homeschooling day. She told the mother that she does not handle schedules well. If she had to schedule in order to homeschool, she could not enjoy homeschooling. Rather her days have a certain rhythm where activities flow one into the other without much pre-planning or conscious thought as to what comes next. It happens. If there is a special activity to accomplish, it gets accomplished without any fanfare.

Our days do have a certain rhythm which is comfortable for us. Whether there were three youngsters, two, or just one homeschooling on any given day, made little difference in the schedule after I had begun to let go of my preconceived notions about how our days should go. We are early risers so the youngsters knew they were expected to get up, dress, prepare their own breakfasts, and complete their other household responsibilities by about eight in the morning. Mornings were spent in learning activities which were usually of the children's own choosing. Many times one or all would go shopping with me. Homeschool support group meetings were in the mornings, as were most field trips. Each child prepared their own lunch when they were ready to eat. Afternoons could be a continuation of morning activities or some other projects.

Jim and Laurie had paper routes in the afternoon. Later on Laurie found it more profitable to babysit. As a homeschooler, she was able to babysit any time of the day without detriment to her learning progress. She spent most of her eighth grade doing child care and cooking, and it was during this time I realized how much she was learning about health, nutrition, economics, a wide range of science and history, along with practical math. Watching her interact with children of all ages, I observed how much she was referring to previous knowledge in these subjects as well as advancing in them, because she was sharing them with the children she babysat. By the end of that school year she was also getting bored because she felt the need for more intellectual stimulation.

We made sparing use of the television. There were certain educational programs the children watched, mainly on PBS, during the day. Evenings they watched other types of programming for a couple of hours. Jim had the most difficult time because television held a strong—but detrimental—fascination for him. At first I had to strictly limit his viewing time and choices because he could easily become mesmerized by it, coming away with a blank look that took some time to dissipate if he had been watching television too long. As he got older he was better able to control his own viewing time, but it was quite a struggle until then. Susan has had the least interest in watching television. Where the rest of us sometimes will have it on but not be paying any attention to it, Susan will turn it off if she is not going to give it her attention.

All three youngsters are avid readers. When they were little they loved to have me read to them. When we first started homeschooling I began reading aloud to all of them for about an hour every evening. They could be doing another quiet project if they wished while I was reading. Laurie, especially, would ask a question about anything I happened to be reading that she did not understand. I did not consider them interruptions; on the contrary I welcomed their questions because then I knew what they were thinking and could clear up misconceptions very easily if needed.

We read a variety of books—classics, mysteries, historical fiction, biographies, stories—just for the fun of it. Some were serious, some were funny. Even today, years later, one of them will mention something we read together. Those were such precious times! At the time I did not realize how precious those times would become. Now I sometimes wish we had not stopped doing this when Jim chose to go to the public high school. I did not realize then that those times were indeed the highlight of our homeschooling adventure.

At the same homeschool meeting where Chris so aptly described our families' days having "rhythm" rather than "schedules," Ginger spoke up. She has three little ones, has come to our support group meetings for over a year, and has considered homeschooling. This year her daughter entered the local public school kindergarten. The major thing that keeps Ginger from homeschooling is wondering how to manage a five year old, a three year old and a baby. Two days before the meeting she had to go to school because her daughter had lost a tooth. I happened to be walking by the school that morning from a Bible study group at church. I stopped and chatted with her for a few minutes then headed home, which was a mile away from the school.

At the support group meeting Ginger related how great it must be for me to have all the children out of the house so I can take a long leisurely walk in the middle of the day. Wistfully she said she was envious of me. I had to laugh as I told her the only reason why I was walking that day was because my teenagers had the car and I had to go to that Bible study because I was substituting for the study leader. Not only that, but when I saw Ginger, I was thinking how great it would be to once again have my youngsters the ages of hers because the bigger they grow the more challenges they present you!

So many times when I speak with parents who have had the experience of having youngsters in a school and also having them in the homeschool setting, they comment that having the youngsters at home is often much easier. Usually these parents were very involved in their youngsters' schools, spending hours a week at the school doing things that usually did not bear directly on their own youngsters. In our case at one point we had youngsters in three different public schools. This really stretched me out as I was very involved with parent/school committees at two of the schools. When they were homeschooled, I was spending my time with our youngsters directly; I was not wasting time traveling between schools.

Mornings often set the tone for the entire day in our household. The most delightful benefit of homeschooling for us was unharried mornings. Getting them ready to go to school in the morning used to be a hassle—we always seemed to be in a hurry. When we were homeschooling everyone was in a much better mood in the morning. Even after they chose to return to school, we no longer had the morning hassle because they had made the choice for themselves.

Another question I often hear from parents inquiring about homeschooling is how we handle the everyday family responsibilities that arise—both the planned and the unexpected. Along with that goes a question as to how we achieve balance in shared family responsibilities. This is something that every family needs to work out for themselves in a manner that is comfortable to them.

Depending upon the circumstances, I sometimes suggest writing down the family's struggles involved in facing such challenges in order to clarify the situation. This solution has helped me on occasion. Other possibilities include talking about it with other parents and reading the stories of other families. As I have mentioned, I can offer you our family's insights, telling you how we have handled a situation. However, you know your own family. What works for us may not be satisfactory for your family; take only what works for you.

Handling family responsibilities and balancing these responsibilities is an important part of the learning dynamics going on constantly within our family, even today. It is something we just do automatically without giving it a second thought—until someone questions us about how we accomplish it.

We expect each family member to take some responsibility for the well-being and orderly conduct of our family life. I can't say that this was a conscious decision so much as simple expectation that if you belong to our family you will be expected to contribute your share of responsibility. From the time they were little, our children were expected to share in family chores according to their abilities.

We have compromised and discussed among ourselves as to what is appropriate for each individual. Sometimes I have relented, other times I held firm. Occasionally I have eaten my words. I never considered family chores an interruption of my children's pursuits of their learning interests. They are an integral part of our lives.

True, chores or family responsibilities are not always attractive when compared to more interesting projects. At those times it was sometimes necessary to evaluate just how imperative the chore was. There were times (more often than I like to admit) I reevaluated how the task had to be completed, or the time frame for completion. Flexibility came to my rescue. However, this does not mean everything ran smoothly for us.

I now have the advantage of having older children. When they were younger I many times wondered if they would really grow up to be responsible adults. Was it worth the hassle we sometimes experienced? It certainly would have been so much easier to do all the wash, sweep the floors, prepare meals, and wash the dishes. Now I am reaping the harvest as I watch our college-age son handle laundry, shopping, and cleaning as ordinary life events. Our 16-year-old daughter works at the local drive-in movie theater. Her boss told my husband that she is one of the best at keeping the place clean (though to look at her room, I have to wonder!).

Pursuing a project in which one of the children was interested was not an excuse to neglect family responsibilities in our house. We learned to balance our interests with our responsibilities. We constantly reevaluate our priorities as a family, encouraging each other to pursue personal interests in balance with the good of the family.

It seems to me that if we don't constantly question ourselves about what we are doing, we miss out on opportunities to expand our horizons. While I do not find it fulfilling to copy another family unless it fills our particular needs, I do find it helpful and comforting to read or hear how other families approach learning. Some of what I read in homeschooling publications gives an unrealistic view of what actually occurs in families because editors have legitimate concerns regarding balancing uplifting, positive, articles with negative articles about the challenges homeschooling parents face. It refreshes me to read articles that remind me not to take things too seriously. Chris, the current editor of our support group newsletter wrote the following in our November, 1993, issue:

The lessons of work, like the lessons of love, are first learned in the family. These are two of the most important lessons to learn in life. In homeschool we have a lot of opportunities to learn them.

Work is integral to just plain living. In our own homes we deal with work issues a lot. Perhaps this is the biggest issue involved in living together with other people. There are chores to do. There's things we want to have and things we want to do. Work is the trade off. It's the "real world" in our homes.

The difference between the home "real world" and the rest of the "real world" is that parents are provided to help guide in a realistic, caring, responsive way and children are allowed time to assume their responsibilities, overcome difficulties and grow to claim their freedom.

School involves work also; but, work removed from a sense of purpose, which becomes absurd. At home the work we do is related to something concrete, that has meaning in our lives. The clothes on the floor need to be picked up. The dinner needs to be made. A skill develops with care and practice. But, by means of grades and tests, a separation between work and purpose occurs. One works for grades and test scores, abstractions that may or (more likely) may not reflect actual learning or skill.

It can be despairing to deal with the everyday, seemingly neverending work that piles up, detracting from "real" homeschool concerns, creating conflicts with the kids. But the lessons of the family, of the homeschool, are here. These concerns are vital to the education of our children. We are doing important work by honestly grappling with them.

Of course, one of the lessons of work is the satisfaction of earning and accepting time for leisure and recreation. That's the freedom that honest

work buys. The capacity for work is a gift. And, it
empowers the person who possesses it.

One of the more difficult aspects I faced as a parent, whether
our youngsters went to public school or were at home, was
deciding about participation in outside activities and organizations. I watched neighbors, friends, and relatives constantly
juggling time and cars to get their youngsters to many different,
and sometimes conflicting, activities. I wondered how I could
manage it when it came time for our youngsters to get involved
in outside activities. Then I asked myself, "Why? Is it worth the
struggle?"

Our family solution to participation in outside activities was
to limit them. Besides school and church activities, Jim, Laurie,
and Susan could join one other activity or organization. The
choice was theirs. This worked well for us. Jim and Susan are
not "joiners" so they had no problem with this. Laurie likes to
be involved with lots of things so it was, at times, a problem she
learned to live with.

Jim tried Campfire for a short while but did not have a very
good group leader so that only lasted a few months. Next he
tried 4-H and again ended up with a group leader who did nothing. He did enjoy a season with Little League baseball and a
couple seasons of soccer. In high school he became involved with
a local computer bulletin board and several school activities.

Laurie was an enthusiastic Campfire member for ten years.
She joined in every Campfire activity she could. She also played
one season of soccer. Of the three of them, she was the most
active with youth activities at church. While homeschooling,
she often thought of and guided activities for the younger homeschoolers.

Susan gradually became interested in Campfire. It took her
longer to get involved in her group activities, though once she
did she really enjoyed them. She is much more choosy as to
which activities she wants to do. Candy sales, an unfortunate
part of belonging to Campfire, were torture for her while Laurie
quickly entered into that activity. Since that is only once a year
and Susan's leader did not push the issue, it was a minor incon-
venience. An unexpected advantage to belonging to Campfire is

the wide variety of projects a child can do to earn numerous beads and patches; both girls found they earned beads because of activities we did in our homeschooling. That also worked the other way around: their project book gave us many ideas of interesting learning projects. The project book had hundreds of suggestions which also earned beads or patches and became a spring board for pursuing their own interests. Topic headings included science, health, government, history, sports, the arts, and human relationships. Because of this we often combined their Campfire projects with homeschooling, achieving a balance in activities.

Looking through Susan's Campfire Adventure Trails book, I see some of the activities for which she earned beads. Under the heading "Action Crafts on the Trail to the Great Outdoors," Susan earned beads for the following:

> Watch a sunrise, a sunset or a gathering storm. Express your feelings in words or a drawing about what you see.
>
> Learn what annual plants and perennial plants are. Find two examples of each in a yard or park.
>
> Find out what plants in your area were used for food, clothes or other purposes by American Indians and early settlers. Tell how these plants were prepared for use.

Under "Create Your Own Activity to Help You Know About Nature," Susan wrote: "Watch a frog lay and guard eggs. Watch the tadpoles/polliwogs grow up."

Under "Create Your Own Activity to Help Your Environment," Susan wrote: "Helped plant city trees project."

One project heading was "Creative Living." This was a favorite heading for both Laurie and Susan. Activities included:

> Tie-dye an article such as a shirt, curtain, table-cloth, scarf or napkin. Use at least two colors.
>
> Weave an item using a loom such as a cardboard, soda straw, flat frame, floor or back strap.
>
> Make up a design. Embroider and/or applique it

on an item such as a place mat, apron, dish towel,
baby blanket or wall hanging.
Make a fabric toy for a child.

Under "Create Your Own Activity Using Fibers," Susan
wrote: "Learn to quilt."

One of Laurie's favorites was "Make your own paper. Use
your paper as stationery. Or, make a sculpture or wall hanging
from paper you have made."

Under the "Smart Shopper" section the girls wrote a business
letter stating their dissatisfaction with a moldable wax we
bought that would not mold as easily as the description stated
it should. To earn the bead they had to use correct business
style and clearly state what happened. Not only did they earn
their beads, the wax company sent us an apology and another
generous supply of moldable wax, because the directions were
wrong.

Campfire was an outside activity, but it was also one we could
easily incorporate into our homeschooling. This certainly made
our days flow more smoothly. The girls shared the same leader
but had their own separate groups which met at different times.
In this way each girl had her own friends and activities most of
the time yet we could also combine some activities so the family was not spread too thinly. Both Laurie and Susan independently chose to be in Campfire. Had Susan chosen another
group, such as 4-H or Girl Scouts, that would have been fine
with me as I felt it was important each one choose which group
she preferred.

We felt that by limiting ourselves to one extra outside activity per family member, we recognized the needs of other family
members. Each of us had to realize how our activity affected
others in a way that did not cause conflicts. This recognition of
needs also carried over into the learning activities each family
member chose. interest-initiated learning projects needed to be
adjusted to family circumstances.

I can't imagine a family that does not have to make choices
(sometimes difficult ones) about individual activities, but you
know your family the best. Trust your own instincts. No one can
tell you what choices to make because what is comfortable for

them may not be comfortable for you. That is why I hesitate to tell someone how we do things.

We did find our family getting caught up in too many activities and had to learn for ourselves how and when to set limits. Circumstances determined who made the decision to set limits and what the financial limits were. In our situation, if I felt stress from an activity, that indicated that the activity was not good for our family. We constantly are reevaluating our commitments. Sometimes we make a wrong choice, but that, too, is a learning experience. Over the years I have become much more comfortable with accepting things in our life that do not match up with someone else's goals (which often are unrealistic for us).

The most difficult balance for me to achieve was how active I should be in the homeschool movement on the local, regional, state, and national levels. I have come to the conclusion that this is a highly personal decision which only I can make because I am the best person to judge what this involvement is doing to me and my family. Pressures can be very subtle to become involved to the detriment of my family, but there is also the temptation to begin to view myself as an "expert" who has most of the answers.

Thank goodness I have the privilege of listening to the stories of new homeschoolers, because I hear some of them telling the very same story I related when we first became involved in homeschooling. This serves to vividly remind me how many other families live out my family's story even today. As the years pass I watch some of these same families grow educationally. I hope to continue listening to the lessons these families can teach me.

I do strongly feel that every family should be well informed as to local and state homeschooling requirements. This generates a greater confidence that homeschooling is a legitimate educational alternative. Involvement in homeschool groups creates a sense of community and eases the feeling of aloneness. Every family has a positive contribution which they can make to the movement.

For several years I was very involved with many different homeschool organizations, in a wide variety of capacities. I kept myself informed as to the latest developments, particularly on the state level. At one point I was involved on local, regional, state, and national levels all at the same time. Then I began to realize I was too involved and began to seek the level of involvement which I felt would do the greatest amount of good. I needed to balance my involvement with my family's needs.

When I was puzzling over the depth of involvement I should have in homeschool organizations, I wrote to a very good friend who was also struggling with this:

> Sounds like you have a very busy schedule lined up for November. It is not easy at times to decide where you should concentrate your energy and especially which activities would be best dropped. You are so right that those who are actively working with their children are not in the best position to handle administrative details in particular. I am finding that it works best for me to have flexible activities without a long-term commitment because the needs and interests of my youngsters do change. We are in a very different year this year and I'm not sure where it is taking us, but I know that in the end it will turn out to be the right course. Laurie and Susan's needs have really changed.

I had served my time. Now we needed to have new insights, people who were fresh. It was hard to relinquish some of my local, regional, and state responsibilities, but the rewards were also there, as I watched people take over with enthusiasm and renewed vigor. The mother who took over guiding our local support group was fantastic. I had watched her grow from a hesitant homeschooling parent to a confident one who inspired this confidence in new homeschoolers.

Things do not always work out the way we would like. I've been involved with groups who were at first accepting of differing educational philosophies but then became rigid and exclusive. That hurts. I have also watched some organizations become too "political" where power plays became rampant within homeschooling ranks. This happens. Change and growth can be painful, but sometimes it is the means by which a new or revised grassroots movement is spurred into action.

Another aspect of balance in our homeschooling adventure is how to achieve a balance in our studies. At first this was my big concern. When Jim first came home I had visions of having to provide a balanced day, covering all of the subjects the state expects us to cover. As I relaxed more over the years I realized that I did not have to balance subjects day by day. Looking over the quarterly reports I wrote, I began to see how over a period of time we painlessly did cover the wide spectrum of topics required by the state. It was not necessary to do it every day.

I deliberately chose a year-round configuration of taking attendance. Since we were always studying in our very portable classroom (wherever we happened to be) I never did mark the youngsters absent. I had no qualms about recording activities done on Saturdays, Sundays and holidays as well as the hours outside 8 am to 4 pm. One of our quarters ran from July to September and that was always my favorite one because I relaxed more psychologically that quarter. Looking over the summer quarterly reports, I can't help but note how much learning took place during a time that seemed academically barren. Another thing I noticed was that the youngsters achieved a natural balance among their subjects during any given week. I wasted time and effort worrying about that.

Despite a seeming lack of structure to our learning activities, all three youngsters had no problem entering into the public high school. They had not covered the same class work, but had no problems catching up on the materials presented. Jim, Laurie, and Susan frequently comment that their attitude toward learning is what made the difference. So many of their classmates were in classes only because they had to be and they were determined they did not have to learn.

From a variety of sources over the years, I gathered some more effective questioning techniques which stimulated learning, rather than so many of the typical questions used which either suggest there is a "correct" answer or suggest that the learner is assumed to be stupid. I found that open-ended questions often led to new insights even for me, the questioner. Actually I rarely ever questioned my youngsters. Usually I intended to start or to stimulate discussion among all of us. Sometimes I succeeded, sometimes I won those pained/disgusted "Oh, Mom!" looks or comments. For what they are worth to you, here are some questions I used the few times they were needed to stimulate discussion:

When I needed more information:

> What do you mean when you say ___?
> Why do you say ___?
> How is your idea similar to or different from ___?
> Give some examples of ___.
> Please explain more about ___.

When I wanted them to dig deeper for themselves:

> What are the advantages or disadvantages of ___?
> Which is the best?
> Which is the worst?
> Why?
> What are alternatives?
> When is the best time to ___?
> What is the best place to ___?
> Why?
> What do you have to do first? Second?

When I wanted them to verify information for themselves:

> What could you do to find out if ___ is true?
> Where could you locate information?
> What makes you think ___?
> Is ___ true in every situation?

When I wanted them to test their theories:

> What are the consequences of ___?
> What will happen if you ___?
> What effect did ___ have?
> Will ___ work?
> Why or why not?

Please do not think for one minute we had an ideal family. Our youngsters have been rebellious, bored, cranky, and ever testing of limits. We had all of that and more. There were times I would snap back, "Well no one ever died of boredom!" when I was pushed too far. Helplessly I watched tears stream down a face because I was insisting on my way of approaching a subject (usually writing). Many times I compromised on what had become a task. Even today we still are an imperfect family. Dale and I still make mistakes.

A good friend told me I did her a marvelous favor one particularly harried day as she and I were visiting. Laurie had come up to me with a seemingly endless list of requests, to all of which I told her, "No." Finally in desperation I looked at Laurie and said, "Laurie, please ask me something to which I can say, 'Yes!'"

I can truthfully say that we had some hearty disagreements within the family. But I cannot give you details, because I don't remember many specific events. It is far easier for me to recall the pleasant times we had. These are what I treasure. I don't dwell on the negative times other than to regard them as times of growth and change for all of us. We had them just as any other family does. I must have put them into perspective in that these events helped to form us into the people we are today—still flawed and imperfect but striving to become better people.

One of the best methods I have discovered for achieving balance in my life as a homeschooling parent is to allow myself to doubt. Listening to these doubts and then observing my surroundings closely, I can turn these doubts into growth as a person as well as a parent-educator. Doubting can be healthy if it allows me to put things into perspective. This has been a topic for our support group discussions several times. Chris summarized one of these discussions in our group newsletter:

> Homeschooling is as individualistic as each family practicing it. We have a wide assortment of options about how we structure or allow homeschool into the pattern of our home life. But, there are times when it feels like we were left in an unfa-

miliar landscape without a map or a compass. And, in many ways it is like that. It's a lot like life itself. There are no assurances. There's no ready made path with direction signs. You're ultimately left with yourself and your family and your own decisions and the consequences of them. And, one of the consequences is that we have doubts.

Doubts can be teachers. They come with the territory of homeschooling. All the homeschooling parents I've talked to have the worry that they aren't doing enough. That seems to get less with time, but to some extent it's always there in the back of a homeschooler's mind.

We worry about how we are doing in comparison to other homeschoolers and to conventional schools. We have the regular parental worries as well. There's plenty to think about. This is natural. Many of us are new to this. Most of us didn't grow up homeschooled or even know anyone who was homeschooled.

Our children's education is important. The consequences matter a great deal. A questioning honesty can keep us from the mistakes of arrogance. We question ourselves because we care so much, because we're attentive and responsible.

To evaluate ourselves periodically is healthy. It provides self-checks on how we're doing. We have to be honest and secure to do this. But, a healthy self-questioning, as opposed to a paralyzing sense of self-doubt, depends on our accepting ourselves as the reference point of all our questing. We each are the final authority in our own lives.

The problem is that most of us went to conventional schools. And, while we may have forgotten a lot of what we "learned" there, we remain entrenched in the thinking that is taught by the underlying curriculum of compulsory schooling: that we trust not our own minds, but in what others tell us; that we find the answers others want us to find to the questions others pose; that the reference point for answering our doubts is not the self, but the institution.

We've inherited the legacy of that system and we have the challenge of uprooting the effects that schooling has had on our sense of security, self-trust, and self- authority.

Fortunately, homeschool is not like school. It is a reclaiming of what we love, finding security in doing what we are. It is a declaration of owning our own minds and the valuing of that so that we raise our children to own their own minds as well. We have a deeper securing in finding and following, with a rigorous honesty, our authentic selves. This is the nature of real education. This is an education for powerful, free and responsible people.

Chapter Six

Jim

We discovered that getting into college takes as much family effort whether the student goes from public high school or from homeschool. Either way, the parents and the students need to do a lot of research and preparation. We found that we could not rely on high school counselors as if they had privileged access to the information which makes the process easier. The information is available from many sources. I personally uncovered general college information as well as scholarship information which was more valuable to us than what Jim's high school counselor provided. The need for college and scholarship information continues throughout the college years, although learning the ropes the first year is the hardest.

When Jim was a sophomore, I began exploring college options in earnest. The most valuable resource I found at that time was Herbert Kohl's *The Question is College*. I understand it is out of print, but hope that it will be reprinted because of all the important information he offers. He reminds the reader that college is an expensive investment. The decision to go should be made carefully and with a sense of purpose. Herbert Kohl then guides the reader in assessing the need for college for the individual student. Then he offers specific alternatives to college, especially during the first year after high school graduation. Jim also read this book, finding it helpful; the author believes that education is broader than schooling, that self-fulfillment and service to others can be central to life, and that work can be more than a job.

Once Jim decided on college, Dale and I were dismayed at how intensely our privacy was invaded because of the required financial and personal disclosures (worse, we felt, than when we applied for our mortgage). The forms must be filled out unless the family can completely cover all college expenses—

which are considerable. It pays to have assistance in filling out these forms. Many high schools have a college financial aid officer present a session on filling out these forms. Usually notices of these sessions are placed in local newspapers. You can inquire at the local high school counseling office as these sessions are often open to the public.

The best written guide which I have found for accurate information regarding filling out the principal standardized need analysis forms (the Financial Aid Form (FAF) and the Family Financial Statement (FFS) sometimes also referred to as FAFSA) is *Paying for College,: A Princeton Review Student Access Guide*, by Kalman A. Chany with Geoff Martz (Villard Books, New York). They expect to print yearly updates—a necessity as financial information is quickly out-dated.

Finding college scholarships takes a lot of research and knowing who to ask. Financial Aid Officers helped us greatly once Jim was enrolled in a specific college. The services of a scholarship research company can be costly and many times are not worth the expense; we found that we could locate the same information—and sometimes more scholarships—on our own. We have talked with friends who paid for the scholarship research service and regretted doing so.

When Jim was a junior I bought a copy of *The Scholarship Book*, third edition, by Daniel J. Cassidy and Michael J. Alves. This thick book lists thousands of scholarships. Combing through it, we easily located several for which Jim qualified. It was well indexed, making it simple to locate specific scholarships.

This fall I bought an updated book of scholarships, *Cash for College*, by Cynthia Ruiz McKee and Phillip C. McKee, Jr. (Hearst Books, New York, 1993). Laurie is eager to begin exploring scholarship possibilities, and maybe Jim will find something in it for him, too. I like this book even better than *The Scholarship Book* because the authors devote the first 71 pages to helpful explanations about the scholarship process. The Appendix offers a high school timetable beginning in the freshman year, forms which you can copy for keeping track of scholarship applications and financial assistance analysis, sample high school resumes, plus other useful sample forms and letters. I find the sample letter of recommendation form very helpful.

Another resource I have is *Making A Difference In College Admission: A Step-by-Step Guide for the Secondary School Counselor*, by Kenneth W. Hitchner and Anne Tifft-Hitchner (The Center for Applied Research in Education, West Nyack, New York, 1989). A brochure came in the mail along with other educational offers; it looked intriguing so I ordered it. While it was expensive, it gave me a sense of confidence that I could guide my children through the college maze. In fact, comparing what I read in this book with what I observed our public high school counselors saying and doing, I realized that I could do better with the information in this book. It is a thick, dry-reading book, but I gained insights into the college application process. I ignored the sections bewailing lack of parental involvement on one hand and deploring over-active parental involvement on the other; the tone of the book tends to inflate the counselor's role and deflate the family's role. While I do not specifically recommend this book, I do want to encourage you to watch for similar publications and to consider whether you wish that information.

Richard Nelson Bolles frequently updates his book *What Color Is Your Parachute?* This book puts career planning and job hunting into perspective. He cautions against going into college without a specific reason for being there. Methods for identifying a person's strongest skills and most meaningful interests are clearly outlined. He emphasizes that one third of all careers require less than twelve years of schooling, one third require at least a high school diploma, and only one third require a college degree or beyond. Plan accordingly, he advocates. I find this book a valuable resource.

Both Jim and Laurie had a public high school English teacher who emphasized preparation for the SAT (Scholastic Achievement Test—used to be called Scholastic Aptitude Test). Almost any student planning to go to college can expect to take either the SAT or the equivalent ACT as a requirement for entrance. Test scores can make a big difference in admission and in scholarships. Jim and Laurie's teachers encouraged students to have copies of Barron's SAT preparation books as it did help improve scores. Taking the practice tests eases some test day jitters. There are now newer editions which prepare for the revised SATs.

Taking the PSAT (Preliminary Scholastic Achievement Test) in the sophomore or junior year places students on college mailing lists. Often the student improves test scores by taking the PSAT a second time, thus becoming eligible for more college financial aid. Many students take the SAT itself in both their junior and senior years for this reason. Jim scored highly his first time so he chose to take certain Achievement tests instead.

We watched for local scholarships. Jim won a $500 scholarship from a local Portuguese organization because my mother was Portuguese. He also applied for a small scholarship from La Leche League of Southern California and a newscarrier's scholarship. While he did not get those two, he was not faced with large numbers of applicants so he stood a good chance of winning them. Because he wants to go into church work he was given a scholarship from our congregation and several others from the college as well as from the church district.

Deadlines are critical when applying for financial aid and scholarships. Usually there are no excuses allowed for lateness; Jim lost out on some because he did not heed deadlines.

I am learning the truth of Herbert Kohl's statement that once the student graduates the helpfulness and resources of the local high school suddenly dry up. Special teachers still remember Jim and the counselor asks about him simply because Laurie and Susan are still on campus. When we need Jim's records now, we have to deal with the impersonal files in the district office. Unless a student is making a name for him or her self in academics, business, or sports, he is no longer mentioned on campus. Nearly all the graduates have gone into oblivion despite all the hoopla of the high school years.

Another thing that had become very apparent is that very few former public high school students have gone on to accomplish the extraordinary. Most are leading humdrum, unexciting lives. They have a piece of paper called a high school diploma which does not define who they are in the least. So why are we worried about our homeschooled youngsters?

Dale's cousin who has a Master's degree in music told us

about being a substitute for an English teacher in his town's community college. It was a basic college English class. All the students, except the three foreign exchange students, had high school diplomas. Immediately he discovered that most of the students in the class had low reading and writing ability. He had to give a test the third class session so he prepared a very easy test, telling the students exactly what questions he planned to ask, with appropriate page numbers to study. Only four students passed the test: the three foreign exchange students and one student much older than most of the class.

Jim has told us stories about some of the college classes he has attended that corroborates what Dale's cousin had told us about that English class. Jim dropped out of one college biology class because it was simpler than his high school freshman biology (from a weak teacher). For him it was a waste of time to attend that college class so he waited until he changed colleges and found a much more interesting college biology class.

Jim was not at all impressed by many of his fellow college students because of their lack of interest in learning. Several were there because they had nowhere else in particular to be. There is no sense of direction or purpose. College is expected of them, with parents or grandparents paying the way hoping something good will come out of it. Naturally, not all the students were that way, but Jim was surprised at the number who were not there to learn.

Jim wants to go into church ministry. This requires him to have four additional years after a Bachelor's degree. For his freshman year he obtained a full tuition scholarship to a college in Oregon which is part of his chosen preseminary program. We were able to afford his room and board, which were quite inexpensive at that college. Travel expenses meant he could only come home for Christmas. However, he soon realized that this college did not have the high academic standards he expected. The campus was in a high crime area so that students could not find jobs or easily participate in off campus activities unless they had a car—which few did.

There were high points in Jim's experience at this college. His Latin classes were superb. He had a few other classes he liked. The highlight of his experience there was being in the spring play. He had never acted before, so he was surprised at how enthusiastic he became over playing the lead role. Originally he had signed up with the class to get arts credit by being behind the scenes in some capacity, but the director encouraged him to try reading for a part just for the experience. He is now hooked on theater.

That summer Jim was a camp counselor for a summer youth camp. The counselors were responsible for the campers from Sunday noon to Saturday noon; their only free time was from Saturday noon to Sunday. He loved this experience. When Dale and I drove him home at the end of the summer he floored us by declaring, "Now I understand why you and Dad did and said the things you did when I was growing up. I was saying and doing some of the same things with the campers!"

Last fall Jim changed to a college in California which offered the same preseminary program as the Oregon college. At last he found a college setting with high academic standards in a much safer community. For the fun of it he had a part in the college's fall play and we were able to see him act.

The problem became finances. Scholarships and financial aid at this college were much lower while expenses were higher than the college in Oregon. He was able to complete one quarter but then had to return home, hoping to find a job while picking up basic classes at our community college.

Jobs are scarce. With so many military cuts, engineers at the local base have been forced into finding any work they can find. Jobs college students were filling are now held by college graduates. Jim has only found occasional babysitting and odd jobs. He is taking classes at the community college and searching out scholarships which will enable him to return to the preseminary program.

We don't know what the future holds, but I feel he can turn this experience to his future advantage. If he is determined to pursue his dream he will find a way to do it. This experience may also point him in an entirely different direction, but it is his decision; as his parents we can no longer direct his life. We stand ready to assist him but we do not think it is in his best interest to do everything for him. We've given him the roots, now he has to use his wings to fly. He wants to get out of the house and we want him to do so also. It has not been easy for either him or us to have him back home, and that is the way it should be.

Before we began homeschooling with Jim, he was miserable in school. Now when he recalls those sad days, he comments that the worst part was thinking he had no alternatives. The homeschooling experience taught him that people, even young people, do have choices. He reached the point where he hated school and everything he connected with the school experience.

After we brought Jim home he did not read for pleasure for more than six months. He only read what he had to during that bleak period. Before that he read voraciously. It took a long time, but he eventually regained his love of reading. My friend Laurie's son, Sam, refused to read for almost a year after they started homeschooling even though he had been and is once again an avid reader. For a solid year all Sam did was wander in their orchard after they brought him home, and Laurie was able to allow this to happen with little concern, but I was very concerned about Jim ever reading again. It was an effort on my part to allow him time for healing. I had days when I almost gave in to nagging him into reading.

Jim insisted upon going into high school. I had no idea what kind of a reception we would receive when I made the appointment to enroll him several days before classes began. In preparation I gathered what few books we used in our studies. In particular I took along the algebra book he used in the Young Scholars Program at the University of California Santa Barbara and which we continued using at home with tutoring from a local high school senior.

When I wrote to John Boston about enrolling Jim in high school I related our experience and reactions to the high school enrollment:

> You may have been contacted by the high school for Jim's records. He and I registered on Tuesday and spoke with his counselor. The counselor seemed quite impressed with Jim's background and made certain he was put in with the best teachers and the best classes. (This I know is a fact

from talking with people in the know about the high school.) It was a definite plus enrolling him late like this as he got personal attention from the counselor whereas all those transferring from the Middle School are mere names and statistics. Dale and I went to the parents' orientation the next night. We were not at all impressed by that—all the emphasis was on extracurricular activities and nothing at all was said about academics! Jim is really looking forward to this high school experience and we have noticed a big change in him. This seems to be a right move for him. It will be interesting to see what happens next. The last two and a half years have been invaluable to him and I have no reason to doubt he will now be able to make the best decisions for his own future.

John wrote back asking what records I wished him to include in the transcripts he was sending to the high school. I replied:

I guess I will play the "school game" and have you include the Student Record for a transcript. They only seem to understand that kind of language. Besides, all they have to do is look at their own past records of Jim's performance to see that all the A's fall right in.

So far it seems like Jim has made the best choice for himself in choosing to go to this school. He seems quite satisfied. My main impression is that the primary attraction is being with friends. He has gotten a lot of homework but it does not seem to bother him like it did in middle school. All this past weekend he and I have been quite sick with flu yet he went off to school this morning with no hesitation although he is still not back to his normal energy level. In past years he would have begged to stay home.

I suspect that the two and half years of breathing space was healing for him and he no longer

feels trapped, as he knows he has educational
options. My feelings are very mixed but I rejoice
that suddenly pieces in his life are coming together for him.

Dale and I went to Jim's first high school "back to school
night" in mid-September not expecting Jim's teachers to know
him as they all have to teach six classes with no breaks and the
average class has so many students. However, we learned that
he was in many small classes (an advantage of registering him
just a few days before school started).

He was placed in advanced classes as they didn't quite know
what to do with him; he was one of two freshmen in his geometry class. His teacher told us Jim should have gone into a more
advanced class. The teacher wondered just what Jim's background was because very few freshmen take geometry to begin
with and to be able to handle an advanced geometry class was
even more unusual! When I said he had been homeschooled the
teacher's eyebrows flew up in surprise but there was nothing
negative about the gesture. The amazing part to Dale and me is
that Jim did what seemed like very little in algebra when he
was being tutored—that is, he never touched the book unless
the tutor was there. Made us wonder what goes on in school!
His reading teacher was full of praise for Jim and for his love of
reading, yet, of our three youngsters, he read the least!

In general Jim's whole attitude about homework and school
had changed radically. He made his own choices and they
seemed beneficial for him. I think the fact that he knew he did
have a choice is the biggest factor. Previously he felt there was
no choice.

As a freshman he took a computer programming class—
again only one of two freshmen allowed that semester because
of a pre-algebra requirement. There are only 12 students and
they worked independently. He came home and applied what he
learned on an Apple computer to our Tandy TRS-80. Before this
he used the computer at home primarily for games.

He thoroughly enjoyed his Spanish class; the teacher's
strength was the use of unorthodox methods. Jim even chose to
get up in front of his class to recite on the second class day. A

very atypical reaction for him. But not all of his teachers were of such high caliber. All in all, Jim fared well in his freshman year.

For the first two and half years at high school, Jim insisted on coming home for lunch. He covered the two and half miles on his bike speedily so he ended up with about twenty minutes for lunch. This gave him an opportunity to drop off or pick up books or assignments as he needed. As he gradually began making friends, he found a reason to remain on campus during the day. Otherwise he did not get to school a minute sooner than he had to and he left as soon as possible after classes.

During Jim's sophomore year I wrote to John Boston:

> Jim's counselor asked all sophomore parents to come in for a visit so we went. He could not say enough good about Jim's background of home-schooling and how it has enhanced his current studies. He reiterated what we already know that the parents can greatly influence a student's love of learning. He feels that Jim will be able to get some rather hefty scholarships for college just based on his academic record. I've done quite a bit of research into college attendance and sure hope he is right but won't be surprised if he isn't. Actually from what I have observed homeschoolers have an advantage when it comes to college attendance because they necessarily have to do the background research that most parents whose students are in public schools think is being done for them by high school counselors!

We entered the phase of parenting which I least like: the driver training period. From the moment Jim and Laurie got their driver's permit until they passed their driver's license exam I was wishing it was all over. When they learn to walk, not too much damage can happen, but when they get behind the wheel of a car I can imagine all kinds of horrible things happening. It will be an enormous relief when Susan finally gets her license, too.

California requires all high school students to take a semester of drug education and driver's theory. Dale and I were dismayed to discover that Jim's teacher devoted most of the time to drug and alcohol education and very little to driver's theory. (Laurie's teacher, on the other hand, devoted about equal time to the two segments.) Jim then had to take ten hours of simulated driver training which the students all regarded as a big joke because it does not realistically portray actual driving situations. He got a total of an hour and a quarter of behind-the-wheel training. Because of state budget cuts, many California high schools no longer can offer the simulation and behind-the-wheel training required unless the individual school district can find an alternative source of funding. Our district has chosen to do this through the Adult Education program which charges parents a $110 fee.

I wrote about this milestone in Jim's life to a friend:

> Jim now has his driver's license and that opens a whole new aspect to parenting, doesn't it? High school is still where he wants to be though sometimes he seems to wistfully watch his sisters. I have become very aware of college opportunities—more due to homeschooling than to the high school—and doing my own research to back up what the counselor is telling us (which is not that much!). Because of his time at home, he is using high school to his advantage rather than letting them tell him what to do!

Another friend wrote asking how Jim was doing in high school and if he regretted either homeschooling or going to high school. I replied:

> Jim has chosen to go to public high school and uses his experience to serve his needs. Normally he does not talk much but he has said at times that the two and a half years he spent at home were the best years of learning he has had. And he knows he has an alternative in case high school no longer

satisfies him—having a choice is the greatest advantage.

Laurie, 13, is content at home for now—Jim tells her that it is where she should be!—with the idea she may go to the local high school. Susan, 11, also is content and is talking about homeschooling until college. She is brilliant in math and uses her time to explore quietly mathematical concepts that scare her brother—who is considered a math whiz himself by his teachers!. Sure am glad I don't have to know more than my students!!!!

Jim's junior year in high school was a continuation of his using his high school experience to his advantage. I wrote to a friend:

Jim is a junior in high school (just told us this weekend he is sixth in his class of 255) and using his high school experience to his own purposes. He does not have much use for most of what goes on there, so spends as little time on campus as possible, unless it is an activity that really appeals to him.

One mother contemplating removing her son from high school up in the Bay Area drove down to talk with us (she is a friend of my Mentor who encouraged me to write my book). Catherine asked Jim if his two and a half years at home were of any advantage to him. His reply was quick and definite. He told her that because of that experience he learned he could control his learning activities and that it gave him freedom to choose. Previously he never realized he had any choices in schooling. He said he would do it all over again. Right now high school is serving his purposes (just what this entails, I don't know as he never has been a great talker!).

When Jim was a senior, Laurie chose to enter the same high school. I wrote to John Boston about my reactions:

> Jim also has the same teacher as Laurie but he has Mr. Fisher for physics and has also been chosen as Mr. Fisher's TA (Teacher's Assistant). Crazy what the system allows for credit—Jim gets credit for the period he spends as TA, yet let another student (I know several who tried and have been turned down) ask for credit for some different activity that is very meaningful and they are refused. Mr. Fisher makes science live for the students. He has all of them eating out of his hand. At "back to school night" Dale and I were very impressed with him but we both had the same reaction—he is so good that he won't last (ala you, John Holt, John Taylor Gatto, etc.). At least Jim and Laurie are getting to experience him and his teaching methods. This is his second year of teaching.
>
> This is also Jim's first really happy beginning of a school year. He is so pleased with his teachers and classes and looking forward to college (how he will finance that is something else!). I gave him Herbert Kohl's book *The Question is College* and have been very pleased to see that he is reading it carefully. He has developed a small circle of good friends. It sure goes to show you that whether you are in the school system or homeschooling socialization is what you make of it! He never has had a wide circle of friends nor has he had much grasp of who he is. This has evolved over time and I am convinced that being "in the system" had nothing to do with his development. When he was ready, he was ready. However, I do believe the two and half years he homeschooled did make all the difference in that he learned to accept himself without devastating peer pressure or premature pushing by adults.

Mr. Fisher left our high school this year; Susan was so disappointed because she wanted to be in his class. It was no surprise that he left because of his innovative ways of teaching science. We still have some outstanding science teachers at the high school, thank goodness for Susan's sake. Soon the high school science teachers will be forced into an integrated science teaching method that does not recognize the differing abilities and interests of students. The idea is to teach every high school student the same material so they are "well rounded" in science. The teachers are resisting the change because they firmly believe in matching the course to the students' interests and abilities as much as possible.

Susannah Sheffer (*Growing Without Schooling*) wrote asking Jim to respond to a question concerning setting educational goals for himself. I empathized with her because I, too, wondered how he would respond. I wrote Susannah explaining that I was encouraging Jim to answer her query:

> James is the least likely to respond but I've learned the hard way never to speak definitively for any of them!! He is now going on 17 and has chosen to go to the local public high school. Currently he is putting up with nonsense as he has a certain goal in mind that he feels includes some of what the local school can offer him. The best part is that he realizes he has choices, unlike most of his classmates who have no idea that there is any educational alternative at all.

When Jim was a senior, I wrote to John Boston:

> Jim graduates from Lompoc High in June. From what I see he would never have made it to his senior year in one piece if he had not taken those two and a half years off at home. Since he is a bright student he got the better teachers and classes at high school (something that makes me mad because I feel every student deserves the "better"

teachers and classes). Of course, some of these
"better" teachers he had were not that great. But
Jim felt he had to attend the high school, even
though looking back as his mother, I really wonder
how he benefited. He is grateful for his time at
home, though.

After Jim's graduation I wrote again to John:

Jim graduated with honors from high school on
Thursday. He also obtained enough scholarships to
make private college affordable for us. This experience proved (not that I needed the proof personally) that parents/students can do as well (if not better because they have a personal interest) as high
school counselors in locating the appropriate colleges and sources of scholarships. The only thing
the high school counseling office did for us was provide a list of local scholarships available (which the
general public can obtain from the high school).
Jim was awarded a $500 scholarship from the
Portuguese Association (I am half Portuguese).
The rest of the scholarship money we obtained
entirely on our own—the school was not even
aware of them. He has chosen to attend a college in
Oregon, taking preseminary courses.

Most of his senior year, in my view, was a waste
of time because he could have done the required
work (seniors aren't apparently expected to do
much) in just a couple of months and then gotten
on with his life. He definitely felt it was a drag and
now acts like life really can begin.

For the summer he has enrolled in an astrono-
my class at the community college. Dale works
with the instructor on base during the day. From
everything we hear he gives a tremendous class—
it fills up just as fast as it is offered. Besides that,
Jim is working every night at one of our three
movie houses (all owned by the same people so he

can work in all three). He found this job because he made friends with one of the managers through being on the local computer bulletin board. And he realizes how fortunate he is since there are very few jobs available in town. Many businesses are closing.

Jim went on to his first college experience in Oregon. As a final in his Speech class he had to give a speech defending some educational method of his choosing. All during high school Jim rarely talked about homeschooling or his experience with it. Apparently at college he got into interesting discussions about homeschooling with other students, and decided to use it as the subject of his final speech.

He called home for some background information. He was pleased when I asked him for a copy of his speech, telling him I wanted to submit it to various homeschool publications. It is a homeschooler speaking out for himself and his perceptions of his experience.

I am not even certain that he had completely read my book, *I Learn Better by Teaching Myself*, before he wrote this speech. I suspect his first time reading it was during his speech preparation.

I Was a Homeschooled Student and I'm Fine, Thank You!
By James Leistico

"Never let your schooling get in the way of your education,"
—Mark Twain

Most of you didn't know that I was homeschooled from the 6th to 8th grade until just now. In this speech, I'd like to give you a little background information about my experiences and then defend the pro-homeschooling stance from common arguments and point out homeschooling's benefits.

Interest initiated learning is what my mom calls

the system she used with my two sisters and me. Interest initiated learning is that learning which the learner himself controls and initiates according to her interests. When it is interest-initiated, learning is guided by internal personal priorities not imposed from the outside. The learner himself chooses when and how to learn about a given topic or skill. It is entirely self-directed. The teacher only enters into the learning process when invited to do so." Mom would introduce topics for us to study. If we were interested in them, we would pursue the subject further, if not, then we wouldn't. That was fine with her.

Mom was not the originator of this concept. The noted author, educator, and homeschool pioneer John Holt advocated allowing children greater freedom in choosing what to learn when they were ready. Observing how young children learn to walk, to talk, and to function in social settings, he reasoned that this was a natural process and that later learning should flow just as naturally. The old saying, "You can lead a horse to water, but you can't make him drink," expresses this in a more familiar way.

Due to decreasing lawsuits and relaxing laws, homeschooling has grown as an acceptable option in the past few decades. In 1970, there were only 10,000, which increased to 50,000 in 1980. In 1990, one percent, or 500,000, of American children homeschooled, a number which continues to increase as parents decide to formally educate their young.

A recent Gallup poll indicated that 70% of the American public is against homeschooling. Many of them believe that the socialization of the children will not be "normal." However, they overlook the fact that socialization at a traditional school is hardly natural. "Social contact limited strictly to 'peers' (defined as everyone of the same chronological age) is a fraud. The world for which we have the responsibility of preparing young people is not full of their peers. It is full of people both older and younger, from social status both higher and lower. What are we teaching children about this very real world?" states Bob Pike, a public school teacher and homeschooling parent.

Stephen Moitozo says, "Normal isn't the same kids in the same room doing the same thing at the same rate in the same way to achieve the same results because they're the same age."

The 70% also don't realize that compulsory school attendance laws as we know them today were not widespread in the United States until about the middle of the last century and before then it was thought that if children were forced to be educated outside the home, parent's rights were being taken away. Homeschoolers are truants from one perspective, but, from another,they are following in the footsteps of Thomas Jefferson, Thomas Edison, Woodrow Wilson, Margaret Mead, and Andrew Wyeth. Today, many take for granted that government has a right to require attendance in school, and we stand amazed at any parent who may challenge that requirement. "To challenge the universal necessity of schools is not merely eccentric, not merely radical, but fundamentally un-American," says David Guterson, another public school teacher/homeschooling parent.

There are many problems with schools now such as school administration, testing, large classes, grading, and the entire reason for schools, i.e. learning, that homeschooling attempts to fix. Many school officials aren't concerned about the students' education and lives when they complain about homeschooling, but about protecting teachers, funding and the imposition of a particular philosophy on students.

In her book, *The Dispossessed,* science-fiction

author Ursula Le Guin writes about a man teaching at a school in a foreign land. "He was appalled by the examination system, when it was explained to him; he could not imagine a greater deterrent to the natural wish to learn than this pattern of cramming in information and disgorging it at demand."

"Standardized tests do not measure what they claim to measure. They are biased and have long term negative effects on students, especially creative thinkers, minorities, women, and anyone who does not possess the same values or experiences as the testmakers... What real purpose do letter grades serve? My grades in high school have had little influence on my lifetime activities," writes my mom in her book, *I Learn Better By Teaching Myself*. (She was the valedictorian of her high school.)

"Why do we allow adults greater freedom to learn according to individual learning styles than our children?" my mom asks. These conditions can contribute to lowering the student's self-esteem. Eighty percent of students entering school feel good about themselves. By fifth grade only 20 percent feel good about themselves. By twelfth grade the average student has received only 4,000 positive statements and about 15,000 negative statements in school.

In addition to giving alternatives to the above conditions, homeschooling offers another benefit. "Even on days when they are sick, they continue learning according to the energy available. While they were in school, I noticed that sick days were 'do nothing' days. Now sick days are quiet activity days in which learning continues," writes my mom.

Like any system, homeschooling has its drawbacks. Parents have to be able to be both a loving parent and an objective, evaluating teacher all year round. Not every child or parent is suited for the freedom of homeschooling as a means of education. Some need directed and controlled learning. Even my mom didn't agree with homeschooling in 1983, when she first met a homeschooling family. She was unimpressed because, as she writes, "The youngsters seemed to be doing nothing. 'Schooling' meant to me blackboards, texts, worksheets, schedules, tests, and a certain amount of boredom."

In some cases, homeschooling may turn out to be a mistake. But, argue some homeschooling parents, public schools already are disasters. Homeschooling is not an easy route; those who go down this road successfully deserve respect.

In conclusion, I'd like to share with you the results of my interviews with Dustin Kunkel and Mukkove Jacobs, two other Concordia students who were also homeschooled. Dustin's homeschooling experience was very formal. It was just like being in school. He had books and assignments that he had to complete by a certain date. Mukkove's experience was not that strict, but she had to complete work in books before the year ended. When asked if they would homeschool their children, both answered yes. Mukkove said that it would depend on how good the available schools were and the age of the kids. Dustin said he would do it because it teaches self-reliance and the ability to think for yourself. But he leans toward a mixture of traditional and homeschooling—he wouldn't homeschool a child for their entire education. None of us believe that homeschooling is for everyone. Dustin said it depends on the parent. I agree with him, but would add that it also depends on the child and the relationship the two of them have. My children will have the opportunity to follow in their father's footsteps when and if they want it.

I was particularly intrigued by his final statement. That is the first indication he has ever given me as to how deeply affected he was by the experience.

Chapter Seven

Laurie

A Montana mother who had read *I Learn Better By Teaching Myself* wrote asking me if I had any doubts about homeschooling, since Jim had chosen to go to public high school after two and half years of relatively unstructured homeschooling. She wondered what the girls were doing. I replied:

> Laurie chose to also go to the high school this year (after homeschooling since fourth grade), though her reasons are mostly social. Her friends at school tell her she is crazy to be there when she has the choice to be there or be at home. She told me that if something happens she does not like, she knows what she can do, and she will come back home.

For the record, all that time of unstructured learning did not cause her to fall behind her peers in the least. Even in algebra— she struggles with math and always has (having a father, brother, and sister who come by math concepts naturally is no help— now me, that's a different story, I can understand what Laurie is going through!)—she tested in the very middle of sixty-seven students her teacher had the first day of school. And this was a girl who spent very little time at home "doing" any math at all! Who says they have to sit in classes for eight years to be able to go into an algebra class? She got a B as her semester grade from a teacher who gives very few As. (Grades—another thing that really grates me—more than ever now that I've homeschooled and haven't had to use grades.)

An explanation of that algebra test Laurie had to take is in order at this point: only seven students even passed the test. It was supposed to be a basic placement test and the teacher expected more than half the students taking it to easily pass. Laurie scored 27 out of a possible 44; more than half of the students scored less than 25.

She was crushed at first as she was not used to failing any test. She had taken her last test in fourth grade because I did not use tests with my youngsters. I strongly feel tests are detrimental to learning if used to judge a student. Tests can be useful if they show a student what is already mastered and where gaps in learning exist. We spent the weekend discussing tests and how they are used. All the other students in this algebra class had already taken pre-algebra in middle school and had obviously forgotten what they had learned as a good grade was a prerequisite for this class.

At the end of the first semester the teacher gave the same test. This time Laurie scored a 38. The teacher embarrassed her by using her progress as an example, as no one else had shown that much improvement. She ended the second semester at the top of her class. It was not so much because of her math ability as a determination to master algebra and her attitudes toward learning. Many other students could care less if they learned any more than necessary to pass the course.

She was not thrilled about taking algebra. Geometry the next year was better once she got to understand how her teacher taught. He made math more interesting than her algebra teacher had. This year, her junior year, she took algebra II because it is a college requirement. Her teacher was an English major who was not interested in teaching math, so Laurie claims she learned nothing new. The teacher would tell the students they could skip certain problems in the text because she herself did not understand how to do them. Laurie also came down with mononucleosis so missed a whole quarter of her algebra classes and still made an A in class. This semester she is taking college algebra at the community college to fulfill her math requirements because she cannot get a good high school math teacher. The advantage is that this class will give her both college and high school credit. Ironically, both Jim and Laurie are taking this college class.

Grades mean a lot to Laurie. She will do anything to get a good grade in class; she prefers to get As but will accept Bs. College scholarship possibilities spur her on to maintain a good grade point average, but she has to work harder than Jim to maintain her grades. I have learned from Jim and Laurie that it is not that hard to get good grades from most of their high school teachers. If a student pays attention to the teacher's "point system," you are usually assured of a good grade. The "system" has more to do with class behavior and turning in homework or extra projects than it has to do with academic abilities. I am so very grateful Laurie had five years at home where grades were not even mentioned.

Laurie had mononucleosis most of the second quarter of her first semester in her junior year of high school. Morning classes were next to impossible for her to attend. She did find enough energy to go to her afternoon class and her work education (also in the afternoon). Through her friends, she handed in homework assignments for the morning classes. Only her algebra teacher caused a few problems because of her absences, which we were able to straighten out. On the basis of her attendance, classwork, and attitude during the first quarter, teachers were willing to work with her so she maintained her grade point average. One morning class was chemistry, but the teacher did not test on lab work so Laurie was able to get a good grade just by reading her text. So why should homeschoolers worry if they don't have access to chemistry labs?

The choices Laurie has made while in high school have been different than Jim's choices. She surrounds herself with people and is very active on campus, though she does not want any student government positions. Her aim is to go into teaching as she loves working with youngsters. This was quite evident when she was homeschooling. Her grade point average is important because she saw how it opened up greater possibilities of financial aid and scholarships for Jim. She is carefully choosing college-track classes while at the same time including activities she enjoys.

This year she is in the work-education program, for which she gets high school credit. For an hour and a half she is assigned to be a teacher's student aide at one of the elementary schools. She chose to go to one of the year-round elementary schools. By doing this she could work in two different classrooms during the summer, doubling her hours for which she is paid as well as receiving high school credit. This means that during the school year she also gets breaks from work education when the elementary school is on break but the high school isn't. She enjoys this periodic respite from a hectic schedule; I do, too, because it means I have use of the car for a change.

This semester she is only taking three morning classes at the high school: English, chemistry, and social studies. Then she goes to the elementary school, getting home about 12:30. One night she has college art appreciation class and the next night the college algebra class. Two nights she works at the drive-in. This makes a busy, but satisfactory schedule for her.

On Sundays Laurie teaches the fifth and sixth grade Sunday School class at church—the only teenager doing this. She is no longer involved with Campfire because the group has disintegrated. She is planning for an annual teen-age Search weekend where teens of many different Christian groups meet for an intense weekend of discovering how God fits into their lives. Only certain people are invited to be in on the planning of this event; her leadership skills are in demand.

Of our three youngsters, Laurie is the clearest as to where she is heading, how she is going to accomplish it, and who she is. She has a lively, outgoing personality which sometimes leads Dale and me on a merry chase. She collects people and objects readily, and living with her can at times be a challenge. One feature about her we all wish we had is her ability to let go of anger. Just give her time to explode; it can be a noisy explosion, but when she has released her strong reaction, she puts it behind her without looking back. She does not let a grudge smolder.

After Jim had started high school, a homeschooling friend wrote asking how Laurie was doing because she knew Laurie would miss having Jim home. I replied:

As for Laurene and Susan, they are very happy

> where they are at home. Laurie (12) has no desire
> whatsoever to attend the local middle school. What
> I find the most encouraging is that even though we
> do not cover specific planned topics at home when
> I listen to her talking with her friends who do go to
> the middle school, I often realize Laurie has cov-
> ered similar topics far less painfully and certainly
> with a lot more fun. And we did not even "plan" it
> that way!!

Laurie is the most likely one in the family to come up with a variety of interesting projects. When she was about twelve years old a neighbor got her interested in flower arranging for the local annual Flower Festival. She won a couple of ribbons in the beginner class. This spurred her to try for entries in the county fair. Here she won more ribbons and a little cash. Was she ever proud of that! By the next year she had started to lose interest in flower arranging, but there were other projects which caught her interest.

While homeschooling, Laurie often planned events for young-sters in our support group. In a letter to longtime friend I wrote:

> Laurie has arranged this month's field trip for
> our group. She even gets a Campfire bead for doing
> it. On Monday she arranged a tour of Domino's
> Pizza. Apparently they let the youngsters make
> their own pizza and then later on they deliver the
> pizza and drinks to a designated spot for us to eat.
> If the weather is nice enough we will meet at
> Beattie Park (the one near us) to eat our pizza.
> Otherwise we will meet at our house.

Laurie told me early during her last year at home that she intended to go to public high school. This did not surprise me since I knew how much she liked to be surrounded by people and to be involved in numerous activities. One aim she had was to become a cheerleader. She bought a baton at a garage sale and often practiced with it as well as made up her own cheerleading routines. While a freshman, she ended up trying out for the tall flags drill team. To her disappointment she did not make the team. However in her sophomore year she was grateful she was not in tall flags because she became involved in activities which were more interesting to her; tall flags would have interfered.

In November of Laurie's eighth grade I wrote to a home-schooling friend in northern California:

> Laurie, 13, intends to go to high school next year and I have no doubt that they will know that she is there and that she will do things her way! She is our socialite. She is highly competent and, more than her brother and sister, highly confident in her abilities. She, too, will work the system to her advantage (and if she can't, she will probably tell them they can go whistle while she returns home to do things her way). She will do fine!!

After Laurie went to high school, I wrote to John Boston:

> Laurie has made a very smooth transition into high school. It really makes a person wonder what the schools are doing with the youngsters when they have them captive for so many hours and so many days a year. Laurie spent very, very little time in "formal" learning situations. Yet on her very first math test (a subject she avoids when she can!) the first day of high school she placed in the upper middle section. And in the few short weeks she has been in algebra she is close to the top of her class. She is making it a point to do well in algebra because she is in a special science classs that has an outstanding teacher. She realizes she needs every bit of algebra she can get to do well in this pre-chemistry/pre-physics class. She now has motivation to learn math!!

A few weeks later I wrote John:

> Laurie going to the public high school has
> turned out to be the right thing for her at this time.
> Like she says, if it does not work out for her she
> knows what she can do about that—she doesn't
> feel trapped in the situation.

Several months later I again wrote to John:

> Laurie continues to do very well as a freshman
> at the public high school. A lot of it has to do with
> her attitude. She freely admits she is going for the
> social aspect but also to learn from a couple of out-
> standing teachers she has. She told me that if it
> ever becomes a poor experience she knows what
> she will do—come back home. She gets lots of ques-
> tions from both teachers and fellow students as to
> why she did not choose to stay home this year. One
> day she amazed me by sitting down and writing an
> article about it for *Home Education Magazine.*

Laurie's story is not unusual. We have good friends who live
about seventy miles away. I have known Laurel since 1979
because we were both La Leche League Leaders. Laurel started
homeschooling her girls before we began homeschooling,
though we did not discuss this until much later. Our contacts
with each other were through La Leche League activities. Her
older daughter is Laurie's age but the two girls did not really
get to know each other until after Laurie began homeschooling;
then Laurel started bringing her girls to our homeschool support group activities because she could not find that support in
her town; the homeschoolers there were very structured in
approach. Laurie and Missy developed a close friendship that
still is important to them.

Missy has a different personality than Laurie. She needed
Mom's presence much longer than Laurie needed mine. Missy
waited until it was time to register to announce to her family

that she was going to public high school. Laurel had misgivings but Missy insisted. Like Laurie, Missy had experienced interest initiated learning while homeschooling. Laurel had an even more relaxed approach to homeschooling than I had. She also had faced adamant disapproval from her husband's parents, where I faced unspoken uncertainty from my parents and in-laws, which later turned into approval as they saw the benefits of our approach to learning.

As with Laurie, Missy had few problems adjusting to the public high school routine. The advantage she had over her peers was that she still loved to learn. Teachers remarked about her positive attitude. Laurie and Missy still compare notes and both agree that high school for now is right for them. They also note that this is not necessarily true for every student.

Laurie loves to write, if she can write when she wants and about what she wants. Otherwise, she strongly dislikes writing. In particular she hates being assigned a topic. Many of the struggles she and I had during homeschooling were over writing. Once I had the bright idea to sit all three youngsters down for ten minutes of journal writing each morning. After a couple of weeks of protest and "I'm only doing this because you are making me" glares, I noticed Laurie filling a page with writing. "Ah, success!" I gleefully thought. That is until I read two pages full of the same words, "I hate writing" repeated over and over. That was our last journal writing session!

It is not unusual for her to draw a blank when told to write. Her sophomore English teacher routinely assigned essays. These were a struggle for her. Even when he gave students a choice of certain topics, she often could not find a reason for writing the essay. Yet she writes lively, fascinating letters prolifically. I love to be the recipient of one of her letters. Therefore, I was really surprised the day she announced she had written an article about her homeschooling experience for *Home Education Magazine.*

She was quite pleased when *Home Education Magazine* published this article as a Letter to the Editor soon after she sent it in:

When I am asked (as I am often) if I think being homeschooled has benefited me in any way, I don't hesitate for a minute before I answer, "Yes."

I am often asked by my friends why I decided to be homeschooled and why I chose to go to high school when I had the chance to stay home. They all say that they wished their parents had given them the option of being homeschooled and they would have STAYED at home instead of going back to school.

The reason my parents pulled me out of school was because of the teacher I had in the fourth grade. No one liked her because she did not believe that children should be on different learning levels. She kept all except one of my classmates on the same levels for all the subjects. The only reason she allowed this girl to work ahead was she had done the things we were doing in the previous year. Many of us (including myself) were advanced students who were capable of doing work for at least a grade higher than the one we were in.

My parents talked to her about giving me a higher level of work, but instead of that she gave me more work. It had no point to it, except it was to keep me busy. By the end of the day, I was expected to turn in two to three times as much work as the other students.

After only a month and a half in her class, I was taken out and placed into homeschool. It took awhile to get used to the unstructured (compared to the public school system I was used to) way of homeschooling. My parents did not force anything on me right away. I am thankful for this because I really think it helped me a lot. All children need "adjustment time." You might not realize how much of a change this is for the child, but from experience, I know it is a lot.

After this, I began to enjoy homeschooling

because of the way my mother did it. We didn't use textbooks for all of our lessons. Instead we used things you might not think of using...board games, for instance...we have a large assortment of these, many of them educational. Monopoly is a great way of improving basic math skills.

The thing I am most thankful for is I was never really forced into anything. I struggled with my math as a sixth grader so my mother decided I should put it aside for awhile, and come back to it later. For about a month I was overjoyed because I didn't have to do my math. However, a neighbor who is a good friend of mine, talked to me about the need for good math skills later in life. After this I decided to resume my math. Totally on my own I picked it up and figured it out.

Another question I am asked is how I made friends. There were many children in our home-schooling support group, but only one around my age. I still have a few friends from school, but I was involved in Campfire so I had many friends.

Now I am almost a straight A student. I made the Principal's List my first semester at high school. I was one of only 11 freshman (out of over 250 freshmen) who received this honor. I received the highest grades in both my English and science classes. The only class I did not receive an A in is Algebra. But I still managed a B in that class.

So thinking about it, I realize that my home-schooling background had helped me a lot more than I sometimes realize.

Chapter Eight

Susan

Susan is a conceptual specific learner. She wants to understand, explain, predict, and control her realities. Problem solving is her strength. Self-motivation is important to her learning. She prefers long-term independent projects and values intelligence and wisdom. Along with this style of learning she has difficulty relating to her peers and has weak social skills. Sometimes her preference for solitary activity springs from finding it uncomfortable to interact with others, or difficulty understanding them. Nevertheless she has a deep need for developing friendships. Logical subjects such as math and science tend to be her major interests.

When I observed her learning methods I discovered that she prefers hands-on involvement, with full control, in whatever she is studying. She can tolerate lectures on a subject if there is some teacher and student discussion allowed. Long-term projects suit her better than short-term projects, as long as she has freedom to act as she sees fit. She will seek to work independently of a group when possible.

She definitely does not like to waste time on previously mastered material or lots of written work. I already knew that she refused to do some activities for her kindergarten and first grade teachers. Once she came home for studies, I quickly learned it was utterly useless to try to demand work she refused to do. Now that she has chosen to go to the public high school she is making some compromises because she sees she must in order to survive in that atmosphere. But she has rebelled more than Jim or Laurie at high school—to the point of refusing to continue a couple of classes when she realized they did not interest her at all.

Our student interest initiated approach to learning appealed most to Susan, though Jim and Laurie mention their gratitude for that opportunity also. Susan needs more independence and control over her learning, avoiding materials that use busy work and repetition. She particularly likes to design her own course of study in a way that allows her free time to pursue her own interests. For the most part she is not overly concerned about social interaction because groups often make her feel uncomfortable. She likes to understand the reasoning and logic behind ideas.

When Susan was younger I often found little notes in places she knew I would find them. The depth of her thoughts as expressed in these notes often surprised me. Sometimes she expressed a deep caring concern for the family that surprised me, because outwardly she gave no indication she was even aware of the rest of us. As she got older, she wrote fewer notes until now they are very rare. Laurie had numerous pen pals around the world as well as the United States, and she still writes many of them. But Susan could not get interested in writing to pen pals; she tried a few times and lost interest. Once in a while she would write a short note to someone, especially to grandparents. These notes were fun to read because she has a clever way of writing.

One October, when Susan was 10, I wrote to John Boston:

> Susan has written very little over the last several months. You'd think I would learn, but I was beginning to doubt when suddenly this week she has exploded into a writing mood. She asked for a spiral bound notebook on Tuesday evening. Now it is Friday. She has filled over ten pages with small writing on narrow lined paper and calls it her journal. I have not been invited to read it and don't know if I ever will be, but that is ok with me.
>
> She does share some of what she is writing and the depth of her thoughts astounds me. Some of it is observations of nature, some is observations on life. She even decided to start a newsletter called "Think Peace." But, like I said earlier, all this came after a lengthy barren period.
>
> I cringe when I think of how she reacted when

forced to produce in school and am convinced she
would be burned out by now if she had continued
there. But now is the time she is really beginning
to blossom and she needs so much time to just let
it simmer yet.

A couple of years later I wrote to John:

> Did you see Susan's item in GWS? Susannah
> had written asking Laurie and Susan to submit
> something on how they learn from their peers or
> from others. Neither could think of anything to
> write about that but Susan sat down to write about
> her experience with the field trip to the Braille
> Institute. She does not ordinarily like to write
> much at all so I was delighted when she did that.

I wrote the following explanation to Susannah:

> Susan (10) usually writes with a depth of feel-
> ing. However, she does not write unless she has
> what she calls her "writing mood." You will notice
> that she did respond to your request although not
> in the way you anticipated.
>
> Three weeks ago she went with several other
> homeschoolers to the Santa Barbara Braille
> Institute and it sparked an almost passionate
> chord in her. Prior to the tour she had no thoughts
> or feelings one way or the other regarding the blind
> person. Now she can't seem to learn enough. She
> has taught herself Braille from the handout she
> was given on the tour and even wrote part of her
> thank you note to the tour guide in Braille.
> Imagine her delight when she received a letter in
> Braille from the tour guide in return!
>
> This shows the importance of letting our young-
> sters have a variety of experiences. Never in my
> wildest imagination would I have thought she
> would have more than a mere passing interest in

Braille. Therefore, what she tried to express to you in her response to your request was that you can learn from anyone, no matter what their age or abilities.

Susan and I spent two years homeschooling together once Jim and Laurie were in high school. She was content. I watched her develop. She directed her own activities.

During the spring of Susan's seventh grade, I wrote to John:

> Our homeschool support group meetings and our Friday swim nicely fills Susan and I up. We enjoy our quiet activities at home the rest of the time. Susan babysits every Tuesday morning for the Ladies' Bible Study and twice a month for their occasional Friday morning crafts session. She has her Monday afternoon Confirmation class (will be confirmed on Pentecost). Her Campfire group meets about twice a month. Other than that she is very content with her activities and does not seem to need anything else.

The next fall I wrote to John:

> Susan is beginning to come out into her own. No matter how I tried to alleviate it, she has always felt in the shadow of Jim and Laurie. Now she is trying new things she was hesitant to try before. One thing is that she is getting comfortable with the computer without having Jim and Laurie hanging around her. She is even tackling learning the database *Alpha Four* we recently got. I have spent quite a bit of time trying to learn how to use it myself. Every other spreadsheet intimidated me as they required too much computer background knowledge. This one I just may conquer! I really don't have too many occasions to use a spreadsheet but it is handy knowledge to have.

In a letter to another friend I wrote:

> The other day Susan sat down at the computer
> and started going through the tutor manual for our
> powerful new *Alpha Four* database program. I
> spent four long, intense, days on that manual yet
> in less than an hour she was competently breezing
> through the first few chapters. Susan is the least
> comfortable of our three youngsters around the
> computer. I was amazed to see her even thinking
> of tackling Alpha Four.

As time went by, both Susan and I lost interest in Alpha Four
because it did not serve a purpose for either of us. We did purchase a few other computer programs when Susan showed an
interest in them. Most of them are still sitting on the shelf
unused because they did not hold her interest. She is picking up
some WordPerfect for some of her high school projects. I am able
to guide her into learning to use what she needs from this program. Her biology teacher provides a study guide on a disk
which she uses quite often. There are a few games she enjoys on
the computer and she still gets on the local computer bulletin
board, though not as often lately.

Susannah Sheffer continued to send queries to Jim, Laurie,
and Susan. Most of the time none of them chose to respond,
although I encouraged them to do so. One of the last times she
sent a query, I responded myself:

> I really admire your persistence in proposing
> topics for our youngsters to have the opportunity to
> give us adults better insight into their interests
> and needs. It is not easy to express these topics in
> a manner to which they will respond. My young-
> sters do read them and no doubt you have stimu-
> lated their thoughts. One of these days you will
> actually get a response from either Laurene or
> Susan so please continue inquiring! And don't be
> discouraged when you don't receive many respons-
> es, please keep it up.

Susan almost wrote you a response on this issue's topic. Right now she is not in one of her writing periods. She is in her dreaming stage. I never know what to expect out of her when this stage comes to fruition. Sometimes there is a quiet advance that can easily not be noticed unless I am specifically observing. Other times she outwardly starts working on a project. I have no doubt whatsoever that it came from the dreaming stage. I honestly do not think she is even aware of what the end result of her period of dreaming will be.

The few times I question her as to what she is thinking about I almost never receive a concrete answer. Usually it is something like, "Nothing in particular." And my impression at that time is that she is being totally honest with me—even to her nothing seems to be happening.

But neither Laurie nor Susan would have thought to write about this in response to your letter. They just do not consider it a "difficult" path to their goal. It was just something that had to be gone through to reach their goal of getting the modem to connect.

Susan taught herself basic Italian a couple of years ago because we happened to find a book that taught Italian through simple songs. It just came naturally to her. She has not pursued it much lately, but I think it will come up again in some way later on.

She also fell in love with Shakespeare at age eight and read several of his plays in a huge complete book of Shakespeare that sits on our bookself. She thoroughly enjoyed seeing a stage production of "The Tempest." She was the envy of her older brother and sister because she and I had had fun reading and rereading "The Tempest" prior to seeing it performed. She would gleefully whisper a couple of times who had just entered the stage at appropriate times. She did not have the difficulties they were having with understanding the plot as it happened.

Thinking about it, no wonder Susan had a "difficult" time responding to your query because she does not consider her accomplishments as "difficult"! They are simply a part of her everyday life.

One day we received an advertisement in the mail for *Provoking Thoughts* magazine. Susan expressed an interest so we subscribed to it. This magazine literally turned Susan on to exploring new things and expressing the depth of understanding she has of the world around her.

That summer she was in a prolonged dreamy stage. It was so prolonged I began to get my usual "worry" about trusting Susan to direct her own learning in a meaningful way. (In a way I guess it is a good thing I do have my own periods of doubt because then I don't become too complacent and I also observe what happens more closely.)

Our second issue of *Provoking Thoughts* arrived on Friday afternoon. All day Saturday Susan sat at the typewriter composing six different ways to finish a story that was started in that issue. She would periodically giggle then type faster. That evening she shared her work with me (I try to not read anything the youngsters write unless they invite me to read it).

As I read her different versions of the story ending I marveled at her vocabulary, at her clever twists of words and thoughts, and her skill at entering into the emotions of the characters involved. I was seeing a side of Susan that she does not often reveal to anyone. That day of writing was worth more than a full year of sitting in a classroom writing "compositions"!

It was a sad day when we were notified that *Provoking Thoughts* magazine had ceased publication, but the issues we received are within easy reach in the file cabinet as their contents will never become out-dated.

Jim and Laurie started earning their own money at a quite young age. However Susan was reluctant to find ways to earn money of her own. Occasionally a neighbor would have her count out flyers she needed to distribute for a class she taught.

As long as the job could be done quietly and at home, Susan would do it. When Susan was twelve I wrote a friend:

>Susan is finally earning her own spending money. Jim and Laurie started sooner because they were willing to take on newspaper routes. Susan wants nothing to do with a paper route. She won't even substitute. She does not yet ride a bicycle although she has made a few attempts—she is just not ready to do it. Both Jim and Laurie use their bikes to go shopping, to the movies, to go visit friends.
>
>Laurie has always been advanced for her age, so confidently started babysitting much sooner. Susan acts like an ordinary twelve year old. I think it is hard on Susan to have to follow Laurie because of this and it takes her longer to have confidence in herself.
>
>Last year Laurie had a weekly babysitting job for the Ladies Bible Study every Tuesday morning. Now that she is in public high school Susan has taken over. There are only a few youngsters that come for this and she is paid very well. The nursery room adjoins the room where the women meet for study.
>
>With Laurie I could just drop her off and pick her up a couple of hours later. To help Susan gain self-confidence I sat in the nursery reading for the first few weeks until she let me know she was comfortable if I'd be in the next room with the women. So that is now what happens. Twice a month on Friday mornings they also meet for crafts.
>
>This means I have every Tuesday morning tied up from 9 to almost 12 and two Fridays a month. Unfortunately this is my most productive time of the day. It is easiest for me to write and work on heavy duty projects from early morning until about noon. Afternoons are harder for me and evenings -- forget it! But right now Susan is my priority and

she needs my presence. She is usually only comfortable babysitting when I am nearby. At the
moment I am typing this we have an adorable two
year old here at the house that she occasionally
babysits. She did have one regular job every
Monday afternoon for a neighbor two houses down
from us. But she was not comfortable yet with
being in that big house alone with a four year old
so decided not to continue that job. One of these
days she will be ready, I just have to remember not
to push her too soon and respect her for the individual she is.

To another friend I wrote:

Just yesterday morning Susan took a big step
forward because she was ready to do so. Jim (16)
and Laurie (13) have opportunities for pet sitting
during the summer. They also have paper routes
and pick up babysitting jobs so have access to earning money.

Susan (11) is beginning to obtain pet sitting jobs
but has been reluctant to accept them because of
not being comfortable with entering empty homes.
My husband and I offer to accompany her and stay
with her throughout her pet sitting duties. She has
accepted our offer for three jobs (but still with a bit
of reluctance).

Yesterday morning I could not accompany her
because of preparing breakfast on a tight schedule
and she did not want to ask Dale. Without saying
anything to us she got the neighbor's house key,
went to take care of the dog. Coming back home
she had the great big grin she has when she is
especially pleased with herself.

After church she went back to the neighbor's
house to take the dog for a walk around the neighborhood. Ordinarily she will not stray far from our
property. But now she is feeling so much more self

confident. This is just one of many indications she
is becoming much more independent.

In a few days she will stay over a week by herself with friends in another town and is eagerly
looking forward to it. She has worked up to this
point by gradually staying overnight at friend's
homes when it was her choice to do so.

This past year she finally learned to swim and has quickly
developed into a strong swimmer after years of being afraid to
get out of arm's reach of the pool side. Another indication of
growing independence is her ability now to talk comfortably
with adults.

None of these accomplishments have come easily for her
because she sees her older brother and sister doing their activities with apparent ease. Sometimes their impatience with her
lacks understanding of the fact that they, too, had to stum-
blingly take those same first steps. They don't always remember their own reluctance to risk moving forward.

Of our three youngsters, I thought Susan would be the one to
choose to homeschool through high school. In letters to several
friends I mentioned this:

Susan, 11, will probably be the one who will continue to homeschool through high school. She is
very quiet, like Jim, and very quick to learn. But
she has a difficult time bucking the crowd. She
prefers her own quiet little corner of the world,
preferring peace and quiet for reflection.

She runs circles around me with her depth of
understanding of mathmatical concepts (of course,
that is not hard to do!). Jim is a math whiz (like
Dale) but they shake their heads at what she
comes up with without any formal training whatsoever.

She was in public school through first grade.
During first grade she wanted to learn to write
cursive so badly. Her teacher let her do a little but
not much as the second grade teachers disap-

proved of letting first graders learn cursive. However, Susan's interest in cursive left and to this day she will not write cursive, preferring to print instead. Since she is at home that is no big deal. And Jim says that in high school his teachers want them to either print or use the computer on anything they hand in anyway!

While in eighth grade Susan began to miss having friends. Our homeschool support group only had a couple of boys her age. The other, larger, homeschool support group now had many older students, many of whom Susan knew but none of whom were friends with her.

She did have one special homeschooling friend whom she saw less and less frequently and then not at all because of seeming scheduling conflicts. Eventually the mother (with whom I had been very good friends previously) explained to me that she could not allow her daughter to see Susan because Laurie (16) was dating boys. She did not want her thirteen year old daughter to start thinking about boys yet. This was hard on both Susan and her friend because they had really enjoyed being in each other's company up to that time. In reality Laurie was only going on a few dates and nothing was serious. Laurie does not want to be tied down by dating as she is having too much fun with all her varied activities. But the mother would not listen to this.

So Susan chose to go to the public high school to find friendship as well as to have some of the classes Jim and Laurie had. She is making friends slowly and enjoying their company. The one teacher she wanted most to have is no longer at this high school. Susan has also been having a struggle with her health that would have stopped other people in their tracks. She is determined to make this experience work for her benefit and overcoming great odds while doing it. She also refuses to put up with some of the school rigamarole, which could cause some difficulty later on. Already she has dropped out of classes which she felt were unsuited for her

Several months before high school started for Susan, I wrote to John:

Susan has decided that she wants to try the local high school this fall. Part of this is she feels confident within herself. And she also feels isolated from other teens.

Her interests are different than Laurie's (who naturally gathers people around her). While we do have quite a few homeschooling teens now (which we never used to—Jim and Laurie were always the oldest around), they belong to the other support group and tend to stay to themselves.

One mother even told me she did not want Susan associating with her daughter any longer (both are 14 and have been close friends ever since we started homeschooling) because Laurie (16) has started dating! Had nothing to do with Susan and she did not bother to even ask what type of dating Laurie is doing—casual and infrequent! She did not want her daughter to be introduced to thoughts about boys.

Both my girls laughed when they heard the reason. How do you stop a 14 year old girl from noticing boys anyway? Makes no difference that the mother knows we are regular church goers as she now is.

Susan is also interested in some of the classes her brother and sister have taken. There are certain teachers who are outstanding and she has a very good chance of getting those teachers because the counselor now knows me well (and our youngsters). She also realizes she has to take the bad along with the good and is willing to do so.

John Boston had turned Home Centered Learning over to Susan Jordan and her husband David. I wrote to Susan Jordan:

Susan is choosing to enter the public high school this fall. In my experience with both Jim and Laurie, it is to our advantage to wait to enroll her just before school starts. The schedules are firmer and the counselors are fresh from their summer break. This assures better placement in classes than if we enroll her now.

As with both Jim and Laurie, we are reserving the option that Susan can choose to return to her learning at home should it become more attractive to her for any reason. Jim now is in college and apparently not only writing papers on his home-schooling experience but also chose to give his final speech for this quarter's English class on home-schooling. So far I have not seen any of his papers, but he has promised to share his speech with me this summer—he earned an A on it! He also has said that I can share it with whomever I wish. So when I get the opportunity to see it, I will read it with the thought in mind that it might be some-thing you might want to put in your newsletter as coming from a former School of Home Learning/Home Centered Learning student.

A major factor in Susan choosing to go into the high school is the lack of companionship with stu-dents her own age. She misses that and there is lit-tle we seem to be able to do to remedy that. There are several other similar aged and older girls in the other support group but they have never real-ly included Susan in any of their activities. Therefore, Susan has no friends with whom to associate. She does belong to the church youth group, but that is mostly boys and the few girls in it have entirely different interests (the same is true with her Campfire group). Lately I've been talking with other homeschooling mothers with similar problems.

However, I trust Susan to find her way and to choose what is best for her. There are some out-standing teachers at the high school. The coun-selor she will have has become very interested in

our children and will do his utmost to see that she
has a positive experience.

I have to eat the last words in this quote. Because of several things happening in our family, including serious illness, I discovered that the high school counselor did not always have Susan or Laurie's best interests at heart. This has been the first year our family has had to rely on people at the high school keeping promises to watch out for our students' welfare and have found them sadly lacking. His intentions were the best, he just never followed through on them. Once again I learned the lesson that parents do know what is best for their children and parental responsibilities do not stop at the school door. No one else has the interest parents do in their students. Susan is having a positive experience because she and her parents are looking out for her welfare.

Chapter Nine

Closing Thoughts

This book is coming to an end; our lives are not. We still have uncharted areas to explore. Who knows where we will be five years from now? Will Jim, Laurie, and Susan have brilliant, star-touched college years that lead to extraordinary careers and worldly success? I doubt that very much. Nor do I wish that for them. What I do wish for them is the continuing love for learning they already have and lives that are fulfilling to them. Dale and I have, as the saying goes, given them roots. Now it is time for them to use their wings to fly on their own.

During one international parenting conference I attended, a noted Canadian adolescent psychologist warned us parents that as teens become adults, parents cannot take the credit for how their children turn out, nor should parents take the blame. Each person is responsible for his or her own actions. Just because Dale and I chose to homeschool Jim, Laurie, and Susan, it does not necessarily mean that they are guaranteed success in life. At most, it showed them that they do have a choice in how their lives are lived. Dale and I now have to accept and respect their choices for their adulthood. This may not be easy, depending on how we view their choices from our perspective and background. We constantly remind ourselves that we had to learn from our own mistakes and so must they.

Opening yourself to others is risky business. Normally I am a very private person, keeping most things to myself. As I get older, I realize how helpful and encouraging it is when people share their experiences. We tend to find that we are not alone in the challenges we face.

Writing *I Learn Better By Teaching Myself* was an enormous risktaking venture for me. I felt I was exposing myself and my family to scrutiny and criticism. Did I really want to do it? I decided to do it because the more I talked with other home-schooling families, the more I realized there were many families just like our family. How true this proved to be.

John Boston helped me print the first hundred copies of the book for trial distribution. These quickly sold and Home Education Press agreed to publish the book, now in its second revised edition. From the beginning of distribution of the first copies, news of the book quickly spread by word of mouth. I began getting letters from families around the United States (and later from around the world) relating their stories. The similarities to our family's experiences proved to me the need to let other families know they were not alone in their struggles to provide the best learning experiences possible for their children.

The most common comment I hear from other families is, "Thank you for reminding me to trust myself when it comes to my children!" When we first started homeschooling, I kept asking John Boston to give me specific, detailed suggestions about teaching methods that work at home. He would gently and quietly tell me to follow the lead of my children. I read every issue of *Growing Without Schooling* to find answers to my questions only to find the same directive: follow the student's interests, but in order to do that I had to learn to trust myself. That was the message I wanted to convey in my first book. According to the letters I have received, that message came through. That is the same message I hope you take from this book.

The hardest part of writing this book is relating specific activities and methods we used while homeschooling. I don't want you to think this is what I think you should do also. Rather, I want to give you ideas from which you can spring into your own approach. What worked for us may not work for you. Something that did not work for us may be the very thing from which you benefit.

Looking back, there are things I would change. It is too late to do that, of course. Maybe another opportunity will come for me or maybe you will take to heart my regret by adapting it in your family situation. Overall I am satisfied with how we home-schooled, though some details I would change.

One thing I regret is not keeping up with a more detailed Quarterly Report. In the Appendix I have included sample Quarterly Reports from my files. At first they were more detailed. As you can see from the last sample included, as time went on I did not include as much information.

At first my motivation for writing Quarterly Reports was to have something specific in writing to show we were meeting California Private School requirements. Along with the Quarterly Reports, I kept samples of the work completed. As the years went by, no one in the district showed any interest in the fact we were homeschooling, so my reports became less detailed.

My regret in not keeping up detailed reports is because I am unable to reread the reports as a reminder of the tremendous variety of learning experiences we had along the way. At the time we were doing them I thought I could never forget the activities because they were actually fun and interesting. I have forgotten so much. Because I did not write them down, it is hard to recall just what we did do. Rereading the reports while writing this book brings back many special memories. I regret that I did not continue writing the reports in the way I did when homeschooling was new to us.

At the end of each quarter I would look over the calendar to prepare my Quarterly Report. The calendar hung on the wall next to my desk. Weekly, and sometimes daily, I wrote brief words or phrases on the calendar as a memory jogger when it came time for the report. I usually wrote the report during our break between quarters. My intentions were to also write down the titles of the books each child read during the quarter. This I did not follow through on and now wish I had done so. At first I also saved the calendars, but in the interest of reducing clutter, began throwing the calendars away when the year's quarterly reports were written.

I hope I have shared enough of my foibles with you that you realize we are not an extraordinary family. Most of all I want to thank all the families who have shared their challenges with me as a result of my book. You have given me encouragement and solace. You have let me know how many families there are who are like ours.

In conclusion I want to share with you a letter from a long-standing friend from my pre-homeschooling life. She has given me permission to use her letter. Her story is our story, with different twists. She expresses the struggle of parenting in a heartwarming, positive manner. To protect her family's identity I am changing their names.

Mary and her husband, Tom, have four boys, ranging in age from six to almost eighteen. As the years went by Mary became increasingly worried about what she saw happening to the education of her boys. She enthusiastically encouraged me when I was writing *I Learn Better by Teaching Myself*, even buying one of the xerox copies John ran off for me. Later she won a copy of the edition published by Home Education Press. She says she constantly reread both copies, but did not start homeschooling until this past fall. Now she has her two youngest boys, Bob and Tim, at home and is so glad she made this step. The local schools had placed Bob into a special education program. Mary could see he was miserable and not learning. What a turn around in his attitude when he came home to learn, even though he did continue some of the special education classes at first.

Recently she wrote me a letter updating her situation:

> I'm thrilled that you'll be writing another book! When I think of how many times your first book has bailed me out of self-doubt and worry, I can't wait to read your second! We've had some good news and some bad news regarding education these past few weeks. If there's one thing I can be sure of, it's that life is never dull!
>
> Last week Bob officially "graduated" from the speech and language program in the public schools after six years of special education! We really celebrated—I let him pick the menu for dinner (pizza, of course!), and I surprised him with streamers, a

mylar balloon, a cake, and flowers. We'd been eating for about ten minutes when he noticed the car-
nations on the table and asked where they'd come
from. He looked so surprised when I told him they
were for him. I suspect Tom thought I was overdo-
ing it a bit, but I see this as such an accomplishment for a little boy whose prognosis suggested
he'd have to learn sign language because he'd
never speak normally. Bob told me that our celebration was better than a birthday!

Bob's speech clinician, Laura, told me before
Christmas that she felt he had met his goals
already for this year and that she'd like to test him
to exit the program. By that time he was beginning
to chafe at having to go for speech twice a week, so
I agreed. Bob finished the anticipated three hours
of testing in half that time, and Laura told me he'd
done very well, that he's so bright he was able to
compensate for difficulties in a way that other kids
couldn't.

I went in two weeks ago to sign papers for his
special education to end. I met with Laura and
Bob's former speech clinician, Judy. They went
over test results with me and gave me some hints
for things that I can do to help Bob build on weak
areas (he'll always be apraxic—at this point, most
deficits are in word finding and short term memory which affect writing). Judy commented that
when Bob comes into school now, he seems so confident, that he's comfortable with adults and other
children, and that he initiates conversations with
her instead of waiting for her to speak first (this is
a change from last year).

It seemed the perfect opportunity to tell them
both how wonderfully relaxed he is now. Last year
he'd come home a bundle of nerves and explode (or
retreat to a quiet corner with his cat) after having
stuffed frustrations and feelings all day. His teach-

ers thought things were fine because he didn't let those frustrations out around them.

This year (with homeschooling), if he's frustrated about not understanding a new concept, the tears come right away, and we can either put aside the frustrating activity for awhile or talk about what's making him upset. Also, I've learned that Bob needs absolute quiet when he's doing an activity that requires concentration or something that he finds especially difficult. Poor Tim often winds up doing his math in the living room because he makes too much noise for Bob.

When I mentioned this to the teachers, Judy nodded and said, "Can you imagine how much energy it must have taken for Bob to fight all the distractions in his classroom?" We left the meeting with both teachers stating that they thought bringing Bob home this year was really good for him. I suspect Judy felt this way all along, but for Laura, it was a real change. Both assume I'm sending Bob back next year, and I haven't dispelled that notion. I don't want to make any decisions this early in the game.

I expected that middle and high school conferences for the two older boys would be pretty routine. Wrong! Mark came to me at 11:30 one night and asked if we could talk (pretty rare unless he's got something heavy weighing on him). As he began to talk, I realized that he was preparing for a bad parent-teacher conference. He told me he has several assignments overdue and doesn't really have any intention of completing them. We talked for over an hour, and I really tried to listen without jumping in. It seems the classic burned-out-on-public-school syndrome I've read so much about. He's rebelling against the control and against being told what to do and what to think. We don't see this at home. Whether he likes some of our family rules or not, he abides by them and is a cheerful, terrific person to have around. He says he works hard on group projects because he doesn't think it's fair to let down the other group members, but he doesn't see the value in many of the individual assignments.

I asked whether in making these choices he was letting himself down, and he said that he may be making mistakes but that he has to make them and learn from them himself. He said that many of his friends are always chasing the almighty "A" and that the frantic chase controls their lives. He told me he doesn't stand a chance with his English teacher because he's a white male. Apparently this woman is very much into political correctness and is very liberal. Mark, while quiet and respectful and not a "redneck," has very conservative views. He told me that during the reading of a piece of literature, one boy in the class referred to a character as a "bum." The teacher made the boy repeat "homeless person" over and over many times in front of the class.

Mark says he needs to make his own mistakes and make his own decisions. He's nearly eighteen, I can't say that I disagree or that I don't remember feeling that way myself at his age (though I was too much of a "people pleaser" to act on those feelings). We talked about short term and long term consequences of decisions he makes, and he agreed that he needs to consider them, but he also repeated that he needs to learn from his own mistakes.

He talked about life a hundred and fifty years ago (he's always loved history), and about how hard it was but that people had more control over their own lives. He said that today society gears everything toward earning the almighty buck. He said that while he's appreciative of technology and comforts of modern life, he wishes life would go slower. He mentioned going up north and just living for awhile, where he could think and relax. I bit my tongue and didn't ask how he'd live because that's exactly what he'd been talking about—chasing the almighty buck.

We did talk about what he wants to do after high school. He said he'd like to graduate just to have it done. Then he wants to take a year or so off from school to "decompress" a bit. I asked about the military, and the way he looked at me confirmed that he's been thinking about it. We discussed control and how if he's chafing at control right now that the military would be a hundred times worse. I think Mark's under the impression that boot camp is the only time control would be a problem. We also discussed how being enlisted differs from being an officer and that if he wants to be an officer he has to have a college degree. We discussed education levels and how he might find a steady diet of people with a high school education (many barely able to read) difficult when he's been with very bright people all through school. I explained that that's not elitist but a reality he needs to be aware of.

I was so grateful for my La Leche League background during that discussion. It was one more example of the value of trusting my instincts. No matter what I was thinking inside, I was able to let Mark talk and express his opinions without butting in and trying to change them. While the choices he's making aren't the ones I'd choose, I do respect the maturity of his arguments and how carefully he's thought things through. When we went to bed in the wee hours of the morning, I really felt at peace with things.

The next night we went to conferences, and things were indeed bad. His Russian and band teachers were the only one who felt things were going well. English was a disaster, but I felt comfortable telling the teacher that Mark has decided not to complete outstanding assignments. I told her how he felt about his chances in the class (the liberal-conservative thing). She listened respectfully and said that public school teaching methods only work with one learning style. What an admission! She had Mark for English part of last year and has seen his ups and downs. I do think she really cares about him. She said that his body language lately had suggested that he feels really restricted. I told her that I wouldn't be surprised if Mark wanted to drop out and that we'd respect any decision he made, whether we liked it or not. We talked about homeschooling a bit and I told her we'd pulled the younger kids out of school this year. She looked at me with a bit of wonder on her face, and she said, "You're really devoted to your kids." I told her it's my job to be!

The Algebra II teacher was downright disgusted with Mark. This is Mark's second time around in that class (he flunked all three trimesters last year because he didn't do daily assignments), and the teacher said Mark has about two more weeks to show improvement before he gets tossed out of the class mid-trimester and put in a study hall (which would result in an F) for the rest of the year. His disgust, he said, comes from the fact that on a recent district-wide test to determine how the new math curriculum is working, Mark pulled the highest score in his high school of more than two thousand students. His PSAT scores were very high in math, also. Of course, all the teacher is seeing is laziness.

I was surprised at how willing Tom was to consider alternatives for Mark. We spoke with Mark's counselor and she said that Mark is "brilliant," and if things had been different, he'd be valedictorian.

She also mentioned what a fine young man he is and how lucky he is to have parents who care and set high standards for him. I told her about his comment about living up in the woods, and she said that Mark's a square peg in a round hole, that he reminds her of Thoreau—a deep thinker who needs to throw off the constraints of modern society to find himself. We talked about a lot of options for Mark—quitting school now and getting his GED, accelerating his program with basic classes he needs so he can graduate early, a work-study program, or homeschooling. I said the thing that would be most difficult if we pulled Mark out of school was the fact that our district doesn't allow homeschoolers to participate in band (a real creative outlet for Mark) beyond eighth grade.

A couple of days later Tom and I took Mark out for dessert and away from family distractions to talk to him. He says he doesn't want to quit school just yet, that he thinks his attitude may improve as the weather gets nicer. He does seem to have cyclic swings in school and always has. So we'll see... I'm happy that Mark knows he can talk to us and that we'll support him emotionally.

As I've thought about all of this since conference time, I've remembered all the teachers who said Mark was a "selective learner," or worse yet, lazy. I wish I'd taken him out of school in middle school when things began to go downhill so he could study the things that interested him most. Perhaps he'd have discovered the joy of learning instead of feeling closed in. There's always hope for the future, however. If we give him space, maybe there's still a possibility.

Outcome Based Education is a big issue in our state right now. Several parents have begged me to speak at a public hearing about the reasons I'd taken Bob and Tim out of school. Some know the struggles we've had with Mark's education and wanted me to tell the OBE task force how whole group instruction and the haphazard OBE methods have hurt him. Part of me wants so much to do this. But our state homeschoolers association has advised us to keep a low profile and not rock the boat. Local newspaper reporters attend these public hearings and quote citizens in the paper. I can only imagine how Mark would feel to see his name and his school performance published for all to see. So I declined.

One school board member must have heard from someone that I was against OBE because he called me. When I expressed my concerns about the direction our school district is taking (watered down standards, elimination of grades, rewarding of mediocrity, equal outcomes whether kids are struggling or gifted, the whole group instruction) he told me that the state board of education is likely to mandate OBE whether our district wants it or not and that there's not much we can do about it. I did write a letter to the OBE task force and I've spoken with the offices of state legislators who have some control in this area, and at this point, given the sensitivity of the homeschooling issue and Mark's feelings, I think that's the most I can do. Our district is facing mandated cross-district bussing for racial quotas, and the thought of putting my kids on buses to travel to districts where violence is ten times worse than in our high school is more than I can bear. The metropolitan districts have also been charged with closing the gap between test scores of different racial groups. All anyone is looking at is test scores and no one seems to recognize that much of the problem with low achievement in many communities is the result of what's happening (or not happening) in society and the family.

Several months later Mary wrote that Mark has chosen to finish high school at home. He is currently enrolled in the Clonlara School Home Based Education Program. Things are definitely better for him though many rough edges need to be smoothed for Mark and his family.

For three years I edited our support group newsletter. Two other editors have carried on since then. Our most recent editor, Chris, often shares her reflections about homeschooling. In the January, 1994, issue she wrote that homeschooling is "no big deal."

> I have certain things I tell myself frequently throughout the day when I'm home all day long with my children. One is that homeschooling is nothing like school. That's not so much a reminder to me that I can deviate from the conventional structure that's been officially sanctioned by the government schools for dispensing education, what people normally mean when they talk about "education," but a joyful affirmation of what education really is and how we are free to follow through on that affirmation when we homeschool.
>
> Lately, what I've been telling myself is that "It's no big deal." Of course it is. It is important. We care a lot about our children's education and put a lot of time and energy and attention into it. But, as I become more comfortable with what we are doing and I feel more in tune with what works for us, it does become less of a big deal.
>
> It's "no big deal" in the same way that feeding a family, making a living, creating a home, living your life is "no big deal." Yes, all these things are important. But we do them matter-of-factly. There are conflicts at times and sometimes disasters. But, that's a part of life. Life is constantly presenting challenges or opportunities, depending on your

perspective, to grow, learn or change something that doesn't work anymore.

It's not "no big deal" because we default on our obligations in the education of our children, but because we align ourselves with that obligation and it feels right.

I was talking on the phone with a good friend in Texas. She is not homeschooling. But she did tell her son who is about to graduate from high school that anything she has truly learned, she has taught herself. School only exposed her to getting along with all sorts of people and to a wider variety of educational experiences than she would have had on her own. When it came to the truly important things in her life, she taught herself what she had to know to be successful in those endeavors. Her words nicely summed up my own sentiments.

A few short weeks from now 1994 will end. Jim is working a few part time jobs while attending local community college classes. He expects to return to his four year college in the fall, financing permitting.

Laurie has arranged four community political forums in preparation for November state and local elections as part of her American Government project. In this process she has utilized many skills she picked up while homeschooling. Academically she is at the very top of her senior class primarily because of her continuing love for learning.

Susan has discovered a hidden interest in drafting and architecture. Both girls are involved in publishing the high school yearbook—learning new skills from a teacher who believes in hands-on learning and student responsibility.

In our family, we are still teaching ourselves.

Appendix

Quarterly Reports
&
Selected Resources

Sample Quarterly Reports

Summer Quarter

July 6, 1987–September 4, 1987

Jim (13)

PE: Jim participated in tennis and diving classes through the Parks and Recreation Department. They were small classes where he received individualized instruction.

Science: Jim worked extensively with the "Science Kit" from *Weekly Reader* studying chemical reactions. He also continued working in his garden, concentrating on sunflowers and pumpkins as well as techniques of pruning on several bushes. He watched many episodes of the "Mr. Wizard" television science program. He joined the family on our monthly visit to Ocean Park, noting the changes on the beach according to the seasons.

Jim went to the Space Week Exhibit at the Veterans Memorial Building. He learned water conservation techniques when our city water treatment plant had a serious fire.

Social Studies: Jim submitted a design for a WE THE PEOPLE banner sponsored by "Spin Off" in *Gifted Children Monthly*. He participated in our family study of various holidays throughout the world. This involved map study as well as discussions on different cultures involved in the holidays. This quarter we studied Dominion Day in Canada, our Fourth of July, the Chinese Dragon Festival, the Moslem Ramadan holiday, and the French Bastille Day celebrations. Jim also helped prepare for our celebration of the Bicentennial of the Signing of the Constitution program which we presented as a family to other homeschooling families. Jim participated in discussions of the thirteen original states and the development of the US Constitution.

Computer: Jim continues use of the computer. With the assistance of Dale, he developed a program for his newspaper carrier bill that records the checks he receives. He did some other programming projects as well as improved his skills with his favorite computer games. Jim often uses the word processor for writing purposes.

Language Arts: Jim wrote an essay entitled "Why the 1987-88 School Year Will Be My Best Year Yet" for the *Family Circle Magazine* contest. He corresponded with pen pals and wrote business letters. He read books about favorite cartoon characters, The Great Brain, and novels based on movies he has seen. Jim thoroughly reads both the *Lompoc Record* and *Santa Barbara News-Press* daily.

Math: Jim keeps his accounting records for his paper route current. He also daily checks the stock market reports, keeping track of his "practice" stock portfolio (a selection of stocks he would like to own someday). He became quite interested in logic puzzles this quarter, working through many Penny Press logic puzzle books from the supermarket. He constructed several paper geometric models from Dover publications. Jim also used scale representations to propose a rearrangement of Laurie and Susan's bedroom. He continues to sharpen his comparison shopping skills.

Vocational Education: Jim participates in newspaper sales crews as often as possible, increasing his salesmanship skills. He also prepares meals or parts of meals for the family. He is responsible for his own breakfast and lunch on weekdays.

Jim assisted Dale with removing the fiberglass panels from the covered patio roof. He built an elaborate cardboard box bunk bed for Laurie's small dolls.

Laurie (10)

Science: Laurie worked with *Weekly Reader* "Kid Kits" of Science, Planets, and Gardening. She also constructed several "exploding volcanoes" using vinegar, baking soda, and red food coloring, using papier mache mountains. She also watched "Mr. Wizard" television science programs. She went with the family to study environmental and seasonal changes at Ocean Park. Laurie went to the Space Week Exhibit at the Veterans' Memorial Building twice. She went with Dale and me to Santa Barbara Water Gardens to select water lilies for our fish ponds. She learned water conservation techniques when our city water treatment plant had a serious fire.

Art and Music: Laurie continues to improve on playing the recorder. She worked with the *Weekly Reader* "Kid Kits" for paper crafts and for hidden puzzles. She made some bead crafts from Susan's Hama bead kit.

Social Studies: Laurie submitted a design for a WE THE PEOPLE banner sponsored by " Spin Off." She participated in the family study of various holidays throughout the world. This involved map study as well as discussions on different cultures involved in the holidays. Laurie also helped prepare for our celebration of the Bicentennial of the Signing of the Constitution program which we presented as a family to other homeschooling families. Laurie participated in discussions of the thirteen original states and the development of the US Constitution. Laurie participated in the Summer Reading Program at the public library where sessions included the theme "Around the World" which included dances, art, puppetry, literature, storytelling, costumes and a karate demonstration. Laurie also participated in our church's two week Vacation Bible School. She joined in the "Pop Into The Past" celebration of the Bicentennial of the Signing of the Constitution at La Purissima Mission. She made a dipped candle and won a prize for her Chumash Indian costume during the celebration.

Computer: Laurie often uses the word processor and a newsletter publishing program. She also creates her own computer programs.

Language Arts: Laurie wrote an essay titled "Why the 1987-88 School Year Will Be My Best Year Yet" for the *Family Circle Magazine* contest. Laurie regularly corresponds with her numerous pen pals and wrote some business letters this quarter. She has added a Japanese pen pal whom she met at the NCACS conference in April. She wrote a letter to our local newspaper editor. The first I knew of her letter was when it was published. She was protesting the removal of the cartoon "Marmaduke" from the comics section. Laurie continually reads a large variety of books. Right now *Sweet Valley High* and *Babysitter's Club* books are her preference. She loves to have me read aloud in the evening. This quarter we read *Moby Dick*, *Freedom Train: The Story of Harriet Tubman*, and *Hello the Boat*.

Math: Laurie worked on some math cards from the "Individualized Mathematics Drill and Practice Kits". She improved her understanding of the concept of multiplying numbers with multiple digits. She worked some with Cuisenaire rods. She did a lot of baking where she changed some recipe amounts and ingredients. She substituted on a neighbor's newspaper route temporarily, including collection of receipts for him. She is a careful comparison shopper. She measured her room and objects in preparation for rearrangement of the bedroom she shares with Susan.

Vocational Education: Laurie continued Campfire activities throughout the summer. This involved craft work, particularly where she taught the others to make plastic canvas needlepoint frogs. She also taught herself to make other plastic canvas needlepoint creatures. She is teaching herself to knit and is working on a special sweater for me. Laurie often made dinner for the family—sometimes for a whole week. She is responsible for her own breakfast and lunch during the week. Sometimes she makes pancakes or waffles for the family on Saturdays.

Susan (8)

Art and Music: Susan made several projects with her Hama Beads. She loves to make up songs of her own. Usually they have to do with nature but she made one up about the United States Constitution, too. She practices on her xylophone and has tried to teach herself how to play the recorder. She often creates imaginative sewing projects.

Science: Susan worked with *Weekly Reader* "Kid Kits" about science, planets, and gardening. She assisted Laurie with constructing several "exploding volcanoes" using vinegar, baking soda, red food coloring, and hand crafted papier mache mountains. She also watched "Mr. Wizard" science programs. She was the most observant of the family in our monthly trips to Ocean Park. Susan went to the Space Week Exhibit at the Veterans' Memorial Building three times because she was fascinated by the exhibits. She went with Dale and me to Santa Barbara Water Gardens to select water lilies for our four fish ponds. She learned water conservation techniques when our water treatment plant had a serious fire. She accompanied Dale and me on a naturalist guided tour of the gardens at La Purissima Mission State Park. She daily spends time outside "studying nature." She avidly reads books of a scientific nature.

Susan's biggest project this quarter was to construct an electronic "Quiz Board" from a battery and wires with minimal help from Dale. From this she discovered how light switches work—including two-way ones, and eagerly and clearly explained her discovery to me.

Social Studies: Susan submitted a design for a WE THE PEOPLE banner sponsored by " Spin Off." She won for her age division. Her design has gone on to former Chief Justice Warren Burger. The book *Kids America* was her prize. It is packed with ideas for projects with which she constantly experiments. She participated in the family study of various holidays throughout the world.

Susan also helped prepare for our celebration of the Bicentennial of the Signing of the United States Constitution program. Using ideas from her *Kids America* book, she made up a game, using a game colonial children played, for our celebration. Susan participated in discussions of the thirteen original states and the development of the US Constitution.

Susan participated in some of the sessions at the Summer Reading Program offered by the public library. She particularly enjoyed the session which included puppetry, story-telling, and a karate demonstration. Susan also participated in our church's two week Vacation Bible School. She joined in the "Pop Into The Past" celebration of the Bicentennial of the Signing of the Constitution at La Purissima Mission. The dipped candle she made at the mission is her prize possession. She won a prize for the authentic Chumash Indian costume she wore.

Language Arts: Susan was thrilled by the money she received for her vacation trip journal excerpts published by *Home Education Magazine*. Susan wrote an essay entitled "Why 1987-88 School Year Will Be My Best Year Yet" for the *Family Circle Magazine* contest.

Susan continually reads a large variety of books. She listens intently to the stories I read aloud in the evening. She made several comments while I was reading *Moby Dick*. On her own, she has started reading Shakespeare and thoroughly enjoying it. She has read parts of *Taming of the Shrew*, and *Romeo and Juliet*. At times she wants me to read some of the parts aloud while she reads other parts aloud.

She often makes up stories on her own which she then types up.

Math: Susan worked on some math cards from the "Individualized Mathematics Drill and Practice Kits". She constantly makes up her own math puzzles. She worked with Cuisenaire rods. Math is her favorite subject.

Winter Quarter

January 4, 1988 to March 4, 1988

Jim (13), Laurie (10), Susan (8)

PE: Jim, Laurie, and Susan participate in the homeschool support group weekly swimming at the Municipal Pool. Jim delivers newspapers to 56 customers six days a week on his bicycle. Since we live at the top of the hill, he gets good exercise on his mile long route. Laurie often substitutes for Jim or other carriers. Both frequently bicycle around town. Susan is not comfortable riding on her bicycle, but she tries. She often goes for walks with Dale and I. Laurie loves to roller skate.

All three are active participants in neighborhood games as well as activities involving physical movement with other homeschoolers. Laurie and Susan participated in the Campfire trash-a-thon, which involved a lot of walking around town. We enjoyed watching the Winter Olympics, learning about several unfamiliar winter sports. The details given of the sports as well as the equipment involved was interesting and informative. We discussed the merits of competition for the sake of winning or for the sake of the challenge. Our favorite Olympian was "Eddie the Eagle" Edwards from Great Britain as he so aptly reminded us not to take ourselves too seriously.

Science and Health: This quarter we studied body systems. Topics studied included: the brain and central nervous system; the respiratory system; the circulatory system, the digestive system; the sensory system; and the reproductive system.

We used hands-on participation through use of both the "Visible Man" and "Visible Woman" plastic models. Supplementary materials included Inside Harry's Brain; textbooks *Building Better Health* levels 3 and 5, *Health: Focus on You* level 8 , *HJB Health* level 5; The Fold Out Atlas of the Human Body; *Human Anatomy for Children*; and *Your Body and How it Works*. We also used the *Human Anatomy Coloring Book* from Dover Books.

We did an in depth study of AIDS. They were able to discuss intelligently all aspects of the problem from origins of AIDS to transmission to treatment and prevention. Even Susan had a good understanding of the problem. We focused on diabetes, what it is, how it is treated, and symptoms. Many of our relatives on both sides of the family have diabetes. Jim continues with his gardening enterprise. In February his grandfather taught him how to graft the apple tree in our front yard. Grandpa was quite pleased with how Jim picked up the technique. Already most of the grafts are budding.

We continued our excursions to Ocean Park. The ocean succeeded in breaking through the built-up sand bar so we observed an interchange of tidal waters. What was especially interesting was watching the force of the small waves that came into the estuary. The ocean birds were more varied than we had seen before. We have been noticing several dead birds lately and are speculating as to the cause.

Jim records our rainfall in his notebook. He compares his notations with readings his grandfather has on his ranch 250 miles away.

Susan has taken great interest in electronics. We purchased a Radio Shack electronic lab kit which she frequently uses. She makes notations on the pages of various experiments whenever she is either not able to do simple troubleshooting, or when the kit does not work properly. Once in a while Laurie will also work with this kit. We have taken a subscription of *Popular Science Magazine*. Jim is quite interested in several of the articles.

Social Studies: This quarter we followed the progress of the Coast Guard tall ship, "Eagle," in the *Weekly Reader Magazine*, plotting its course and learning about some of the countries and Pacific Islands on its course. We also used some of the "Mystery Country" games in *Scholastic Senior Edition News* to become better acquainted with our world—particularly South America. From *The Whole Earth Holiday Book* this quarter we studied the holidays of New Year's, Epiphany, Martin Luther King Day, Feast of St. Anthony the Abbot, Tu B'shvat (Israel), Chinese New Year, Groundhog Day, Lincoln and Washington's birthdays, Valentine's Day, and Mardi Gras. These took us into many different parts of the world so we did lots of map work. We spent considerable time discussing Australia's 200th birthday. We used the Winter Olympics to learn more about different countries and different cultures. All three youngsters found television's "Passport" views of different athletes and their countries fascinating. This made our world smaller and more comprehensible for them—showing we are all inter-connected and important to each other. History was also a part of this event. What fun to see some of the athletes from Holland contrasted with the story of Hans Brinker which we had read as a family just recently.

Weekly Reader sent us a United States map on which to follow the Presidential Primaries. This is up on our bulletin board. The youngsters eagerly fill in primary results as they occur. They are watching the various candidates closely. Jim outlined the states on the map that are involved in Super Tuesday (March 8) so that they stand out. Jim also uses the IBM computer game "President Elect" to forecast presidential election results based upon current events. For the fun of it he "ran" his politically savvy grandfather against one of the chief presidential candidates. Grandpa won, according to the computer. We play the game "Hail to the Chief" frequently to sharpen our knowledge of American History and to remind us of the presidential elections.

Our field trip in February was to the local newspaper. We were there at press time although we got to only see the tail end of the press run for that day. Our guide went into great detail about each department at the newspaper office. In March our support group toured a large bakery. Unfortunately the day's work was completed before we arrived but we did get to see the enormous equipment used to produce bread, cakes, and cookies. Because of a serious employee morale problem several workers refused to show us their work when the tour guide asked them to. Our guide covered as well as possible. This experience provided me with the opportunity to discuss with Jim, Laurie, and Susan about less than ideal working conditions.

All three youngsters daily read the newspaper—all sections. Jim participated in World Almanac's "US Rand McNally Valentine's Massacre." This year the contest involved maps of parts of Canada as well as the entire United States. (Last year the maps went into parts of Mexico.) He enjoys the challenge of these contests and is preparing to enter the 1988 World Almaniac this month.

Language Arts: All three continue writing their pen pals. Jim and Susan only write to a couple of pen pals whereas Laurie has several. They read a wide variety of materials—from newspapers to novels. Jim reads *Popular Science, 3-2-1 Contact, Family Computing, Rainbow Magazine* (for our TRS 80 computer), and has started keeping up with baseball card catalogs and books. *Reader's Digest* is a family favorite magazine that is read cover to cover each month. Laurie and Susan borrow lots of books from the library. They often order books from the Scholastic Book Clubs or Troll. We have many, many books around the house from different sources, including garage sales.

Susan has grown to love books on mythology. She read *Jason's Argonauts* in just a few hours. Her interest in Shakespeare continues. One day she, Laurie, and I sat down and read parts from *Macbeth* after reading an explanation of the plot. Books we read as a family this quarter were: *A Little Princess* by Frances Hodgsen Burnett, *The Light In the Forest* by Conrad Richter, *Voyages of Dr. Dolittle*, *Peter Pan* by J.M.Barrie; and *King Arthur and His Court* by Howard Pyle.

Laurie published two more issues of her *Monthly Star*. She has several subscribers to her newsletter. Susan contributed articles for it. All three are using Scholastic's computer program, "Success With Typing" to learn typing skills. They are expected to put in daily practice on the computer. Jim is working up a computer program to sort his extensive baseball card collection. Laurie often uses "Bank Street Writer" for word processing.

Math: Jim continued studying advanced algebra with his math tutor two hours a week. They are close to completing the algebra book Jim started last spring in the University of California Santa Barbara Young Scholar's program. Because of scheduling problems, the tutor will be unable to continue next quarter. Jim also works in the *Scholastic Math Magazine*. Susan and Laurie work in *Scholastic DynaMath Magazine*. Susan is working with the Cuisenaire rods to study area, volume, and multiplication. She loves the challenge of the game "Math Craze," playing it frequently with me. Laurie and I finished the geoboard book and are now going into dot paper geometry using a book and task cards for geoboards. All three youngsters process the homeschool support group Scholastic Book Club orders each month. They gain practical experience in filling out order forms and distributing the books to customers. Some of the orders get quite complicated.

Art and Music: Laurie is still teaching herself to play the recorder. Susan is mastering the xylophone. Susan was able to translate one of her favorite pieces from the xylophone to the piano with no problem last week. Our January field trip was to a music store. It was time well spent. The manager showed us the band instruments they had on hand. This part was disappointing as the instruments were unassembled. No effort was made to demonstrate those instruments. The woman handling the guitar department demonstrated several types of guitars for us. The youngsters were fascinated by her explanation, asking her many questions. Another gentleman demonstrated pianos and organs, clearly explaining how pianos and organs are constructed, took us to the pianos, showing the insides and how they work. He demonstrated the capabilities of modern keyboard instruments by playing a variety of selections on each. His demonstration ended with electronic keyboards, showing how they can duplicate the sounds of every other instrument in existence as well as do things undreamed of a few years ago. The highlight of the tour came when he allowed each youngster to use the "sampler" where their voices became the music. Laurie is putting together a magic show to be given March 15 to homeschool friends. Susan is her assistant in this venture. They are doing it all themselves from invitations to show to props and refreshments. Other activities: Jim has started tutoring other homeschoolers on a weekly basis. Laurie has started to babysit. This has become a learning experience for Laurie. She plans activities for the children and actively interacts with them more than is ordinarily expected from a babysitter. Jim has varied activities in the church Confirmation class. In early March he helped plan, cook, and serve the congregation's Wednesday night Lenten Soup Supper. He made the apple cake that was served as dessert. Susan joined Campfire this quarter. She started an informal "Science Club" with her homeschooling friends. They come to our house for science activities which they plan for themselves.

Fall Quarter

October 3, 1988 to December 2, 1988

Laurie (11) and Susan (9)

PE: Laurie and Susan participate in the weekly support group swimming at the Municipal Pool. Both are gaining confidence in water activities. Laurie is now swimming well and has started diving. Susan is beginning to feel free to leave the side of the pool. Laurie has plenty of exercise riding her bike delivering papers in our hilly neighborhood. Susan loves to be out of doors and often goes on walks with Dale and meI. Both look forward to spending time in a nearby park, especially with other homeschoolers. We watched the Summer Olympics. This stimulated discussion about the various Olympic sports. We discussed the abuse of steroids and other drugs and their effects on our bodies as a result of Olympic athlete drug violations.

Science and Health: We worked with experiments from the Backyard Scientist. The local television weatherman visited our support group for an afternoon of weather related activities. He described what it was like to be a weatherman. He explained weather patterns in our area. One day during our monthly outing to Ocean Park we watched a pod of dolphins come in close to shore. Many shoreline creatures, including little crabs and live barnacles, were on the beach that day. We have been observing the way the Santa Inez River is getting ready for its annual breakthrough to the ocean itself. The sands have done a lot of shifting and we are noticing that there is more plant life nearer to the shore line than previously. Both girls continue to find fascinating scientific experiments to try. Susan explains a lot of scientific facts to her friends to the amazement of their mothers. We watch the television series "Wild, Wild Animals" and "3,2,1 Contact" regularly. Both girls often prepare meals. We use this opportunity to discuss good nutrition practices.

The entire family attended a two hour drug awareness workshop presented by a woman who works with teens having problems with drug and alcohol abuse in the school district.

Social Studies: Our emphasis has been on the presidential election. In fact this occupied most of our time until Election

Day. Laurie conducted a poll among other homeschoolers about both the presidential and mayoral candidates prior to the election. We discussed both national and local issues, including state ballot initiatives. The girls went with me to the polls where the officials graciously explained their duties and the importance of voting. We used two different workbooks from *Weekly Reader* publications for our study. The game "Hail to the Chief" was a favorite method for learning about our history and our government. We have continued using this game after the elections.

One ballot issue we focused on concerned the city proposal to sell the property where the town tennis courts are, in a run down condition, relocating the tennis courts to one of our parks. We visited the courts in question as well as the proposed relocation site. We wanted to see for ourselves their run down condition. Jim provided us with some insights because he was using those courts each week when he played tennis with friends. We even had the opportunity to discuss the issue with the mayor, who was running for re-election, when he came to the house passing out his campaign literature.

Our favorite support group field trip this quarter was a walking history tour of the downtown area of our town. It was conducted by the head of the Parks and Recreation Department. He has eagerly researched background history of the town and loves to share his findings with anyone who will listen. It was a fantastic look into our past. There are many interesting people who lived here. The youngsters loved his story about the flag pole that used to be in the middle of the main town intersection. People in horses and buggies would race around the flag pole just for the fun of doing it. At another intersection two different churches were built across the street from each other. As time went by the congregations began feuding until one group abandoned their church building to build another church in another part of town. So the remaining congregation moved the empty church over next to their building. The two buildings were joined and now serve a large congregation. A large three story building was moved from the country into town, where it still stands, by rolling it on logs for three miles. The two hour tour stretched into three hours because the children had so many questions to ask. Susan commented one day that it really helps her to learn history by using her dolls. She puts plays on with them and discusses things with them. Later on she added that this method helps her learn other subjects, too. She also uses time with her homeschool friends in the same way.

Math: We concentrated on math this quarter. Susan is working in the *Hayes Mastery in Arithmetic*, book 4. Laurie is using the Cambridge pre-GED program *Math Skills*. At least two mornings a week had specific time allotted to math. Another important math activity continues to be filling out the book order forms. This is complicated sometimes since we order from four different book club levels and a few times from two different book clubs. Often we shift books from one to the other when necessary for credit or for meeting minimum order requirements.

A favorite television program is "Square One." I find that the math skills they learn by watching this program stays with them much longer than what they do in workbooks. After watching the program one day Susan concocted her own Fibonacci chart. Susan enjoys math challenges because of the depth of her understanding of math concepts. She will pull out the advanced math skills cards to work on for the sheer enjoyment of it. On the other hand, Laurie expresses a deep dislike for anything having to do with math work.

Language Arts: Laurie continues writing to several pen pals. She is still publishes her *Monthly Star* newsletter. She has started a new combined newsletter with a good friend: *Kids Monthly*. A third girl joined the effort but did not remain long. Laurie wrote an effective business letter complaining about a piece that broke too easily off a glider she bought. The company sent her two replacement parts in case she had more problems with it. Susan does not care to write letters but occasionally will write to a pen pal or thank you letters (which are truly delightful to read). I encourage her to enter interesting writing contests—like in *Ranger Rick Magazine*, which is her favorite magazine.

At the beginning of the quarter I attempted to set aside just ten minutes each morning for journal writing. Both girls vigorously protested so eventually I gave up that idea. They hated it. Both girls constantly read. This is the greatest benefit of continuing the book orders despite the work involved. The book orders have been a source of many free books. Two outstanding examples of free books we received are *Lincoln: A Photobiography* and the new book of poetry *Sing a Song of Popcorn*. We order a large variety of inexpensive books this way. The girls have discovered different authors and book series, some of which have become their favorites. The girls also read a variety of magazines. Susan seems to favor *Reader's Digest* and *Ranger Rick*. We also subscribe to *Kid City, Three, Two, One Contact* (both published by Children's Television Workshop), *Penny Power* (now called *Zillions*), *Popular Science, Smithsonian, Home Education Magazine*, and *Gifted Children Monthly* (no longer published), and several computer magazines.

The biggest event for us this quarter was the girls being in the civic theater production of "The Best Christmas Pageant Ever." This involved long hours of hard work with extensive use of language and reading skills. We learned firsthand what is involved in live theater. There were nine performances. What an experience for Laurie and Susan! Besides her own part, Laurie was understudy for the main character.

Both girls developed skits to present at the annual home school Christmas potluck supper.

Laurie uses the computer regularly. Susan only uses it occasionally.

We use both the 4th and 6th grade editions of *Weekly Reader*.

Art and Music: Laurie planned a homeschool Halloween party with another homeschooler. Everybody had a good time at the party; however, the other girl claimed all the credit, which upset Laurie as she had done most of the work herself. It was an invaluable lesson in human relationships. Susan planned a Christmas party for her friends during which they decorated Christmas ornaments as gifts for their families. Both girls enjoy learning music. A family friend gave us her daughter's rarely used small electronic organ. The girls learned to play it easily.

Susan had fun composing music on her own. Neither girl will become great musicians, but they are having fun with music on their own terms. Both girls enjoy all kinds of crafts, particularly needlework. Laurie learned to cross stitch. Susan made a grapevine wreath and potpourri with a friend. The girls often draw or paint. Susan especially enjoys working with the hama beads, creating her own designs.

We attended the annual La Purisima Mission Christmas music program and thoroughly enjoyed the choral group that presented the evening's music.

Other Activities: Susan now goes to her friends' homes on a more regular basis. The mothers report back that this benefits everyone because of all the learning that spontaneously occurs among the girls. Laurie babysits for several families. Other homeschoolers love to come to our house to collect tadpoles from our fish ponds. One boy claims Susan knows the best way to catch frogs! Both Susan and Laurie are active with their Campfire groups. I help out regularly with Susan's group. In October I presented a unit on the meaning of "peace." In December we talked about peacemakers during which I discovered that Susan was the only one who knew anything about American Indians or about slavery. Susan shared with them what we had read about Harriet Tubbman and the Underground Railroad. Laurie has her newspaper route well under control. She knows each of her customers and preferences or idiosyncracies. The customers appreciated her attention to detail and she was selected "Newspaper Carrier of the Month."

She is also involved with her Confirmation classes at church. Both girls regularly attend Sunday school classes. Susan's class rebelled because of uninteresting materials. Parents asked that no homework be given as there is so much pressure for homework from the schools. The teacher is now concentrating on craft activities.

Fall Quarter

October 2, 1989 to December 1, 1989

Laurie (12) and Susan (10)

The first day of this quarter, we discussed what each girl wanted to accomplish. However as the quarter progressed we did not follow through on several of our decisions because of circumstances. Susan wanted to do some community volunteer work. We contacted Campfire, even actually visiting the local office, but never heard back from them. So we tried other volunteer agencies with the same result. I do not know the reason why these organizations did not respond to our offer. Susan lost interest in volunteering after a few attempts.

Susan has begun babysitting when the child is in our home so that Susan knows I am available for her. She enjoys being able to earn her own money. She has no interest whatsoever in delivering newspapers, not even being a substitute carrier.

An activity I suggested to the girls was to read an article in *Newsweek* to report about on Monday mornings. The girls were not at all enthusiastic. They chose not to participate in this idea.

This year I subscribed to several different magazines for us to use—*Newsweek*, *U.S. News and World Report*, *Natural History* (which Susan came to enjoy reading as time went on), *Smithsonian* (which Susan will look at and Laurie did glance over an article on the history of the Barbie Doll), and *American History Magazine* (which no one read). *Freebies Magazine* is the only new one they eagerly look for when the mail comes.

We renewed our subscription to *Weekly Reader* but the articles no longer appeal to the girls. We like some of the posters included with the subscription.

The girls eagerly read the calendars from *Learning 90* and *Instructor Magazine* each month because they usually can find some interesting information on them. They sometimes like the posters that come with these magazines.

Susan reads each issue she receives of *Ranger Rick* and *World*. She also likes to read *Kid's Art*. Both girls read *Penny Power*. They have missed receiving *Gifted Children's Monthly*.

Sometimes they glance through *Home Education Magazine* for articles which catch their interest. Laurie enjoys reading *3-2-1 Contact* and has just gotten a subscription to a couple of magazines aimed at teenagers.

Both girls help with the Scholastic Book order preparation. They order and read many books each month.

We thought we would work with foreign languages this quarter. Susan worked some with her Italian book and I unsuccessfully tried to locate more Italian materials for her. Laurie studied some French. However, neither girl was inspired to pursue this very far.

One thing that we did do was get to the library more often this quarter. We also checked out some of the video tapes available. Laurie was particularly interested in cake decorating and copied down a few of the ideas which she then used successfully. The girls helped a young neighbor girl obtain her own library card—of which she was proud!

One day Laurie helped Coral check out some books. The librarian looked at Coral, then asked Laurie, "Why isn't she in school today?" Not a word about Laurie not being in school herself. (She does look older than her age, but I didn't think she looked that old.) Laurie calmly replied, "She's only four years old."

Both Laurie and Susan took swimming lessons in September. They have been putting their new skills to good use during our weekly swimming.

Campfire activities keep the girls busy and happy. They helped all day this year with the October Campfire Carnival. Laurie participated in the Christmas parade with another Campfire group as neither her or Susan's group had entries. Susan chose not to participate.

We went to the annual Mission music program. We thoroughly enjoyed the impression of being back in mission days for an evening of traditional mission times holiday music. This year's choral group performed several selections from the Mission period.

Susan has spent many hours a week this quarter writing in her journal. She goes all around our yard to find perfect spots in which to write. One day she was sitting under a tree on our upper level in the back yard composing a poem about leaves on a windy day. For a while she was writing several poems that she thinks she will put into her own book. She has written several thank you notes and one letter to her grandparents.

Laurie continues writing to her many pen pals. She has made many, many friends. Her Japanese pen pal whom she met in Escondido almost four years ago recently got married. It was interesting to read of the many different wedding ceremonies she went through over a period of about a month. She and her new husband came to the United States so he could run in the New York Marathon this year but were unable to stop in to visit us.

A big project for Laurie this quarter was the Dynamite Club that she has begun. All the other homeschoolers are welcome to participate each month as she leads them through a variety of activities. For her first meeting she presented them with several science projects using Ziploc bags. One was creating a "Wave Machine" using water dyed blue and mineral oil. Her bag remained around the house for a couple of months until one of our cats put a claw through the bag! The youngsters also went home with bags of beans to sprout in different locations. They brought their bags to show the results at the next meeting. For her Dynamite Club, Laurie has made up a banner, a logo, membership cards, birthday cards, opening ceremony and simple rules. Other activities have been puff painting tee-shirts, making Christmas napkin rings, and ornaments. She is very enthusiastic about this project and constantly planning new activities.

During December the girls and I got to go on a special tour of the Marian Theater for the Pacific Coast Performing Arts production of "Peter Pan." First we had an hour and a half tour of the whole theater. We learned that everything we did last year for the "Best Christmas Pageant Ever" is indeed part of legitimate theater—including the "green room" where the actors assemble for announcements and prepare themselves to go onstage. After dinner we saw the production itself and then were treated to a half hour of questions directed to the actors.

Most of the questions had to do with the "flying" several actors had to do during the play. Among other things we learned that there is only one company in the United States who is allowed to handle all flying scenes in any production. They also handle most of the flying scenes in other parts of the world. They have exclusive rights to do the flying scenes for "Peter Pan" anywhere in the world. Another interesting tidbit was that wherever "Peter Pan" is put on in the world a portion of each ticket price must be sent to an orphanage in England that was a favorite project of the author.

Hurricane Hugo was of particular interest to us because Laurie was born in Charleston. Susan was born five months after we left Charleston, so she has roots there, too. We spent a lot of time watching Hugo and the hurricane aftermath. This led to an unplanned study about hurricanes.

But our biggest unexpected study was the Loma Prieta earthquake as my parents live near the quake's epicenter. We saw first hand the effects and listened to stories of those who went through the quake.

After the quake we went up to help my parents in the clean-up efforts. We learned how crucial water is. We are not used to having to take up drinking water, or to very strict water rationing, but the girls quickly adapted and carried home with them some of what they learned about how wasteful we are of water!

That trip we spent most of our time covering up the new pipelines that my Dad had to replace. We also filled in some of the fissures on the property. Fissures were all around us. Before heading home on Sunday morning we drove through several damaged areas and were over-awed with the damage sustained by residents in this rural area!

A few weeks later we returned for more clean-up work. By then a lot had been accomplished. This time we witnessed more clearly the emotional aftereffects of an earthquake. Each of us learned that natural disasters are not just momentary. We have all learned much more about our planet.

As soon as it was announced, Susan started mentally calculating the new earthquake relief quarter-cent state sales tax into our purchases.

Susan read *Little Women* and *Little Men* this quarter along with several other books.

In craft works, both girls used our new lap weave looms for interesting projects and continued with cross stitch projects. Laurie taught Coral how to make dough ornaments for her Christmas tree. Their Campfire art project this year is working with clay so they have been learning pottery techniques. Susan made a lovely bead and wire broach for me with tiny seed beads as a Christmas present this year.

The girls babysit a neighbor girl two days a week at our house. It is often a twelve to fourteen hour day. Both Susan and Laurie keep her occupied. Susan has a quiet way of handling the girl that often succeeds when she becomes obstinate. Laurie also is excellent in handling this little girl. It has been a terrific learning experience for all three girls. Of course, Laurie and Susan love the chance to earn money at the same time.

During this quarter we took our three cats to the vet to be spayed and neutered. This led to a study of reproduction and pet ownership responsibilities. In November we acquired a kitten that had been through the earthquake at my parent's ranch. Now we have four cats. The girls are the primary ones responsible for the cats.

Also under the heading of science, we used the Karol Media videotapes during October. *The Search For Solutions* had three video tapes and teaching guides covering several topics. We found them well done but they moved too quickly from topic to topic.

The girls and I also had a discussion about human reproduction and viewed the tape put out by Tambrands and Tampax. I showed them the many different kinds of feminine protection available. Laurie's Sunday School teacher is using Dobson's book *Preparing for Adolescence* which included a thorough presentation on human sexuality.

Laurie has been attending a weekly youth group meeting at church. They have had many different types of activities. She also went to the Melodrama with her Confirmation class.

In October we spent over two and a half hours at the La Purisima Mission with Juanita Centano learning various Indian crafts. We could have stayed all day (this was a homeschool field trip). Juanita, a Chumash Indian intent on preserving California Indian culture for future generations, kept commenting that this was the way education should be with the children and parents actively involved in activities of their own choosing. She told of her reaction to being forced to go to school.

Susan worked on several math projects this quarter. Laurie is still resisting math although she can keep good financial records when she wants to. She can handle book orders with a fair amount of ease. She likes to watch "Square One," the math program on public television.

Laurie continues to use the computer extensively for her various projects. Susan rarely uses it but will on occasion when she feels comfortable with it. Laurie has also learned to "call forward" a neighbor's phone and does this for her at least once a week, receiving payment for this service.

Laurie helped other youngsters practice for skits which they presented during our homeschool support group's Christmas potluck dinner. She is good at this kind of activity.

Summer Quarter

July 3, 1991 to September 6, 1991

Susan (12)

Over the summer quarter Susan read and wrote extensively. She no longer had much interest in the *Nancy Drew* series but continued with the *Sweet Valley Twins* series as well as several books she had ordered through the Scholastic Book Club. She became very interested in books written by Cynthia Voigt.

We started subscribing to *Provoking Thoughts* magazine. One challenge she accepted was to write an ending to a story six different ways. She spent two solid days at the typewriter responding to this challenge and enjoyed every minute of it.

She enhanced her computer skills through the Granola Bulletin Board activities even to entering the G-Wars competition and adding her own stories to the story board.

She also became more used to acting on her own while Dale and I were away for two weeks. She is skilled at doing laundry and learning to be more comfortable in meal preparation. She planned her own birthday party activities and sleep over.

Susan was chosen as a consumer tester for this year with *Zillions* magazine. They sent her a new microwave popcorn popper (which she was allowed to keep after the experiment) as well as money to cover the cost of specified types and brands of popcorn. Since she was to also provide other "taste testers;" she combined this activity with her birthday party. By the end of the testing Susan and her friends were tired of popcorn!

She went on a weekend campout with friends from church. She had her first experience with riding in a small motor boat.

Susan worked on Saxon math nearly every day without any prompting because she was enjoying what she was doing.

Selected Resources

Homeschooling Books

Child's Work, by Nancy Wallace
Published by Holt Associates Inc., 2269 Massachusetts Ave,
Cambridge, MA 02140; (617) 864-3100

Homeschooling For Excellence
Published by Warner Books. available from John Holt's Bookstore,
2269 Massachusetts Ave, Cambridge, MA 02140; (617) 864-3100

Home Grown Kids, Home Spun Schools, Home Style Teaching
Available from Moore Foundation, Box 1, Washougal, WA 98607;
(206) 835-2736

Magazines

Growing Without Schooling, 2269 Massachusetts Ave, Cambridge, MA
02140; (617) 864-3100 - bimonthly, $25.00 /year, $6.00 current issue, free
catalog

Home Education Magazine, PO Box 1083, Tonasket, WA 98855; (509)
486-1351 - bimonthly, $24.00/year, $4.50 current issue, free catalog

KidsArt News, PO Box 274, Mt. Shasta, CA 96067; (916) 926-5076; (800)
959-5076 - quarterly, $8.00

Ranger Rick, National Wildlife Federation, 1400 Sixteenth St.,
Washington, DC 20078-6420; (800) 432-6564 - monthly, $15.00

Zillions, PO Box 54861, Boulder, CO 80322-4861; (800) 234-2078 -
bimonthly, $16.00

Catalogs

Aristoplay, PO Box 7529, Ann Arbor, MI 48107; (800) 634-7738

The National Center for Fair and Open Testing (Fairtest), 342 Broadway, Cambridge, MA 02139; (617) 864-4810

S & S Arts and Crafts, POB 513, Colchester, CT 06415-0513; (800) 243-9232

Scholastic, Inc., PO Box 7502, Jefferson City, MO 65102; (800) 325-6149

TOPS Science Learning Systems, 10970 S. Mulino Rd, Canby, OR 97013

Usborne Books, PO Box 470663, Tulsa, OK 74147-0663; (800) 475-4522

Miscellaneous

California Coalition-People for Alternative Learning Situations (CC-PALS), PO Box 291786, Phelan, CA 92329; (619) 868-2860

Clonlara School, 1289 Jewett St., Ann Arbor, MI 48104; (313) 769-4515

Home Centered Learning, PO Box 2920, Big Bear City, CA 92134; (909) 584-9540

National Coalition of Alternative Community Schools (NCACS), PO Box 15036, Santa Fe, NM 87506; (505) 474-4312

National Homeschool Association, PO Box 290, Hartland, MI 48353; (513)-772-9580

Saxon Publishers, Inc., 1320 West Lindsey St., Norman, OK 73069; (800) 325-6149

World Almaniac Contest, PO Box 53, La Canada, CA 91011

Indexes

I Learn Better By Teaching Myself

Index

Still Teaching

Ourselves

Index

Our free catalog of homeschooling books and publications is available upon request from:

Holt Associates/GWS
Dept. ILB
2269 Massachusetts Ave.
Cambridge, MA 02140
(617) 864–3100

To request a copy of the current issue of *Growing Without Schooling* magazine, write to the above address and enclose US $3.00